Michał Głowala
Singleness

Philosophische Analyse/ Philosophical Analysis

Herausgegeben von/Edited by
Rafael Hüntelmann, Christian Kanzian,
Uwe Meixner, Richard Schantz, Erwin Tegtmeier

Band/Volume 70

Subseries: Books Edited by the International Center for Formal Ontology

Editorial Board of the ICFO
Miroslaw Szatkowski (International Center for Formal Ontology, Warsaw, Poland), Tomasz Bigaj (University of Warsaw, Poland), Michał Głowala (University of Wrocław, Poland), Christian Kanzian (University of Innsbruck, Austria), Uwe Meixner (University of Augsburg, Germany), Joanna Odrowąż-Sypniewska (University of Warsaw, Poland), Roger Pouivet (University of Lorraine, France)

Michał Głowala
Singleness

Self-Individuation and Its Rejection in the Scholastic
Debate on Principles of Individuation

DE GRUYTER

ISBN 978-3-11-061170-0
e-ISBN (PDF) 978-3-11-046388-0
e-ISBN (EPUB) 978-3-11-046301-9
ISSN 2198-2066

Library of Congress Cataloging-in-Publication Data
A CIP catalog record for this book has been applied for at the Library of Congress.

Bibliographic information published by the Deutsche Nationalbibliothek
The Deutsche Nationalbibliothek lists this publication in the Deutsche Nationalbibliografie; detailed bibliographic data are available on the Internet at http://dnb.dnb.de.

© 2018 Walter de Gruyter GmbH, Berlin/Boston
This volume is text- and page-identical with the hardback published in 2016.
Printing: CPI books GmbH, Leck

♾ Printed on acid-free paper
Printed in Germany

www.degruyter.com

Foreword

An earlier version of this book was published in Polish as *Pojedynczość. Spór o zasadę indywiduacji w scholastyce* (Wrocław 2012). A number of important revisions have been made in the text; most of them have been intended to focus the whole book on the issue of self-individuation and the contrast between primitive and derivative individuality.

What remains unchanged, however, is the main source of inspiration which has been the magnificent work of Elizabeth Anscombe and Peter Thomas Geach on ancient and medieval philosophy. I think they managed to show clearly what doing philosophy is, and why old philosophy, and Aquinas in particular, matters so much.

I would also like to express my deep gratitude to Prof. Mirosław Szatkowski, the Director of the International Center for Formal Ontology in Warsaw, for his support and encouragement that made the preparation of this book possible.

Contents

1	Introduction —— 1	
1.1	The Problem of Principles of Individuation —— 2	
1.2	Singleness. A Brief Survey of Notions Concerning Individuality —— 8	
1.3	The Importance of the Scholastic Problem of Individuation —— 13	
1.4	A Brief Historical Survey of the Scholastic Debate on Individuation —— 14	
1.5	The Method of the Study —— 16	
2	*Entitas.* **Nominalism and Self-Individuation —— 23**	
2.1	Main Nominalistic Theses —— 23	
2.2	Standard Arguments for the Strong Self-Individuation Thesis —— 26	
2.3	Ens et Unum Convertuntur —— 27	
2.4	The Immediacy of Individuality —— 28	
2.4.1	The Immediacy of Attributes in General —— 28	
2.4.2	The Immediacy of Distinction —— 30	
2.4.3	The Immediacy of Individuality —— 33	
2.5	The Individuality Thesis and Simple Entities in Nominalism —— 34	
2.6	General Features of the Nominalistic Standpoint —— 37	
3	*Haecceitas.* **The Scotistic Rejection of the Strong Self-Individuation Thesis —— 39**	
3.1	Main Theses of the Scotistic Standpoint —— 39	
3.2	Standard Arguments for the Scotistic Theses —— 40	
3.3	A Weak Sense of Individuality —— 42	
3.4	Avicenna on Instantiable Natures —— 46	
3.4.1	Some Details of Instance Ascription —— 49	
3.4.2	Natures and Instances, Parts and Wholes —— 52	
3.4.3	The Scotistic Interpretation of Avicenna —— 56	
3.5	Can Things be Differentiated by What They Have in Common? —— 58	
3.6	The Scotistic Way of Rejecting Self-Individuation —— 60	
3.7	What Individuality is Not? —— 62	
3.8	Scotism and Nominalism —— 65	

4	**Forms and Self-Individuation** —— 67	
4.1	Forms as Principles of Individuation: the Main Thesis and Standard Arguments —— 67	
4.2	Effects of Formal Causes —— 69	
4.3	Formal Causes, Kinds, and Singleness —— 70	
4.4	Formal Causes and Self-Individuation —— 72	
5	**Subjects as Principles of the Individuation of Their Accidents** —— 73	
5.1	Aquinas's Main Thesis Concerning the Individuation of Accidents —— 73	
5.2	Being in a Subject and Singleness —— 76	
5.2.1	Various Senses of 'Being in a Subject' —— 76	
5.2.2	Being in a Subject, Parts, and Wholes —— 78	
5.2.3	Being in a Subject and Individuality —— 80	
5.2.4	The Two Senses of the Subject-Individuation Thesis —— 81	
5.3	The Individuation of Human Virtues —— 82	
5.4	Subjects of Accidents and the Thomistic Way of Rejecting Self-Individuation —— 86	
5.5	The Subject-Individuation Thesis and the Formal Individuation Thesis —— 88	
6	**Matter: Noninstantiability and Self-Individuation** —— 93	
6.1	Matter and Individuality: Aquinas's Main Thesis —— 93	
6.2	Subjects of Substantial Forms: Matter —— 96	
6.3	Prime Subjects and Noninstantiability —— 98	
6.3.1	Matter as a Prime Subject —— 98	
6.3.2	An Old Objection and Various Responses to It —— 101	
6.4	Matter and Noninstantiability of Forms —— 105	
7	**Quantity and Self-Individuation** —— 109	
7.1	Quantity and the Individuality of Substances: Aquinas's Main Thesis —— 109	
7.2	Material Difference, Matter, and Extension —— 112	
7.3	Division into Pieces, Position, and Individuality —— 115	
7.4	Aquinas on the Self-Individuation of Quantity —— 117	
7.5	Matter and Quantity. What is *Materia Signata*? —— 121	
7.6	The Two Aspects of Individuality —— 124	
7.7	Quantity and the Individuation of Parts of Substances —— 126	

7.8	The Individuality of Human Souls. Commensuratio animae ad hoc corpus —— 128	

8 Actual Existence and Individuality —— 131
- 8.1 The Existence-Individuation Thesis and Some Standard Arguments —— 131
- 8.2 Actual Existence and Individuality —— 133
- 8.3 Ultimate Actuality, Ultimate Distinction, and Noninstantiability Again —— 136
- 8.4 Actual Existence, Accidental Unity, and Individuality —— 139
- 8.4.1 *Per se* Unity, Accidental Unity, and Individuality —— 140
- 8.4.2 *Per se* Unity, Accidental Unity, and Existence —— 142
- 8.5 Is Actual Existence a Principle of Individuation? —— 143

9 Concluding Remarks: The Thomistic Theory of Individuation —— 147
- 9.1 Main Features of the Thomistic Theory of Individuation —— 147
- 9.2 The Thomistic Theory of Individuation, Scotism, and Nominalism —— 149
- 9.3 The Thomistic Theory of Individuation from a Historical Point of View —— 149
- 9.4 The Problem of Individuation: a General Framework —— 150

Bibliography —— 155

Index —— 161

1 Introduction

The topic of this study is the scholastic debate on principles of individuation (*principia individuationis*); more precisely, I focus on various ways in which self-individuation, being individual of itself, is accepted and rejected within the main standpoints of the debate. This, I hope, will be a sort of unifying perspective that will help to see the core of the problem and various relationships between its solutions, and finally to evaluate particular theories of individuation. On the other hand, it seems that self-individuation (of various sorts) has not received the sort of attention it deserves in the contemporary literature. So the aim of this book is, on the one hand, a presentation of one of the most important strands in the scholastic debate that, as I hope to show, sheds much light on problems of individuation and their solutions; on the other hand, my aim is to sketch and advocate a Thomistic theory of individuation in this light.

Since 'principle of individuation' is used in various ways, it is necessary to sketch preliminarily the way it is, as I claim, used to identify the object of the scholastic debate by its participants (the details of this sketch will be discussed in due course). Suppose there are five houses in a street. Now one may ask what makes a given building *a house*; the answer is roughly clear: it is the way the building is arranged as a place to live in. But one may also ask what makes it a *single* house (in the sense relevant for counting and identifying what counts as a single house). This question is much more difficult than the former one. It is not even clear whether the answer should be different than in the former case: after all, does not anything that makes it a house make it a *single* house? In a way to be a house is to be a single house. At any rate, we usually know what counts as a single house, a single roof tile, a single tree, a single leaf and stalk, a single man, a single action, a single hour of life, a single breath, a single rosary bead, a single bell or a single bell stroke. Being single (being something that counts as a single F) is an important feature ascribed to things, so the question about the basis of this feature is an important one. It is just the question of a principle of individuation (of houses, roof tiles, men or their deeds) in the sense that I am interested in here. A principle of individuation is a principle of being single (in the sense of being something that counts as a single F), something in a thing in virtue of what it is a single thing. So what I am interested in here is *not* the epistemic sense of 'a principle of individuation' – the way in which *we* individuate or single out something, but instead the *metaphysical sense* of 'a principle of individuation'. I neither presume here that there is a single sort of principle of individuation in all the cases (for example, in the case of roof tiles and human actions), nor even that in a single case there is only one thing that may rightly be called *the* principle of individuation.

The scholastic debate on principles of individuation, conducted during some centuries by many generations of the best thinkers, sheds much light on a number of metaphysical issues invoked more or less directly by the question of principles of individuation; and all of these issues are important ones. It also sheds much light on a number of important and well known standpoints concerning unity and plurality, identity and distinction, number, parts and wholes, extension, and universals. It is just this debate that I am trying to present here in a systematic manner.

In my preliminary remarks I will proceed in the following way: first I offer a general formulation of the question of a principle of individuation (1.1); then I sketch the very concept of an individual (*individual*) and the background of some related concepts (1.2) and give main reasons for the importance of the issue of individuation (1.3). Then, from a historical point of view, I show the main stages of the scholastic debate on principles of individuation (1.4). Finally, I sketch the way in which the debate is presented here (1.5). These preliminaries are restricted to the minimum that is necessary to grasp the subject of the debate. Various important issues obviously involved in the preliminaries are postponed and discussed in the course of the book.

1.1 The Problem of Principles of Individuation

To keep trace of an argument exchange or to get involved in it one has to know at least roughly what the subject of the debate is, and what is uncontroversial about that subject. The scholastic individuation debate poses serious problems here, for the very concept of *principium individuationis* coming from the jargon of philosophy may provoke some misunderstandings, and there is a muddle of issues (metaphysical, logical, and epistemic) in contemporary philosophy that are brought together under the heading of "principles of individuation". Moreover, what I am interested in here, is not just a precise formulation of some problem, but a formulation that was in fact accepted by participants of the scholastic debate.[1] This is necessary if we are to learn something from the very exchange of arguments in the scholastic debate on individuation.

---

[1] For example, Anscombe (1981a, 64) suggests that the problem of "principle of individuation" in the Aristotelian context is just the problem of the source of distinction between co-existing individuals of the same species; but clearly this sense of 'principle of individuation' is not

One of the sources of misunderstandings seems to be the very grammatical form of 'individuation' ('*individuatio*') which might suggest that individuation is a sort of procedure, an operation or a process; so, for example, Jorge J.E. Gracia claims that individuation (at least taken in some important sense) is a process of becoming individual.[2] This view, however, at least in its general form, seems unjustified. Admittedly, '*individuatio*' is a noun derived from a verb, but '*relatio*' (relation), '*negatio*' (negation) or '*oppositio*' (opposition) are also derived from verbs and it would be at the very least strange to suggest that relation or negation are (in general or in some central or particularly important meaning) processes;[3] it is similarly strange, I think, in the case of individuation. It seems rather that the Latin verb '*individuari*' means precisely 'to be (an) individual', '*individuum esse*' (they are obviously used interchangeably in most contexts).[4] So *individuatio* is just being (an) individual – or, in other words, individuality;[5] similarly: relation (*relatio*) is just being related (*referri*) to something, opposition (*oppositio*) is being opposed (*opponi*) to something, and motion (*motio*) is just being moved.

The verb '*individuari*' in scholastic texts is regularly accompanied by '*per aliquid*' or '*aliquo*' – 'by something' or 'in virtue of something' (and '*individuari per aliquid*' is clearly used interchangeably with '*esse individuum per aliquid*'). In a similar way you can ask, for example, *per quid* or *quo* – by what or in virtue of

---

enough for a broader reconstruction of the scholastic debate concerning principles of individuation. Gracia (1988, 8–26) proposes some way of singling out the problem of principles of individuation among many other problems concerning individuality, but he himself admits (see e.g. Gracia and Kronen 1994, 513) that the participants of the scholastic debate concerning principles of individuation do not single out the problem precisely in the way he proposes. For an overview of the issues involved in the debate see also King (2000).

2 See Gracia 1984, 19 and 38; Gracia 1988, 4; Gracia 1991, 385. In Gracia 1988, 4 he claims that "'Individuation', like 'universalization' and 'externalization', and many other substantives related to verbs, refers primarily to the process that is carried out by the action expressed by the verb". In 1984, 38 he says that individuation is a process or change that something universal must undergo to become individual, and the principle of individuation is "the principle or cause of such a process or change".

3 Other examples could be '*privatio*' (lack), '*contradictio*' (contradiction), '*extensio*' (extension), '*intensio*' (intension).

4 Aquinas, for example, says of a form that cannot be received in a subject that *ex hoc ipso individuatur quod non potest recipi in alio* (Aquinas 1980, *S. th.* I, q. 3, art. 2, ad 3) which means precisely that it is individual by the very fact that it cannot be received in anything else. Similarly, he often contrasts *habere speciem* (belonging to a species) and *individuari* (being an individual) (see e.g. Aquinas 1980, *S. th.* I-II, q. 63, art. 1, corp.; II-II, q. 4, art. 6, corp.; *De potentia*, q. 10, art. 2, corp.).

5 So, for example, Aquinas, Suárez as well as other authors use repeatedly the phrase '*habere suam individuationem*' which, I would claim, mean 'to have individuality' or 'to be individual'.

what – something is a house, is white or is good, and that is the question about something inhering in an entity in virtue of which the entity is a house, is white or is good[6]. In a similar sense the soul is that in virtue of what we live – *quo vivimus*: something inhering in a human being that makes him a living human being[7]. To be sure, there are many various ways in which such '*quo*' is used, and various senses of, say, 'that in virtue of which the chalk is white'; some of them may well seem unclear and stand in need of further inquiry. At any rate, however, all of them are closely related to the concept of a principle (*principium*) in one of its important senses: something in virtue of what a thing is white is its principle of being white. Similarly something in virtue of what a thing is (an) individual (*id quo individuatur*) is its principle of being (an) individual, that is, its principle of individuation or just its principle of individuality (*principium individuationis*).[8]

In some cases, however, we would say that a true answer to the question 'in virtue of what is something F?' does not yet reveal a principle of being F. We should say so, for example, if someone claimed that something is indivisible in virtue of its indivisibility; or that it is the shininess of a piece of steel that makes it shiny. We could also say so when someone claimed that a thing is (an) individual in virtue of its individuality. Such answers are unsatisfactory – they do not yet reveal a *principle* in question – for at least two reasons. The first is that (as Scotus points out in the case of indivisibility), we should ask at once in virtue of what does the thing enjoy indivisibility.[9] The other is that such answers do not tell us whether something is F and i G in virtue of the same thing or in virtue of two distinct things; for example, in the case of shininess we would like to know whether it is one and the same thing that makes a white shiny thing both white and shiny; or we would like to know whether it is the same thing that makes a given person both patient and resolute. It is clear, for example, that it is one and the same thing that makes a uniformly red shiny apple both red and colourful; but it is far from being trivial whether the same thing makes it also shiny. Settling

---

[6] For some key remarks concerning the scholastic use of '*quo*' see Geach 1969a, 42–64.
[7] See Aristotle 1961, *De anima* 414a5–15; Aquinas 1980, *In Sent.* II, d. 17, q. 1, art. 2, ad 5.
[8] A similar formulation of the problem of the principle of individuation in the context of the scholastic debate is to be found in Gracia 1994b, 1, King 1994a, 143 and King 2000, 159–162. This general formulation is close to the proposal of Lowe (2005, 75); Lowe thinks, however, that 'to individuate' is a transitive verb that expresses a sort of ontological relationship, and it seems to me that the transitive sense of '*individuare*' is relatively rare in scholasticism.
[9] Scotus 1982, *Lectura* II, d. 3, pars 1, q. 2, n. 48.

such questions concerning the identity of principles seems to be one of the fundamental procedures connected with the concept of principle I have sketched.[10]

The complex of identity statements concerning that which makes various things fall under various predicates (and especially the complex of arguments for these identity statements) constitutes a framework of principles we are able to look for. The question about principles of individuation presupposes such a framework in the background; for the scholastic dispute over individuation such a background is provided by, roughly speaking, Aristotelian metaphysics with its key concepts of substance and accident, form and matter, actuality and potentiality. So the issue of individuation is also the issue of relation between principles of individuation and other principles responsible for other features of things, especially features such as unity, persistence, distinction from other things, extension in space, various forms of activity and passivity, and so on. There are various connections between individuality and, say, unity or persistence, so it seems that there is a close relationship between their principles; it may even seem that the principle of all of them is one and the same.

So that is a general formulation of the question of a principle of individuation that I think can be ascribed to all the authors engaged in the scholastic debate over principles of individuation. The Thomists, Scotists and nominalists do differ fundamentally from one another in their views on unity, plurality, number, universals and related issues; henceforth they differ fundamentally from one another in their theories of principles of individuation. The question they ask, however, is the same: what in a thing makes it (an) individual. So my claim is that the whole scholastic debate on principles of individuation focuses on various ways in which individuality belongs to various sorts of entities.

In this general formulation of the question I leave it open what individuality can be truly ascribed to; at any rate, it is one of the most important topics of this book. Some contemporary formulations of the problem presuppose that individuality is ascribed only to individuals (for example, King says (2000, 162) that the problem of individuation is "what makes a given individual an individual", and Lowe (2005, 75) claims that "what 'individuates' an object [...] is whatever it is that makes it the single object that it is"; in both cases individuality is ascribed to individuals; one of my main points here, however, is that individuality can be ascribed not only to individuals (see in particular 3.4, 5.2.1 and 5.2.4).

---

10 What I have sketched is obviously a concept of a principle in the *metaphysical* sense as opposed to a concept of principle in the *epistemic* sense. For a distinction between these two concepts of a principle see Aristotle 1953, *Met.* 1013a14–15.

Moreover, the general formulation does *not* imply the uniqueness of the principle of individuation in a given case; it does not rule out the possibility that there are some distinct things that all make something (an) individual, each of them in some specific way, or that each of them is responsible for some distinct aspect of individuality, so that they all may be rightly called principles of individuation.[11] Therefore I prefer to speak about *a* principle of individuation rather than *the* principle of individuation. Moreover, the general formulation does not imply that there is one general answer to the question about principles of individuation, holding for all sorts of entities whatsoever. Some participants of the discussion (like Scotus, Ockham, Suárez or Leibniz) do claim that such a general answer revealing *uniforme principium individuationis* is possible and desirable. Some other, mainly Thomists, claim that there is no general answer to such a question, but various answers for various domains of reality. There are, in particular, three kinds of being for which they thought one should expect fundamentally different answers: material substances like human beings, animals or plants; properties of material substances like colours or powers to act; immaterial substances such as created pure spirits, in particular angels.

The question of a principle of individuation sketched above may be distinguished from some other closely related complexes of questions concerning individuality: (i) semantical and logical questions concerning the use of proper names and other singular terms, anaphora, pronouns and bounded variables, identity statements or Leibniz Law; (ii) epistemological or psychological questions concerning the way we individuate objects (in the epistemic sense of 'individuation' as singling out) in acts of ostension, counting or re-identification; (iii) metaphysical questions that are closely related to the question of a principle of individuation, but are distinct from it: for example, questions about identity over time or about identity criteria relevant for a given sort, and, last but not least, about the soundness of the principle of identity of indiscernibles.[12]

There is also a close relationship between the issue of individuation and the problem of universals. From a scholastic point of view, the former concerns the way in which things are individual(s), the latter – the way in which things are universal(s) or kinds having many instances. It is sometimes thought that the

---

[11] Lowe considers such a possibility (2005, 76–77), but tends to reject it; by contrast, plurality of principles of individuation of one and the same thing is a mark of Thomistic theories of individuation.

[12] For a much more detailed typology of these questions see especially Gracia 1988, 8–26, Gracia 1984, 21–54 and Gracia 1994b.

problem of universals is prior to the problem of individuation, so that the question about principles of individuation does emerge only in the context of some sort of realism about universals. It seems, however, that the problem of individuation is a more fundamental one, since individuality is a more fundamental feature of things than universality (that seems obvious unless you accept a sort of excessive realism about universals). In this book I am concerned with the problem of individuation as opposed to the problem of universals (I offer only a general formulation of the latter in 3.4).

In his preliminaries concerning being (an) individual Gracia introduces a distinction between an individual and individuality. Individuality, he says, is distinct from an individual in the way a feature is distinct from its subject: "the former is the feature whereby the latter has its unique character"; so individuality is a feature of an individual that makes it individual[13]. Then he distinguishes between the question of the ontological status of individuality (which concerns the ontological type individuality belongs to and the kind of distinction between the individuality of an individual and its other components, principles and characteristics) – and the question of the principle of individuation (which concerns the principle or cause of individuality)[14]. It seems to me, however, that this proposal might be misleading. The individuality introduced by Gracia on the one hand is something that *renders* something individual; on the other hand it stands in need of some principle or cause. It seems, however, that if individuality really *renders* something individual, it *is* its principle of individuation; we could then ask what individuality is, and this is just the question what is a principle of the individuation of the thing in question.

Gracia and Kronen complain moreover that there is a sort of equivocation in the scholastic use of '*individuatio*' – it is used to mean both individuality and "the process whereby individuality accrues to an individual"[15]. I think that scholastic authors may be defended against this charge. It is clear that '*individuatio*' is used in scholastic texts in the sense of 'individuality'; as for the other alleged meaning, namely "the process whereby individuality accrues to an individual", it seems to be an unclear and dubious concept.

---

13 Gracia 1984, 20–21.
14 *Ibidem*, 34–39.
15 Gracia and Kronen 1994, 513.

1.2 Singleness. A Brief Survey of Notions Concerning Individuality

The general formulation of the question of a principle of individuation introduced above needs some further clarifications concerning the concept of individuality that is used in it and the feature of being (an) individual. Obviously such a feature like being (an) individual in many respects does not resemble features like being white or being a house; '(an) individual' is not a predicate like 'white' or 'a house'. Now for a good account of what sort of feature individuality is, one needs to settle a great muddle of interconnected logical and metaphysical issues. By way of preliminary remarks, however, some points seem quite clear.

(i) Sometimes '*individuum*' is used in the scholastic texts as a noun or as a *predicative* adjective[16]. So, for example, we read that "this hand is an individual" (*haec manus est individuum*)[17]. We could also ask, for example, whether any part of an individual is itself an individual or not, or whether any mereological sum of individuals is an individual or not. In this predicative use 'individual' occurs also in contexts like 'another individual' or 'one and the same individual'.

(ii) What we encounter more often, however, is the *attributive use* of 'individual' in the context 'individual F', where 'F' is a noun expressing some kind; so, for example, we have 'individual man' (*individuus homo*) or 'individual whiteness' (*individua albedo*) – in the sense of a particular instance of man or whiteness or a *token* F as opposed to the *type* F ('individual colour' means not 'a particular *sort* of colour', but instead 'a particular instance of some sort of colour'). In general, '*a* is an individual whiteness' does not split into '*a* is (an) individual and *a* is (a) whiteness'.[18] Used in this attributive way, 'individual' seems interchangeable with 'single'. Therefore I suggest that in an important sense being individual is just being single and individuality is singleness.

(iii) There is a number of concepts in the scholastic texts on the problem of individuation used in a very similar attributive way; so, for example, we encounter '*singularis albedo*' (singular whiteness) or '*particularis albedo*' (particular

---

16 For the logical distinction between predicative and attributive adjectives see Geach 1956 and Rind and Tillinghast 2008.
17 As for the former see Aquinas 1980, *In Sent*. III, d. 6, q.1, art. 1.
18 A clear example of attributive use is Aquinas' passage in 1980, *Contra gent*. II, 73, 5: "unitas rei sequitur unitatem formae. Impossibile est igitur diversorum individuorum esse formam unam". This cannot mean that distinct individuals cannot have a common form, for according to Aquinas the two hands of one and the same man have one and the same form; what Aquinas means is precisely that distinct individual Fs cannot have one and the same form of F.

whiteness) or even '*haec albedo*' (this whiteness). In the case of the demonstrative pronoun it is noticeable that no actual ostension or identification is needed for the correct use of '*haec albedo*' in this sense – 'this whiteness' here is just a whiteness that might be identified by ostension, and not necessarily one that is actually so identified. Moreover, sometimes we encounter the demonstrative pronoun used in a predicative way '*est haec*' ('is *a* this'),[19] and there is an abstract noun derived from this sort of use, namely '*haecceitas*', 'thisness', 'being *a* this'. My suggestion is that the predicative use of '(an) individual' is strange in the way in which the predicative use of 'a this' is; more generally, that the predicative use of '(an) individual' is derivative from the attributive one.

(iv) Explaining the meaning of 'being individual' the scholastics say that to be individual is to be internally undivided (*in se indivisum*) and to be divided or distinct from other individuals (*ab aliis divisum*); and the question about a principle of individuation is the question about something in virtue of which something meets these conditions of being undivided and being distinct.[20] The first condition is close to noninstantiability: to be divided in the relevant sense is to have many instances. So, for example, an individual whiteness is a noninstantiable whiteness (a shade of whiteness is, by contrast, instantiable whiteness).[21]

The best way to grasp the sense of the two conditions associated with individuality is to apply them in the context of *counting*. Something is an individual whiteness (a single instance of whiteness) if it is a noninstantiable whiteness that we should single out or divide from other instances of whiteness. A particular shade of whiteness does not meet the first condition (being undivided), although it meets the second; a particular instance of a given shade of whiteness meets both.

(v) As I have suggested in (ii), the predicative use of '(an) individual' seems derivative from the attributive one; and sometimes when we say that something is an individual, the locution is clearly incomplete and what we mean is that it is an individual F, a particular instance of F. There is a number of metaphysical problems related to the predicative use: is being an individual common to many individuals in the way in which being a house is common to many houses? Are

---

19 E.g. Suárez 1866, *Disp. met.* V, s. 6, 5: "dicendum est formam substantialem esse hanc intrinsece per suammet entitatem".

20 A similar formulation is to be found in other scholastic authors. We find also a similar formula in Lowe who says that what individuates some object is "whatever it is that makes it *one* object, distinct from others, and the very object that it is as opposed to any other thing" (2005, 75).

21 For some clarifications concerning the close relationship between individuality and noninstantiability see e.g. Gracia 1983 and 1988, 43–60, and Lowe 2009, 38.

there individual instances of individuality, and is it possible to distinguish an individual individuality from individuality in general? In general the answer seems to be negative, but it takes more effort to say precisely why.[22] It might seem advisable to ignore the general sense of 'individual' and to say that a principle of individuation is anything that makes a thing the individual it is (as in Lowe's proposal in 2005); I think, however, that is impossible to ignore the general sense of 'individual' in a comprehensive treatment of the issue of individuation.

(vi) As I have suggested in (iv), the main context in which individuality and related notions are primarily used is the context of *counting*. Two points are to be made here. The first is that if we are going to *count* Fs we have to single out what should count as one or single F, so we have to answer the question whether something is a single F or not. In other words, it is precisely in the context of counting that we want to know whether something is *numerically one* (*unum numero*) – that is, whether something counts as one or single. The other point is that we count not only individuals, but also *kinds*;[23] and a single *kind* (for example magpie (*pica pica*)) is a *single* kind, but, as far as it is itself instantiable, it is not *single* in the stronger sense. So there is a clear contrast between two sorts of counting and two senses of being single relevant for them; what we are interested in in the debate about principles of individuation, is being single in the strong sense. More precisely, we want to say what this strong sense precisely consists in, and we want to say what makes things single in this strong sense.

Since I think that it is precisely the context of counting that is the source of the concept of individuality in the sense which is relevant here (as opposed to some other important senses), I assume for the purposes of this study that to be an individual F is to be a *single* F, and that individuality in the sense relevant here is just singleness.

(vii) The close relationship between the notion of individuality and the use of demonstratives (see (iii)) suggests that there is a close connection between individuality and ostension. According to remarks of Boethius and Marius Victorinus "individual is what you point at with the finger" (*individuum enim est quod oculis digitoque monstratur*).[24] We have to keep in mind, however, that the very ostension involves some procedures of singling out or identifying what you are going to point at, and that the same procedures are used when one *counts*. So I think

---

22 For a discussion of this issue see Punch 1672, *Logica*, disp. VI, q. 2.
23 That point is clearly made by Anscombe (1961, 46) who notes that the very notion of numerical identity and numerical difference it their contemporary use misleadingly suggest that "counting of itself implies that individuals and not kinds are being counted".
24 See Marius Victorinus 2014, 82 and Riesenweber's comments *ad locum* in Riesenweber 2015.

the close relationship of individuality and ostension is just some aspect of a more fundamental relationship of individuality and *counting*.

(viii) There is a good deal of *logical* problems closely connected with the notion of individuality; they concern the uses of various sorts of pronouns, anaphora, articles, contexts such as 'the same F', 'another F', 'some F', quantifiers, singular terms or referring expressions in general.[25] In particular, there is a close connection between the logical properties of *singular terms* (as opposed to general ones) and the metaphysical properties of individuals (as opposed to what they are instances of); and there is some close relationship between instantiation and predication. This shows the immense complexity of the issue of individuation. It is possible, however, and obviously commendable, to distinguish between the metaphysical and the logical problems here; I try to do it and focus on the former.

(ix) It is also important to note that many notions related to individuality have other meanings and uses that do not seem totally irrelevant for the very issue of individuation. For example, 'single' is used in contexts such as 'a single thread', and in these contexts being single contrasts with being double or triple (and multiple in general); in this context it tends to mean 'not composed of parts'. Now this sense of 'single' is clearly different from the one connected immediately with individuality; if you count single threads in a piece of fabric, what you single out as numerically one thread might happen to be a double thread. On the other hand, it seems that the opposition of 'single' and 'double' is not just totally irrelevant for the discussion of individuality; indeed, it plays a prominent role in the nominalistic theory of individuation that I focus on in chapter 1. Similarly, the Greek term *'haplous'* which means 'single' often means just 'simple'. In general, such connections make the whole issue of individuation even more complex: although they are not immediately relevant to the problem, they cannot be totally ignored, and they play important roles in some theories of individuation.

(x) Besides the notions of individuality, singularity, particularity, numerical unity and thisness there are also some key metaphysical concepts related to some other aspects of individuality in a broad sense. These are the notions of *suppositum* and *hypostasis* (the notions of a subject in some special sense), and the notion of a person (*persona*). To grasp the difference between these three notions and the former group of concepts related to individuality and discussed above, let us make three points. The first is that the notion of (an) individual is applicable not only to substances in the Aristotelian sense (in particular to plants, animals,

---

25 For a confrontation of some scholastic and modern theories here see e.g. Geach 1980.

human beings), but also to their *parts* (as the left hand or the right eyebrow) as well as to particular instances of their accidents (for example, someone's musical skill or patience, or the shape of a given plant). By contrast, '*suppositum*' and '*hypostasis*' are applicable *only* to substances as opposed to their parts or their accidents, and '*persona*' is applicable only to substances that have rational specific nature. There is some intuitively appealing difference between individuals like Socrates and individuals like Socrates' right eyebrow or Socrates' patience; and the notions of *suppositum* and *hypostasis* are designed just to express this difference (a metaphysical *theory* of this difference is one of the most developed and complex areas of scholastic metaphysics).[26] The second point is that both Socrates and *his humanity* are individuals; there is, however – according to the scholastic metaphysics of substance – a special sort of difference between Socrates and his humanity; the notions of *suppositum* and *hypostasis* are designed to express this difference, too: Socrates is a *suppositum* and a *hypostasis*, but his humanity is neither of them. The third point is that while the concepts of individuality, particularity, singularity, numerical unity and thisness are all related primarily to the context of *counting*, the notions of *suppositum*, *hypostasis* and *persona* are not. Note that, in terms of Lowe's ontological square, the relationship between Socrates and his humanity is neither instantiation nor exemplification (since we are interested here in a particular instance of humanity in Socrates); moreover, Socrates is not characterised by his humanity, since humanity is a substantial universal and Socrates' humanity is not his mode.

The philosophical notions of *suppositum*, *hypostasis* and *persona* stem basically from thinking about the Holy Trinity and the Incarnation, both in the dogmatic formulas and in theology. In the Holy Trinity one and the same individual nature of God belongs to three distinct Persons who are one and the same God because they have one and the same individual nature of God. In Christ His divine person is distinct from the individual humanity assumed by Him, and this humanity in turn is distinct from His nature of God; moreover, this individual humanity is *not* a *suppositum* distinct from the Divine *suppositum*.[27] There are, moreover, some theses of metaphysics and theology showing some crucial relationship between a *suppositum* and its instance of its nature; they state, for example, that it is impossible for a created *suppositum* of human nature to have

---

26 See e.g. Aquinas 1980, *In Sent.* III, d. 6, q. 1, art. 1a; *S. th.* I, q. 29, art. 1–2; *In Sent.* I, d. 23, art. 1.
27 Godfrey of Fontaines 1914, *Quodl.* 7, q. 5, 301: "Filius Dei assumpsit in unitate suppositi aeterni naturam humanam, non autem hominem; unde etiam illi naturae non convenit ratio suppositi creati".

two distinct human natures, and that it is impossible for two created *supposita* of human nature to have one and the same individual instance of human nature.

In this study I focus on the issue of individuality or numerical unity as opposed to the problems of *suppositum*, *hypostasis* and *persona*. The scholastic problem of individuation concerns almost exclusively individuality as opposed to the issue of *suppositum*.[28] I make only some remarks concerning *suppositum* in 8.5.

1.3 The Importance of the Scholastic Problem of Individuation

There are at least six reasons that show the importance of the scholastic problem of individuation.

(i) Individuality or singleness is a fundamental feature of things. It is worth noting in particular that we have a good understanding of some domain of reality as far as we are able to single out individual entities in this area: for example, in the domain of human actions – individual actions and decisions, in the domain of physical objects – individual substances, and so on. So the question concerning the ground of individuality and in general the way in which it belongs to things is particularly important in metaphysics.

(ii) Individuality is closely related to many other features of reality that are fundamental from a metaphysical point of view. To begin with, individuality is a sort of unity and one may ask about its relationship to other sorts of unity. Moreover, individuality is closely related to identity and distinction, number and plurality, and to various aspects of the part–whole relation. Finally, individuality is closely connected with universality and the problem of universals.

---

[28] A systematic distinction between the issues of individuality and of *suppositum* is to be found e.g. in Godfrey of Fontaines (1914, *Quodl.* 7, q. 5, 300–301); he formulates the problem of individuation in the following way: "Quaerere autem quid addit suppositum sic acceptum ad naturam sic acceptam is quaerere de causa individuationis sive quid addit singulare super commune, scilicet haec humanitas super humanitatem, hic homo super hominem, haec albedo super albedinem, hoc album super album"; by contrast, the proper problem of *suppositum* is "utrum homo addat aliquid supra humanitatem et hic homo super hanc humanitatem et quid sit illud". Similarly Suárez who devotes the fifth *Metaphysical Disputation* to the problem of individuation, and the thirty fourth one to the problems of *suppositum* (see in particular 1866, *Disp. met.* 34, sect. 2, 1–3); he says that the problem of *suppositum* concerns the relationship between a man, say Peter, and his humanity ("quomodo distinguatur hic homo Petrus ab hac humanitate"). For Godfrey see also Wippel 1981, 225–254. By contrast, the distinction seems to be rather neglected in the contemporary literature on individuation; for example, Gracia does not mention it in his surveys of questions concerning individuality in the broad sense.

(iii) A metaphysical study of individuality is closely related to various fundamental problems of logic and epistemology indicated above.

(iv) The scholastic discussion of individuation parallels in many important ways some debates in contemporary analytical metaphysics, for example: the Fregean distinction of *Gegenstand* and *Begriff* and some analogies between functions and *Begriffe*; Fregean and non-Fregean metaphysics of number; saturatedness and unsaturatedness in the Fregean sense; the problem of the criteria of identity and Geach's relative identity thesis; the issue of sortal terms; Bergmann's bare particular metaphysics; various forms of haecceitism and anti-haecceitism; metaphysics of tropes; Lowe's ontological square and the four-category ontology.[29] Some of these parallels are investigated more thoroughly in the present study.

(v) A sound theory of individuation is a sort of preparation for a theory of *persons* both in philosophy and in theology. There is a number of questions within metaphysics of persons that are closely related to the issue of individuation (although they are not discussed here in detail). They concern, for example, the relationship between a person and its soul, between a person and its body (and the way in which a body is a body *of* some person), or the problem of personal identity.

(vi) Scholastic metaphysics in general offers a unique combination of precision in philosophy, responsibility in the treatment of fundamental questions, sensitivity to various intuitions, and plurality of standpoints taken into consideration. Moreover, its impact on the later philosophy is difficult to overestimate.[30] As King says, the result of the scholastic debate on individuation "was a thorough and deep understanding of the problems and puzzles surrounding individuality and individuation, unsurpassed in the history of philosophy".[31]

1.4 A Brief Historical Survey of the Scholastic Debate on Individuation

According to Gracia, there are five main stages of the debate on individuation in scholasticism: (i) a stage of absorption (1150–1225); (ii) a stage of consolidation

---

29 There has been a number of very important attempts to integrate the study of the scholastic debate on individuation with contemporary metaphysics; see, for example, Geach 1961, Anscombe 1981a, Gracia 1988, Park 1990, Park 1996, Oderberg 2002.
30 See e.g. McCullough 1996.
31 See King 2000, 159.

(1225–1275); (iii) a stage of maturity (1275–1350), when the problem of individuation becomes, according to Gracia, one of the most central problems of philosophy; (iv) a stage of decline (1350–1450) and (v) a stage of rebirth during the so-called second scholasticism mainly in Italy and on the Iberian Peninsula (1450–1650).³²

Stages (iii) and (v) are the most natural subject of more systematic interest in the scholastic debate on individuation. The issue of individuation is discussed at length in distinct questions devoted to it (by contrast, even in Aquinas remarks concerning individuation occur in questions devoted to other topics, either philosophical or theological). So we find a great number of *quodlibeta*, questions within the *Sentences* commentaries and within XVIth/XVIIth century course-books of philosophy or theology devoted directly and entirely to the problem of principles of individuation³³.

Typically questions devoted to the problem of principle of individuation consider various solutions currently being discussed and examine in detail the arguments in favour of them. What emerges from discussing the solutions and arguments for them is the widely recognised set of canonical solutions that prove in the course of the discussion to be serious enough to be taken into account by anyone who enters the debate; and the widely recognised set of canonical arguments for each of the solutions – the arguments that prove deep and interesting enough to be analysed and investigated by anyone who enters the debate. It seems that these widely recognised sets of canonical solutions and arguments have remained a common background for the debate for many years; and various standpoints in the debate are identifiable only against this common background.

Another important thing to note is that in stages (ii)–(v) there is wide agreement between scholastic authors that a theory of accidental individuation should be rejected *a limine*. According to this rejected solution it is a unique complex of accidents of a thing that accounts for the individuality of that thing and its distinction from other individuals. In some sense it is the rejection of this sort of solution that shows that there is something serious about the problem of individuation. There are various reasons for rejecting that view. For example, it is incompatible with the Aristotelian view of priority of substance (and not the accidents).³⁴ It seems clear that, as Geach puts it, two coins may differ in some accidental features *because* they are distinct coins, so these differences of accidents

---

32 See Gracia 1994d, 545–549 and Gracia 1991.
33 For a survey of quodlibetal questions concerning individuation in the years 1277–1320 see Pickavé 2007.
34 See, for example, Fonseca 1615, lib. V, c. 6, q. 1.

presuppose the distinction of coins and cannot be the ground for it.[35] Finally, note that when we are going to count something – coins or houses – what we have to know is what is to be counted as a single coin or house; and to settle the question what should count as a single coin or house we are not interested at all in the accidental differences between coins or houses.

1.5 The Method of the Study

The main aim of this study is a *systematic* presentation of the scholastic debate showing the core of the problem of individuation and providing some classification and evaluation of its various solutions; in particular, I focus on the issue of self-individuation: the question whether there is something that is self-individuated or individual by itself, what it is, and what is the difference between things that are individual by themselves and those that are not. Focusing on the issue of self-individuation and its rejection, I hope, offers some unifying perspective on the debate as a whole and may shed some light on contemporary debates on individuation and help to integrate the old debate with contemporary ones.

Now this type of systematic presentation of the scholastic debate poses at least three serious problems.

(i) The scholastic debate on individuation is motivated mainly by theological investigations, and, more precisely, by the most advanced and the most subtle theological doctrines of the Trinity and the Incarnation. For example, it is not just an accidental circumstance that most relevant remarks of Aquinas concerning individuation are to be found in his strictly theological questions. Geach insists that "some of the logical distinctions he finds it necessary to draw, in e.g. his treatises on the Trinity and the Incarnation, are of an importance that could hardly be exaggerated"[36]. This suggests clearly that a full account of the scholastic debate on individuality requires a good understanding of the most sophisticated theological doctrines of the period. The discussion of *individuality*, however, can be distinguished from the discussion of *suppositum*; the former, unlike the latter, is clearly a philosophical enterprise; more generally, there is a purely philosophical strand in the debate concerning individuality in a broad sense. So in this study I confine myself to these purely philosophical problems, and I add some remarks concerning the problem of *suppositum* only in 8.5.

---

35 Geach 1961, 73.
36 Geach 1972, 300.

(ii) The scholastic debate on individuation comprises a great number of relatively independent problems, and each of them demands a closer philosophical scrutiny; in other words, from a systematic point of view the debate is extremely rich and complex, and may even seem to be rather muddled. This suggests that the best strategy to learn something from the debate would be a fine-grained individuation (in the epistemic sense) of distinct metaphysical problems and then focusing on just one of them; by contrast, any attempt to present the whole debate on individuation is bound to be vague and futile. I think, however, that in some important respect it is the debate and the problem *as a whole* that sheds very important light on the details. I think, moreover, that the method of the scholastic debate makes it possible to grasp this whole without being vague or futile. At any rate, it is the problem of principles of individuation that is singled out as the main topic of a great number of scholastic texts; so if we grant the scholastic authors the ability to single out philosophical problems in a sound way, this suggests strongly that the problem of principles of individuation might be discussed in general without being futile or vague. So instead of a preliminary taxonomy and selection of distinct questions I focus here on the problem of principles of individuation sketched in 1.1.

(iii) From a historical point of view, on the other hand, there is a striking plurality of views and standpoints; Olivi, quoted by the contemporary editors of Scotus's work on individuation, says that there is an infinite muddle of opinions, *infinita silva opinionum*, concerning principles of individuation.[37] Moreover, many relevant texts concerning individuation have still not been edited. So, Gracia claims, "no single work could hope to discuss fully all the figures involved in the scholastic controversies surrounding individuation". More generally, he claims that "it is difficult enough to try to understand and present a clear exposition of the thought on this issue of any major scholastic figure such as Thomas Aquinas or Duns Scotus, let alone attempt to do so with several of them". This suggests that the best way is either to focus on a single author or even a single text concerning principles of individuation, or to prepare an anthology of papers that focuses on single authors or texts. The latter poses a problem of selection: so, Gracia says, although the choice of *major* scholastic authors was not difficult, the choices concerning minor ones were difficult[38]. It turns out, however, that the very selection of major authors is debatable. For example, it was objected by Rega Wood that the anthology passes over the work of Richard Rufus of Cornwall who

---

37 Scotus 1982, 229.
38 Gracia 1994a, x.

played a key role in the rejection of the theories of accidental individuation[39]. To sum up, it seems that from a historical point of view it is just impossible to give any reliable and non-trivial analysis of the scholastic debate on the principles of individuation as a whole.

This, I think, is a serious objection. It seems to me, however, that it underestimates the role of the canonical sets of solutions to the problem of individuation. These sets have been widely recognised by all participants of the debate since the beginning of the fourteenth century; they are the basis for the identification of the very problem of individuation that is discussed. The standpoints in the debate (the solutions to that problem) are identifiable only within this common context. Moreover, Scotus, whose editors add Olivi's statement concerning the muddle of infinitely many opinions (*infinita silva opinionum*) in a footnote to his text, focuses on just *six* main opinions, and he does not seem to be radically selective in doing that.

The point is that these commonly recognised sets of solutions and arguments are easily identifiable in most of the scholastic texts concerning individuation. So to understand this common context or background is to grasp the very problem of individuation and the spectrum of its plausible solutions in the scholastic debate. In this way one grasps the outline of the debate as a whole. Admittedly, there are many slightly different versions of one and the same standpoint, and there are various formulations of the main arguments; some details of them may vary, and some of these differences may prove to be fundamental from a systematic point of view. I think, however, that it is just a general understanding of the problem and the spectrum of its possible solutions that paves the way for detailed analyses of various standpoints.

So the aim of the present study is to sketch these sets of canonical solutions to the problem and of canonical arguments for them, and in this way to give an outline of the core of the problem and of the debate, focusing on just one of the central issues: various ways of accepting and rejecting the idea of self-individuation, being individual *by itself*. This, I think, offers some interesting unifying perspective on the debate and opens the way for an integration of the scholastic debate with contemporary metaphysics.

The seven subsequent chapters of the study are devoted respectively to the seven main answers to the question of principles of individuation; these answers are singled out according to what they point at as a principle of individuation:

---

39 Wood 1996, 113.

(i)   the whole entity of an individual (*tota entitas*) (the nominalistic standpoint embraced also by Suárez and Lebniz);
(ii) a special type of entity called *haecceitas* (the Scotistic standpoint);
(iii) the form of an individual (the standpoint of Peter of Auvergne and Godfrey of Fontaines);
(iv) the subject of an accident (the Thomistic standpoint);
(v)   prime matter (the Thomistic standpoint);
(vi) dimensive quantity or extension (the Thomistic standpoint);
(vii) actual existence (perhaps Henry of Ghent and some contemporary versions of Thomism).[40]

Some of these seven answers are fundamentally different and mutually exclusive: they differ not only as to what is a principle of individuation; their disagreement concerns also what individuality should be ascribed to and in what way. Some of the seven answers, on the other hand, are not mutually exclusive; instead they show distinct principles responsible for distinct aspects of individuality.

As far as the issue of self-individuation is concerned, (i) claims that everything is necessarily self-individuated in the strong sense: there can be no distinction whatsoever between what is individual and what makes it individual. This claim poses some problems that are solved by assigning a crucial role to postulated simple entities. All the other answers reject the universal self-individuation. There are, however, two utterly distinct ways of rejecting it, namely the Scotistic one ((ii)), and the Thomistic one ((iii)–(vi)). The former is based on the general opposition of natures and haecceities and claims a very special sort of distinction, within any particular instance of a nature, between individuality of that instance and the nature itself. On the one hand, it insists that some sorts of entities do owe their individuality to something distinct from them – although the sort of distinction must be a very weak one, and it is impossible to owe one's individuality to a distinct individual; on the other hand, it admits that haecceities are self-individuated in a way in which, according to nominalism, everything is necessarily self-individuated. The Thomistic strategy of rejecting universal self-individuation considers individuality in the context of forms and matter as well as subjects and

---

40 These principles are often discussed article by article in the scholastic questions concerning principles of individuation; the titles of the articles have often the form 'Whether P is a (the) principle of individuation?'. This is the way in which many scholastic treatments of principles of individuation are composed (for instructive examples see the individuation questions of Scotus, Fonseca or Suárez).

accidents. On the one hand, it claims that some sorts of entities owe their individuality to distinct individuals (for example, that accidents owe their individuality to their subjects). On the other hand, it claims that dimensive quantity is self-individuated and that matter enjoys a sort of primitive noninstantiability, and that both the self-individuation of quantity and the noninstantiability of matter are sources of individuality of things that are not self-individuated. Moreover, the Thomistic strategy assigns some special sort of simplicity (not having parts) to forms which is closely related to their role as individuating factors. The point, however, is that both the self-individuation of quantity and the noninstantiability of matter are utterly different from the nominalistic or Scotistic primitive individuality, and the simplicity of forms in the Thomistic theory is utterly different from the simplicity of the simple entities postulated by nominalism. So in general the main issue discussed here is the problem of various relationships between individuality and natures, form and matter, subjects, and accidents. Some of them are claimed to be self-individuated in some ways, some of them are claimed to be individuated, in a number of utterly distinct ways, by something distinct from them.

To go into the details of the issue, in the case of each of the seven main answers I present its typical formulations known from the history of philosophy and its various senses distinguished from a more systematic point of view. Then I focus on the main arguments in favour of the answer; these are extracted mainly from the most representative texts defending that answer. The arguments are analysed from a systematic rather than an exegetic point of view: my main aim is to show whether they are correct and what precisely they prove. In some cases the answers or solutions are confronted with some standpoints in contemporary metaphysics, as far as it helps to shed some light on the problem. In particular, I explore some aspects of Geach's suggestion that the Thomistic metaphysics of natures and individuals is closely akin, in some key respects, to the Fregean metaphysics of *Begriff* and *Gegenstand*.

In analyses of the arguments I take for granted some fundamental metaphysical theses of scholastic Aristotelianism, in particular concerning the distinction of substances and accidents or matter and forms. Some of them are still defended within various strands of contemporary metaphysics, for example in Lowe's four category ontology; some of them, by contrast, are not widely accepted today. It would be impossible, however, to argue here in favour of them. So I take them for granted or offer only a brief sketch of the argument and focus on the role they play in the theories of individuation.

For each of the main answers there is also the set of traditional objections raised against it, and the set of standard ways of responding to those objections;

in some cases I consider in some detail these objections and responses, but I do not try to offer any comprehensive treatments of those doubts or objections. My main focus is on the arguments *for* the seven main answers.

Finally, I focus on the views and arguments concerning the individuality of *material* substances and their accidents, leaving aside the question of the individuality of *immaterial* substances, although both for the scholastic theologians and, for example, for Leibniz's metaphysics of substance it is the latter question that plays a prominent role. I hope to show that the individuality of material substances is closely related to their materiality, and that this is a reason to expect that the problem of the individuation of immaterial substances requires a distinct investigation.

From a historical point of view, the seven answers considered in this study are to be found in the texts from the years 1250–1325; these texts constitute the first group of sources used here. The other group of scholastic sources consists of the texts of Renaissance and early modern scholasticism. The main advantage of the latter group is that they present various standpoints in the debate against some historical and systematic background.

In the concluding remarks I sketch what I take to be a sound answer to the question of principles of individuation; it is a sort of Thomistic standpoint that may be summarized as follows. (i) *Individuation pluralism*: the nature of individuality varies from one type of entity to another; in particular, the ways in which individuality belongs to material substances, immaterial substances, accidents, matter, and forms, are fundamentally different. (ii) *The individuation of accidents*: The sources of the individuality of accidents are their subjects (in one of the important senses of 'subject'), although there is a group of accidents (namely some geometrical accidents) that are self-individuated in an important sense. (iii) *The individuation of material substances*: Individuality of material substances depends in various ways on their forms, their matter and their extension; what makes the latter two sources of individuality is that matter enjoys a sort of primitive noninstantiability, and quantity is self-individuated in an important sense. I hope to outline the main ideas and intuitions of such a doctrine here, but it is clear that the details of the picture still remain to be worked out.

2 *Entitas*. Nominalism and Self-Individuation

2.1 Main Nominalistic Theses

By *nominalism* in the theory of individuation I mean the following thesis:

> **(The Strong Self-Individuation Thesis)** There is no real distinction between something that is single or individual (*quod individuatur*) and what makes it single or individual (*quo individuatur*) – that is, between what is individual and its principle of individuation.

In other words, the Strong Self-Individuation Thesis states that anything that is individual is *self-individuated* in some strong sense; what is strong about this sense is just the rejection of any real or mind-independent distinction between what is individual and what makes it individual.

The Strong Self-Individuation Thesis has been expressed in various ways, for example: "any individual is individual by itself" (*omne individuum individuatur per se ipsum*), "any individual is individual in virtue of its whole entity" (*omne individuum sua tota entitate individuatur*), or "whatever is individual is individual not by something added to it, but just by itself" (*quidquid est individuum, per nihil additum est individuum, sed seipso*).

The Strong Self-Individuation Thesis can be ascribed to the Dominican John of Naples, to Wilhelm Ockham, Peter Auriol, John Buridan, Francisco Suárez, and Leibniz.[1]

In a contemporary context: having introduced the metaphysical notion of individuation ("what 'individuates' an object [...] is whatever it is that makes it the single object that it is") Lowe says that some philosophers may find this notion strange just because, as Bishop Butler says, "Everything is what it is and not another thing", and it may seem that there is no point in asking what makes an object the very object it is.[2] These philosophers, I think, would embrace the Strong Self-Individuation Thesis.[3]

---

[1] John of Naples 1951, *Quodl.* 3, q. 5, 154, 7–8 and *Quodl.* 7, q. 6, 161, 14–15; Ockham 1970, *In Sent.* I, d. 2, q. 6, 196,2–3; Peter Auriol 1605, *In Sent.* II, d.9, q.3; Suárez 1866, *Disp. met.* V, sect. 6, 1; Leibniz 1930, *De principio individui*, §4.

[2] Lowe 2005, 75.

[3] Denkel (1991, 213) distinguishes between Leibnizian and Aristotelian types of principles of individuation, the latter, as opposed to the former, being some selected aspects of individuals. Nominalism in the sense relevant here is just opting for a Leibnizian type of the principle of individuation.

It may be useful also to compare the Strong Self-Individuation Thesis (or what I call nominalism here) with two standpoints that Gracia calls *Essential Nominalism* and *Derivative Nominalism*. The former holds that everything is essentially individual or individual by itself (which Gracia suggests to be just an equivalent formulation), and the latter claims everything is individual, but (at least in some cases) in a derivative way[4]. On the one hand, it seems to me that, *pace* Gracia, there is a difference between Essential Nominalism and the Strong Self-Individuation Thesis. For example, Socrates is *essentially* a man, but, at least within scholastic metaphysics, what makes him a man (his essence or his substantial form) is in a way distinct from him; so it seems that to be essentially individual does not entail being self-individuated in the strong sense. On the other hand, the Strong Self-Individuation Thesis is just the negation of Derivative Nominalism. In other words, the perspective of self-individuation adopted here seems to me to be different from the one adopted in Gracia.

The Strong Self-Individuation Thesis is usually accompanied by another one:

(The Individuality Thesis) Everything that exists is individual.

The Strong Self-Individuation Thesis and the Individuality Thesis together imply that everything that exists is individual just by itself.

Gracia holds the Individuality Thesis to be the main thesis of nominalism in a wide sense of the term[5]. It is worth noting, however, that the Individuality Thesis is not peculiar to nominalism in any sense of the term; it is embraced by many authors rejecting the Strong Self-Individuation Thesis and not being nominalists in any traditional sense of the term (for example, both by Scotists and by Thomists). On the other hand, there is some way of arguing in favour of the Individuality Thesis which is specific to nominalism.

There is also another thesis closely related to the Strong Self-Individuation Thesis, namely that

> Anything that constitutes a thing being its cause in a broad sense, either internal (like matter or form) or external (like efficient or final cause), does constitute the individuality of that thing or makes it individual.

---

[4] Gracia 1988, 70–82, in particular: "the most extreme interpretation of the general nominalist formulation holds that everything that exists is *essentially* individual or, as others prefer to put it, individual by itself" (70).
[5] Gracia 1988, 69.

It may be found, for example, in John of Naples or Wilhelm Ockham.[6] The fundamental idea of this thesis is the following: there is nothing in a thing that is responsible for the individuality of the thing – as opposed to something that is responsible for some other features of the thing but *not* for its individuality. There is no distinct principle of *individuality* of a thing as opposed to the principles of the other features of the thing.

So here I focus on an analysis of the Strong Self-Individuation Thesis which seems most specific for various forms of nominalism, and on the nominalistic arguments for the Individuality Thesis.

It is sometimes said that according to nominalism there is simply *no* principle of individuation at all.[7] This idea may have its roots in some remarks by authors embracing the Strong Self-Individuation Thesis; as a matter of fact, they tend to say that one should not look for a principle of individuation or that looking for a principle of individuation is just looking for nothing; or they say that as far as a principle of individuation is concerned there is no question to be asked: *questio nulla est*.[8] I think, however, that the Strong Self-Individuation Thesis clearly points at a principle of individuation and does not deny the existence of such a principle. So what the nominalistic claims adduced above mean is precisely that as far as the principles of individuation are concerned, there is nothing to be investigated, because they are obvious at once; or maybe that there is no principle of individuation in some special sense which they may ascribe to their adversaries. There is also another important reason for interpreting the nominalist claims in this way: it is a conceivable view that the question "What makes that apple something individual or single?" (as opposed to the question "What makes that apple red?") is just a sort of misunderstanding. In such a view there would

---

6 See e.g. John of Naples 1951, *Quodl.* 3, q. 5, 154,8–9; 155,1–17; *Quodl.* 7, q. 6, 161,16–18; 163,15–44; Ockham 1970, *In Sent.* I, d. 2, q. 6, 197,16.

7 See e.g. Maurer 1994, 373 and 389; in a weaker version King 1994b, 397 ("Buridan holds that no principle or cause accounts for the individuality of the individual, or at least no principle or cause other than the very individual itself"). In a similar vein, Gracia claims that according to Ockham there is no room for individuation Gracia 1994c, 500; this, I think, reflects just the way Gracia conceives of 'individuation'. In 1984, 38 he suggests that the issue of a principle of individuation arises only when there are universals that "in some way must undergo a process or change in order to become individual". More generally, he suggests (1988, 18–19) that in nominalistic ontologies there is no room for *principles* of individuation, although there is a possibility of an account of individuality providing sufficient and necessary conditions for being individual; I think, however, that in the sense of 'a principle of individuation' sketched here even nominalists may be interested in principles of individuation.

8 See John of Naples 1951, *Quodl.* 3, q. 5, 154,9–10; *Quodl.* 7, q. 6, 162,39–40; Ockham 1970, *In Sent.* I, d. 2, q. 6, 191,15–16; Peter Auriol 1605, *In Sent.* II, d. 9, q. 3.

be *no* principle of individuation in the sense in which there is a principle of being red.[9] The point is, however, that no scholastic nominalist I know accepts such a view. They think rather that individuality or singleness does have its principle or ground in the thing itself, and it is the very thing itself and not anything distinct from it.

It is also sometimes said that the nominalistic theses about individuation are in some way derived from the nominalistic views concerning universals, or, in other words, concerning the sense in which it is true that redness is some kind of colour or something one that has many instances.[10] Admittedly, some arguments in favour of the nominalistic theses are based on premises concerning universals. In general, however, I think that the theses concerning individuality are more basic than the ones concerning universals in the sense that being individual or single is a feature more fundamental than being a universal; and a theory of universals has to be based on some premises concerning individuality or singleness; authors who embrace the nominalistic theses do stress this primacy of individuality.

2.2 Standard Arguments for the Strong Self-Individuation Thesis

There are three main lines of argument in favour of the Strong Self-Individuation Thesis. The first one is based on the principle of convertibility of being and unity: *ens et unum convertuntur*. The second one – on the premise that individuality or singleness and related attributes belong to a thing *immediately* and not in virtue of something else than the very thing they belong to. The third line of argument is based on a rejection of all other (known) theories of individuation, and in particular of the Scotistic theory of individuation; many authors embracing nominalism (for example, Ockham and Auriol) argue in favour of it in the discussion with the Scotistic theory, and using the sophisticated terminology introduced by it.

Some ideas of the third line of argument will become clear in the presentation of the Scotus' standpoint (in chapter 3). Here I focus on the first two sorts of argument in favour of the Strong Self-Individuation Thesis (2.3 and 2.4), and then I present Ockham's argument for the Individuality Thesis which sheds much light on the nominalist idea of individuality or singleness (2.5). Finally (2.6) I present the main features of the nominalistic theory of individuation.

---

9 See e.g. Mulligan, Simons, Smith 1984, 301–302.
10 See e.g. Maurer 1994, 389.

2.3 Ens et Unum Convertuntur

The fundamental premise used (as Leibniz says) by all the authors embracing The Strong Self-Individuation Thesis is the Aristotelian principle that "unity does not add anything real to being" (*unum supra ens nihil addit reale*).[11] This principle, commonly accepted in scholasticism, expresses a deep interconnection between the predicates 'is a (sort of) being' and 'has a (sort of) unity'.

It is easy to see this interconnection by way of the following contrast. The predicates 'is red' and 'is square' express different things; moreover, if something falls under both, it falls under them in virtue of different things: under the first in virtue of its colour, under the other – in virtue of its shape. This is not the case with 'is a (sort of) being' and 'is a (sort of) unity'. The Polish nation is a different sort of being than a musical piece, and it is precisely because the former enjoys a different sort of unity than the latter. So one may concede that what makes the Polish nation something one makes it some sort of entity, and similarly in the case of the musical piece: what makes it something one makes it some sort of entity and *vice versa*. It is in just this sense that Aristotle says: "being and unity are the same and are one thing in the sense that they are implied in one another as principle and cause are"[12]. On the other hand, however, Aristotle states that the predicates 'is a sort of entity' and 'is a sort of unity' are not synonymic; they express distinct attributes of a thing[13] and in the very meaning of the predicates there is something that unity adds to entity: on the one hand it is being not divided internally (*indivisio*), on the other hand it is being divided or distinct from any other entity (*divisio*).[14] It is just because these attributes are negative ones that the addition here is of a very special sort, for what makes both of these negations true is precisely the same that makes true the predicate 'is a sort of entity'.[15]

All these claims are the most fundamental metaphysical truths and, at least in some interpretations, can hardly be objected; but the very *use* of these fundamental truths in the nominalistic arguments for the Strong Self-Individuation Thesis requires two additional important steps. Firstly, we are expected to admit that there is nothing in a being that (in some important way) makes it a being,

---

11 Leibniz 1930, *De principio*, §5: "unum supra ens nihil addit reale. Usi sunt hoc argumento omnes huius sententiae defensores". As for the earlier authors see e.g. John of Naples 1951, *Quodl.* 3, q. 5, 154,1–18; *Quodl.* 7, q. 6, 161, 9–43; Suárez 1866, *Disp. met.* V, sect. 6, 1.
12 Aristotle 1908, *Met.*1003b23–24 (trans. W.D. Ross); see also *Met.* 1003b31–32; 33–34.
13 Aristotle 1953, *Met.* 1003b24–25.
14 Sometimes only being undivided is mentioned in this context. See e.g. Aristotle 1953, *Met.* 1052b16; *Met.* 1016b3–5; Suárez 1866, *Disp. met.* IV, sect. 1, 2.
15 See e.g. Aquinas 1980, *De veritate*, q. 21, art. 1.

and is (in some important way) distinct from it. Secondly, we are to admit that the unity mentioned in these metaphysical truths can be understood as individuality or singleness. As for the latter, John of Naples makes it explicitly and states that "unity in general is numerical unity and individuality"[16]; this enables him to draw the conclusion that anything that makes a thing some sort of being makes it *individual*. Both of these steps, however, are far from being obvious, at least because the notion of unity is notoriously ambiguous: *unum dicitur multipliciter*[17], and we have good reasons to suspect that individuality or singleness is just one of the many senses of 'unity'.

2.4 The Immediacy of Individuality

Another argument for the Strong Self-Individuation Thesis rests on the premise that individuality or singleness is just the sort of attribute that belongs to its subject immediately (*immediate*), and henceforth it cannot belong to it in virtue of something distinct from the subject (*per aliquid aliud*).[18] Ockham adds here another similar premise: what is universal and not single or individual, cannot be made single or individual by something added to it.[19]

I go into the details of this line or argument in three steps; (i) first I contrast attributes belonging to their subjects immediately with ones that belong to their subjects in virtue of something else; (ii) then I consider in detail the nominalistic claim that *distinctness* and *difference* are attributes belonging to their subjects immediately; (iii) finally I conclude whether individuality belongs to its subject *immediately*.

2.4.1 The Immediacy of Attributes in General

A good example of an attribute belonging to its subject *not* immediately, but only in virtue of something else, is the redness of an apple. The apple is red in virtue of its redness inhering in it, and its redness is something distinct from the apple

---

16 John of Naples 1951, *Quodl.* 3, q. 5, 154,10–11; *Quodl.* 7, q. 6, 161,19–20.
17 Aristotle 1953 *Met.* 1052a15–19
18 Ockham 1970, *In Sent.* I, d. 2, q. 6, 196, 4–5: "singularitas immediate convenit illi cuius est, igitur non potest sibi convenire per aliquid aliud".
19 Ockham 1970, *In Sent.* I, d. 2, q. 6, 196,7–12.

itself. So what makes the apple red is not the apple itself, but instead some additional entity inhering in it, namely its redness. On the other hand we could say that the redness of the apple is an instance of this property not in virtue of something else, but rather just by itself or immediately. Moreover, we could say that this redness is a colour immediately and not in virtue of something else inhering in it.

What I have said in the last paragraph obviously may be challenged, and in fact was challenged, in many ways, both within the scholastic, broadly Aristotelian metaphysics and in the later history of metaphysics of properties; some of these challenges will be discussed here in due course. What I claim is that it captures, in an introductory way, some intuitions concerning the metaphysics of properties and the contrast between attributes belonging immediately to their subjects and ones that belong to their subjects in virtue of something else – and that these intuitions are elaborated in very sophisticated ways in various strands of scholastic metaphysics.

Among the attributes that belong to their subjects *immediately* the adherents of the Strong Self-Individuation Thesis list identity (*identitas*), unity (*unitas*) and being distinct from others (*distinctio*). Following the intuitions evoked by the adherents of the Strong Self-Individuation Thesis we may add to that list some other attributes belonging to things immediately. For example, something that is simple (*simplex*) is simple by itself and not in virtue of simplicity which is something distinct from it; and something that is complex (*compositum*) is a complex thing by itself and not by something distinct from it. The same may be said about transcendental relations (*respectus transcendentales*), for example the relation of a property of a thing to that thing (e.g. the relation of an apple's redness to that apple) or the relation of an emotion to its intentional object.[20] These examples, I think, show the sort of intuitions which are fundamental for the nominalistic arguments for the Strong Self-Individuation Thesis.

---

[20] For some introductory remarks concerning transcendental relations in scholasticism see e.g. Elders 1993, 267–268 and Bos 2003. The scholastic concept of transcendental relation is obviously close to the contemporary concepts of formal or thin relations (see for example Lowe 2004). It plays also a prominent role within the Thomistic theory of individuation, so I will return to it many times in due course (in particular in 5, 5.3, 5.5, and 7.8).

2.4.2 The Immediacy of Distinction

The nominalistic application of these intuitions to the case of distinction deserves more careful examination. As Ockham says, "each thing that is really distinct from another thing is distinct from it just by itself [*se ipso*] or by something intrinsic";[21] he adds that if a thing is distinct from some other thing just by itself [*se ipso*], it is also distinct just by itself [*se ipso*] from any other thing.[22] Buridan says that distinct things are distinct in virtue of their whole entities (*seipsis totis*) and that the distinction between individuals of the same species is not something added to those individuals; so Socrates's being distinct from Plato is not anything distinct from Socrates himself.[23] Finally, Suárez says that a thing cannot be distinct from some other thing in virtue of a third thing that is distinct from both: it is distinct from that thing just by itself (*per suammet entitatem*).[24] To sum up: if only *a* and *b* are really distinct, according to the nominalists the right answer to the question "What makes them distinct?" is always "they are distinct just by themselves".

There are two sorts of arguments for such a thesis about distinction. On the one hand, they evoke the obvious absurdity of some ways of rejecting that thesis; for example, Ockham points out that to say that "Sortes differs essentially from that donkey by Plato" is to say nothing.[25] On the other hand, there is a much more sophisticated *reductio ad absurdum*: if what makes *a* distinct from *b* is something distinct from *a* itself, we may ask in turn what makes *a* distinct from that thing; and if what makes it distinct from that thing is again distinct from *a* itself, we can again ask the same question about this distinction, and so *in infinitum*. To avoid an infinite regress here we have to acknowledge that there are things that are distinct from one another just by themselves, and Ockham and Buridan think that these things are just *a* and *b* from which we started our inquiry. Ockham says moreover that if *a* is distinct by itself from what makes it distinct from *b*, it is also distinct by itself from *b* and is not made distinct from *b* by anything else.[26]

---

21 Ockham 1970, *In Sent*. I, d. 2, q. 5, 154,9–11, and q. 6, 184,18–20.
22 Ockham 1970, *In Sent*. I, d. 2, q. 5, 155,16–18: "quando aliquid se ipso distinguitur realiter ab aliquo ibi extrinseco, eadem ratione distinguitur se ipso ab alio sibi extrinseco".
23 Buridan 1987, 169,15–16 and 162,19–21.
24 Suárez 1866, *Disp. met*. V, sect. 2, 13: "in universum enim existimo fieri non posse ut una res distinguatur realiter ab alia per aliam a se distinctam".
25 Ockham 1970, *In Sent*. I, d. 2, q. 5, 184,23: "nihil est dictu quod Sortes distinguitur ab isto asino per Platonem essentialiter".
26 Ockham 1970, *In Sent*. I, d. 2, q. 5, 155,6–12 and 16–20; Buridan 1588, *In Met*. V, q. 6, 30va: "si Sortes est diversus a Platone per diversitatem sibi additam: tunc illa diversitas est diversitas a

The significance of this line of argument lies in the fact that in the Aristotelian tradition answers to the question "What are *a* and *b* distinguished by?" were thoroughly investigated, and these investigations play a prominent role in the debate on principles of individuation. To introduce this tradition let us make three points.

(i) In many cases by telling in what respects *a* and *b* differ we do not reveal the source or basis of the distinction *a* and *b*. To use Geach's example: "Two pennies that coexist may in fact differ in all sorts of respects – one may be in mint condition and the other bent, defaced and stained – but these cannot be what makes the pennies two: if they were not in any case two pennies, they could not acquire these differences" (Geach 1961, 73). These differences may be helpful in *learning* that things are distinct, but they are not what things are distinguished by in a strong sense. And it is a strong sense of being distinguished by something that we are interested in here.

(ii) Aristotle distinguishes *heterotes* (*diversitas*), otherness, and *diafora* (*differentia*), difference, in the narrow sense; in the latter case things are distinguished *by* something in a special sense. Introducing this sense Aristotle says that "that which is different is different from some particular thing in some particular respect, so that there must be something identical whereby they differ"; this common thing they are distinguished by is expressed by a predicate F such that these things are different Fs (one is a *distinct* F from the other). In other words, the predicate F shows what it is a difference *of* that occurs between these things; there is a difference of F between them if one of them is a distinct F from the other. For example, man and god are distinct living beings, there is the difference *of* living being between them; by contrast, a man and his eyebrow, although they are not identical, do not differ *in that way*. Whiteness and redness are distinct colours, and there is the difference *of* colour between them; by contrast, whiteness and sheen do not differ in that way. Generally speaking, Aristotle says, the general term F expresses either a genus or a species ("and this identical thing is genus or species; for everything that differs, differs either in genus or in species").[27] In *Physics* he says that "a triangle differs from a triangle by the difference of a triangle, and therefore they are different triangles", but, we may add, a triangle does not differ in that way from a quadrangle.[28]

Sorte et Sortes diversus ab alia et tunc: vel Sortes et illa diversitas sunt abinvicem diversi seipsis vel per aliam diversitatem: si seipsis pari ratione standum erat in primis. Et si hoc fit per aliam diversitatem procederetur de illa ut prius: et sic in infinitum: quod est inconveniens".

27 Aristotle 1908, *Met.* 1054b26–28 (trans. D. Ross).
28 Aristotle 1983, *Phys.* 224a7–8 (trans. E. Hussey).

The general term F expresses what the distinct things have *in common*. Whiteness and redness are distinct colours, and colour is both something that they have in common *and* something they are distinguished or differ by; both are colours, but the point is that they are *distinct* colours. To grasp this peculiarity is to grasp the nature of general terms that have plural forms and occur in contexts like '*different* Fs'.

Here the question "What are a and b distinguished by?" is a question about the sort of difference between them: what it is the difference *of*. Interestingly, it is also a question about what they have in common in the sense indicated above. It is also clear that it is possible that a is distinguished from b by something by which it is *not* distinguished from c; for example, whiteness is distinguished from redness by something by which it is not distinguished from man.

(iii) The sense of being distinguished *by* something I have sketched is also associated with some narrow sense of being distinguished *by itself* (*se ipso differre*). In this narrow sense these things are distinguished by themselves which are distinct in a primitive way (*primo diversa*): there is no predicate F for them meeting the conditions sketched in (ii). For example, *summa genera* are distinct in this way. I will return to the issue of things distinct in a primitive way (*primo diversa*) many times in due course (3.5, 3.7, 3.8, 7.4).

It seems that there are at least four theses of the Aristotelian doctrine of *diafora* that are incompatible with the nominalistic doctrine of the immediacy of distinction. (*a*) The answers to the question what are things distinguished by, are deeply different in different cases. (*b*) What a thing is distinguished from one thing by, may be not what the same thing is distinguished by from some other thing. (*c*) There is a contrast between things that are distinct in a primitive way (*primo diversa*) and things that are *not* distinct in that way. (*d*) The difference of whiteness and redness is not only the difference *of whiteness* (from redness) and the difference *of redness* (from whiteness), but also the difference *of colour*; the very sense of the genitive form 'the difference *of*' is utterly different in the latter case and the former ones.

This does not necessarily mean that distinction or differences do not belong to their subjects *immediately* in some important sense; but it does show, I think, that if there is such an important sense of *belonging immediately* to a subject, it has to be investigated more carefully than it was investigated by the nominalists.

2.4.3 The Immediacy of Individuality

The contrast (sketched in 2.4.1) between attributes that belong to their subjects *immediately* and those that do not may make one think that individuality is an obvious candidate for an attribute that belongs immediately to its subject. It is worth noting, however, that individuality belongs to various subjects in various ways, and some of these ways may not be "immediate", or be "immediate" in a sense that needs investigation. In a way, the immediacy of individuality poses problems similar to those posed by the immediacy of differences. Two points are of special importance here.

(i) Consider the Royal Sigismund Bell in Wawel Cathedral in Cracow. It is a single or individual bell; but all of the material that makes up the Sigismund Bell is also a single or individual bell. Should we claim that the material of the bell is an individual bell just by itself, and there is nothing distinct from it that *makes* it a single bell? To some extent the answer here depends on what you think about material constitution and identity. But it seems obvious, at least within Aristotelian metaphysics, that the material is *not* a bell just by itself, and there is something *distinct* from it that makes it a bell: it is a form in the Aristotelian sense (which in the bell's case is its shape). It is also obvious that the material didn't used to be a single bell when it was not a bell at all; this seems to imply that it is not a single bell in and of itself, but rather something else makes it a single bell. In other words, being a single bell belongs to the material in a way which is utterly different from the way in which it belongs to the Sigismund Bell; and clearly it does *not* belong to it immediately. So there is something that is a single bell, but is not a single bell *by itself*.

I suppose the nominalist would respond to this sort of reasoning by claiming that when the material is a single bell, it consists in its being single and being a bell; and when the same material is not a single bell, it is not a bell, but it is still single. This sort of analysis of being a single bell (treating 'single' as a predicative and not an attributive adjective), however, is at least controversial and much less convincing than the general idea that individuality is an immediately belonging attribute (note for example that the material may become *two* bells instead of one single bell[29]).

(ii) It seems plausible that when we say that The Sigismund Bell (or the stuff it is composed of) is an individual bell or a single bell, what we ascribe to it is not just being individual or single, but being an individual or single *bell* – as opposed

---

[29] This sort of one-many and many-one changes is given much attention in Brower (2014, 64–66); I think it is very important for various issues related to individuation (see e.g. 6.2, 7.3, 8.3).

to, for example, being a single or individual piece of bronze. As I have said in the Introduction, 'individual', like 'single', seems primarily an attributive adjective. Clearly what is a single bell is typically *not* a single piece of bronze. So we can distinguish the individuality or singleness of *bells* and the individuality or singleness of pieces of bronze, and the genitive 'the singleness/individuality *of*' here has a different meaning than it has in 'the individuality of The Sigismund Bell', and that different meaning seems very important for understanding individuality and requires closer consideration.

2.5 The Individuality Thesis and Simple Entities in Nominalism

The way in which Ockham argues for the Individuality Thesis deserves closer scrutiny; it sheds much light on the issues of the immediacy of differences discussed in 2.4.2 and 2.4.3.

There are two versions of Ockham's argument for the Individuality Thesis.

{*} Anything that exists in extramental reality is either simple (*simplex*) or complex (*compositum*). If it is simple, it does not contain a plurality of things and henceforth is single or numerically one. Why? Because, Ockham argues, such a thing together with another thing similar to it are *two*, so each of them is single or individual. On the other hand, if the thing is complex, we arrive at some definite number of its parts, so each of these parts will be single or individual; in this case either their totality will be single, or it will be a loose manifold of things.[30]

{**} Take a thing that is supposed not to be single or individual; now it either contains a plurality of things or not. If the latter, we take one thing similar to it and really distinct from it; they are in some number which is just 2; so each of them is single or individual. If the former, it contains a finite number of things, so each of them will be single or individual.[31]

---

[30] Ockham 1970, *In Sent.* I, d. 2, q. 6, 196,13–22: "omnis res extra animam est realiter singularis et una numero, quia omnis res extra animam vel est simplex vel composita. Si it simplex, non includit multas res; sed omnis res non includens multas res est una numero, quia omnis talis res et una alia res consimilis praecise sunt duae res; igitur utraque illarum est una numero, igitur omnis res simplex est una numero. Si sit composita, tandem oportet devenire ad certum numerum partium, et per consequens quaelibet illarum partium erit una numero, et per consequens totum compositum ex eis erit unum numero vel erit unum aggregatione".

[31] *Ibidem*, 196,23–197,7: "Et hoc etiam potest argui sub ista forma: accipio illam rem quam non ponis rem singularem et quaero: aut includit plures res aut non. Si non, accipio unam consimi-

At least three aspects of these arguments are worth noting.

(i) One of the main premises of the argument is that if there is some *number* of things somewhere, there must be single/individual things in that number. A closely related premise is that if *a* and *b* are two, then both *a* and *b* are single. Obviously these premises express an important and true observation: number occurs only where something is single. It should be noted, however, that we count not only individuals, but also kinds of something: they are in some number, but they are not individual or single in a strong sense. It is not clear how to square this fact with the arguments {*} and {**}.

(ii) Another important premise of the argument is that things that are distinct are always in some number; and the related premise is that if *a* and *b* are really distinct *simple* things, then they are in number 2. These premises are far from being obvious. There has been a long tradition, from Aristotle to Frege and Geach, maintaining that the real distinction is not enough for being in number. For example, in what number are the right hand and the left thumb, or a single rose and a bunch of roses? The point is that in cases such as these various answers might be right, but it always has to be made clear *what* exactly are we to count. We made it clear giving some sortal term F under which all these things fall: then we can count Fs and determine the number of Fs; it is not enough to say that we are interested in the number of *those things*, namely the hand and the thumb. More generally, counting things requires always giving some general term F under which all of them fall and which the number we look for is the number *of*, and it cannot be just a dummy predicate like 'thing'. If there is not such a general term or *common measure* in some case, then in that case distinct things are not in any number at all.[32] Nothing like this is mentioned in the arguments {*} and {**}. Moreover, discussing what would be a key example of the impossibility of being

---

lem distinctam realiter et arguo sic: istae res sunt distinctae realiter et non sunt in numero infinito, igitur in numero finito, et non nisi in dualitate, manifestum est; igitur sunt hic praecise duae, et per consequens utraque illarum erit una numero. Si autem includit plures res et non infinitas, igitur finitas, et per consequens est ibi numerus rerum, et ita quaelibet illarum inclusarum erit una numero et singularis".

32 See e.g. Aristotle 1908, *Met.* 1088a8–11: "The measure must always be some identical thing predicable of all the things it measures, e.g. if the things are horses, the measure is 'horse', and if they are men, 'man'. If they are a man, a horse, and a god, the measure is perhaps 'living being', and the number of them will be a number of living beings." (trans. Ross); Aquinas 1980, *In Sent.* I, d. 24, q. 1, art. 1, 4: "Deus non est connumerabilis alicui creaturae; tum quia creatura et Deus in nullo conveniunt, quia hoc esset prius utroque; nec inveniuntur aliqua connumerari, nisi quae in aliquo conveniunt; sicut dicimus duos homines vel duos equos"; Frege 1987, §45–54; Geach 1961, 86–87.

in number Ockham says that if there were a universal man, such a universal man and a single man taken together would be in some number : *talis res universalis, si ponatur, vere facit numerum cum re singulari*.[33] Ockham clearly thinks that the problems of number ascription indicated above are just absent when you set out to count *simple* things (that is the key issue I return to in (iv)).

(iii) The third important premise of the arguments {*} and {**} is that in case of a complex thing one must "arrive at a determinate number of parts"; the problem with this premise is similar to the one sketched above. Take for example the whole right hand: how are we supposed to arrive at some number of its parts? Obviously we may adopt *various* correct ways of singling out parts of the right hand, arriving at *various* numbers of parts. And it does not seem that we may single out parts without knowing what *kind of parts* we are supposed to identify – without employing some measure given by a sortal term. Here again Ockham thinks that we get rid of all such difficulties by looking for *simple* parts and arriving at *their* number.

(iv) So in the two last premises the contrast between a *simple* and a *complex* thing (that is, a thing "including" a plurality of things) plays a key role. This distinction is supposed to offer some way of avoiding the problems concerning number ascription or parts identification, since it seems that there are no such problems with counting *simple* things; or, in other words, that problems with singling out units for counting arise always for *complex* units. The way, however, in which Ockham uses the contrast between *simple* and *complex* things may be doubtful in two ways. First, the connection between number and the measure expressed by a sortal term occurs not only in the case of complex entities, but also in the case of simple ones. Secondly, if what I have said in (iii) about singling out of parts is correct, the very contrast between a simple and a complex thing (having a plurality of distinct parts) always has to be relativized to some sort of parts identification; what does not have distinct parts *of a given sort* and is simple with respect to this sort of parts, may well have a great number of parts of another sort.

(v) The contrast between simple and complex entities occurs sometimes even in the very formulation of the Strong Self-Individuation Thesis, for example in Suárez; it is said that simple entities are individual just by themselves, whereas complex entities are individual in virtue of the individuality of their simple parts.[34] More precisely, the *Strong* Self-Individuation Thesis holds for *simple* individuals.

---

33 Ockham 1970, *In Sent.* I, d. 2, q. 4, 113,7–8.
34 Suárez 1866, *Disp. met.* V, sect. 6, 1.

(vi) The doubts mentioned in (ii) and (iii) suggest another line of argument in favour of the Individuality Thesis; its absence in Ockham sheds important light on nominalism. The fundamental idea would be that anything that is a realization of some F, is necessarily a *single* realization of F; you cannot realize F unless you realize a *single* F. For example, any realization of a sort of house is necessarily some *single* house of this sort. This, I think, is a deep metaphysical intuition (see also 8.2), but it requires a closer scrutiny of the ways in which both realization or existence and singularity are ascribed to what is expressed by general terms; and this is the topic that is absent in Ockham's thinking about individuality.

2.6 General Features of the Nominalistic Standpoint

(i) A fundamental trait of nominalism is the conviction that attributes like singleness, being in number or distinction can be fully analysed without *any* examination in the ways in which they attach to measures expressed by sortals. Returning to Frege's example: a pack of cards is a single pack of cards but not a single card; a pair of shoes is a single pair of shoes, but not a single shoe; so something may be single and not single in context of various general terms. Something similar holds for difference or distinction and number.

(ii) In contexts where one and the same thing seems single in one sense and not single in another, and there are various correct answers to the question about number of the same things, Ockham tends to use the contrast between simple and complex entities; this suggests that the well-known problems with number and singleness must disappear in case of *simple* things (by the way, '*simplex*' as opposed to '*duplex*' or '*triplex*', means just 'single' as opposed to 'double' or 'triple'). It seems also that the nominalists tend to think that simple things are individuals in the strongest sense. This solution, however, faces the same difficulties again, for the very contrast of simple and complex involves some use of a sortal; so without a theory of number, difference in the sense of Aristotelian *diafora* and a full-fledged mereology the very contrast of simplicity and complexity is of very limited use at best.

(iii) The basic nominalistic idea is that individuality *must* be an attribute belonging to its subject *immediately*. What is its subject, however, and what is the relationship between its individuality and its other attributes, remains unclear; Ockham seems just to think that there *must* be (*simple*) objects that are individual in an immediate way and in the strongest sense.

(iv) According to the nominalistic standpoint there is a uniform answer to the question of individuation for all sorts of entities; they do not differ, according to the nominalists, in this respect. It is symptomatic that Leibniz in the beginning of his nominalistic work *De prinicipio individui* decides to leave aside the difference between angels and material substances.[35]

---

[35] Leibniz 1930, *De principio individui*, §3.

3 *Haecceitas*. The Scotistic Rejection of the Strong Self-Individuation Thesis

3.1 Main Theses of the Scotistic Standpoint

The Scotistic standpoint concerning individuation, outlined in the second book of Scotus's *Sentences* commentary (in *Lectura* and *Ordinatio* as well as in *Reportata*) and in the *Metaphysics* commentary[1], includes two main theses, a negative and a positive one. Both concern the way in which individuality belongs to instances of natures – for example, the way in which individuality belongs to the humanity of a given man or to the redness of a given rose.

The negative thesis is

> **(The Distinction Thesis)** Individuality belongs to any particular instance of a nature in virtue of some entity distinct from that instance of the nature.[2]

So the Distinction Thesis contradicts the Strong Self-Individuation Thesis. Scotus maintains that the humanity of a given man, as well as the redness of a given rose, are in fact individual, but unlike the nominalists he thinks that they are *not* individual just by themselves – but only in virtue of something that is in some way distinct from them. More precisely, he thinks that an instance of a nature is *composed* in a very special way of something that is individual by itself and something else which is individual only in a derivative way. A detailed analysis of the special sort of distinction that is involved here is one of the main topics of the Scotistic analyses of the problem of individuation. To some extent the Scotists do agree with the nominalists that the idea of two things distinguished by *a third thing* is patently absurd (see 2.4.2), but they think that it is not absurd just in the case of this special sort of distinction (I return to this point in 3.6).

The positive thesis in turn says what the entity is that makes the instances of the natures of things individual; its usual formulation uses the term '*haecceity*' ('thisness'), although Scotus uses that term very rarely and not in his main lectures of individuation. Some other Scotists use other abstract nouns referring to individuality like '*singularitas*' ('singularity') or '*individualitas*' ('individuality'),

---

[1] In my presentation here I focus on *Ordinatio* and *Lectura*. See Scotus 1982, *Lectura* II, d. 3, p. 1, q. 6, and Scotus 1973, *Ordinatio* II, d. 3, p. 1, q. 6. For a general presentation of the Scotistic theory of individuation see e.g. Noone 2003; Wolter 1994; Rudavsky 1977/1980.

[2] Scotus 1973, *Ord.* II, d. 3, p. 1, q. 6, n. 142 and 168; 1982, *Lect.* II, d. 3, p. 1, q. 6, n. 164; similarly Fonseca 1615, *In Met.* V, c. VI, q. 5, sect. 1.

as well as abstract nouns derived from proper names, for example '*Paulitas*' ('being Paul')[3]. So the positive Scotistic thesis on individuation is that

> **(The Haecceity Thesis)** What makes the instance of the nature of a given thing individual is some special type of entity which is the individuality or thisness of that instance; this entity is distinct from others we may know from elsewhere, but it may be characterized using some analogies with *differentia specifica*.[4]

3.2 Standard Arguments for the Scotistic Theses

There are two main arguments for the Distinction Thesis. Interestingly, the first is based on the principle of convertibility of being and unity (see 2.3). Any sort of entity, Scotus says, has some sort of proper unity that belongs to it immediately, and any sort of unity has some sort of entity to which it is appropriate and to which it belongs immediately. So there is some entity to which individuality belongs immediately. It is *not*, however, the entity of the instance of the nature of a given individual (for example, the entity of the redness of a given rose), because, Scotus claims,

> **(The Weak Unity Thesis)** The sort of unity that belongs immediately to the entity of the nature in a given individual is distinct from individuality; it is a sort of unity weaker than individuality (*unitas minor unitate numerali*).[5]

Scotus offers a long series of arguments for the Weak Unity Thesis which I discuss in detail in 3.3 and 3.4.

The second argument for the Distinction Thesis involves some ideas concerning being distinguished by something, and being primarily diverse (*primo diversa*) (see 2.4.2). Scotus claims that in general any difference (*diafora* in the Aristotelian sense discussed in 2.4.2) is ultimately reducible to entities that are primarily diverse; so the difference between the individuals of the same kind is reducible to some entities that are primarily diverse. The instances of the natures of the things in question, however, are not primarily diverse, because they are rather what the things have in common. So there must be some other entities in the things in question that are primarily diverse – and, we may add, they are what

---

[3] See e.g. Punch 1672, disp. 6, q. 9, n. 66.
[4] Scotus 1973, *Ord.*, *loc. cit.*, n. 187–188; 1982, *Lect.* II, d. 3, p. 1, q. 6, n. 179; Fonseca 1615, *In Met.* V, c. VI, q. 5, sect. 1.
[5] Scotus 1973, *Ord.*, *loc. cit.*, n. 169; 1982, *Lect.*, *loc. cit.*, n. 166.

makes the things individual.⁶ I discuss the details of this argument in 3.5. The kind of distinction involved in the Distinction Thesis I discuss in 3.6.

Scotus's argument for the Haecceity Thesis is that individuality or thisness cannot be identified with any other principle, because to each of them one may apply the two arguments for the Distinction Thesis showing that individuality does not belong to it immediately.⁷ I focus on some details of this argument and some doubts one may raise against it in 3.7.

My main claim here is that the three Scotistic theses mentioned above focus on the unity of individual *instances* of natures and *not* of natures they are instances of. By contrast, both Wolter (1994, 273–4) and Park (1996, 281–283) seem to suggest that the Scotistic claims concern just "common nature". In a similar way, King (1992) says that the theses concern "the uncontracted nature" as opposed to "the contracted nature". This, of course, makes a crucial difference for the whole interpretation of Scotus' individuation theory. I think Scotus is clearly referring to the nature of a stone existing in a particular stone.⁸ Similarly, the second argument for the Distinction Thesis suggests also that the whole issue concerns individual instances of natures and not just natures they are instances of.

I use the Fregean distinction of *Begriff* and *Gegenstand* to shed some light on key points of the Scotistic individuation theory. I follow the attempts of Geach (1961 and 1969a) who used it in the context of Thomistic metaphysics, and, on the other hand, of Angelelli (1967, 143–145) and Park (1990) who used it in a Scotistic context. My proposals here, however, depart radically from those of Park in the ways that will be presented in some details in due course.

---

6 Scotus 1973, *Ord.*, *loc. cit.*, n. 170; 1982, *Lect.*, *loc. cit.*, n. 167.
7 Scotus 1973, *Ord.*, *loc. cit.*, n. 187–188.
8 Scotus 1973, *Ord.*, *loc. cit.*, n. 8: "Sed naturae exsistentis in isto lapide, est unitas propria, realis sive sufficiens, minor unitate numerali"; n. 35: "nam ista natura secundum quod ens in isto lapide, prior tamen naturaliter singularitate lapidis, est ex dictis indifferens ad hoc singulare et illud"; n. 172: "in eodem igitur quod est unum numero, est aliqua entitas, quam consequitur minor unitas quam sit unitas numeralis, et est realis". Similarly, he claims in n. 174 that the instance of (the nature of) colour *in whiteness* is not immediately marked by the unity of this particular species of colour: "color igitur in albedine est unus specie, sed non est de se nec per se nec primo". See also Scotus 1982, *Lect.*, *loc. cit.*, n. 176: "alia est unitas propria naturae in Socrate ut natura est, quam sit unitas numeralis: habet enim propriam unitatem, quae minor est quam unitas numeralis".

3.3 A Weak Sense of Individuality

The Weak Unity Thesis that the instance of a nature in a given individual has some proper sort of unity which is weaker than individuality (*unitas minor unitate numerali*) belongs to the well-known peculiarities of Scotism.[9] To avoid some misunderstandings let us make three introductory points connected with my general claim that in the Weak Unity Thesis Scotus focuses on individual instances of natures, and not just on multiply instantiable natures. (i) Scotus admits that the humanity of Socrates, *his* instance of humanity, is something quite individual; similarly in the case of the redness of *this* rose.[10] (ii) So it is not true in *any* sense that one and the same humanity which is in Socrates, *his* humanity, is also in some other man; as he makes clear, the real unity he discusses is not the unity of something existing it distinct individuals, but of something existing in only one.[11] (iii) The main point of the Scotistic theory of individuation is that individuality does not belong to Socrates's humanity *immediately* in the sense sketched in 2.4 and related to the principle *ens et unum convertuntur* (2.3) – because there is some *other*, weaker sort of unity appropriate to it and belonging to it immediately.[12]

What is unity weaker than individuality? I think it can be understood as singleness *in a weak sense*; and we can introduce this weak sense in the following way. One might plausibly say that cadmium red, as opposed to red in general, is something single – and he does not mean any particular cadmium red that might be given a proper name. The details of what he actually means I now leave aside; but it seems that the concept of singleness involved here is at least closely related to what Scotus means by unity weaker than singularity.

The argument for the Weak Unity Thesis is the following: if this sort of weak unity did not belong to the nature of a given thing, this sort of unity would not be anything real at all; the falsity of the consequent, Scotus claims, might be shown in "five or six ways" (both in *Lectura* and in *Ordinatio* we find seven). These ways show some contexts in which, Scotus thinks, we refer to this weak *real* unity.

{i} Scotus appeals to the Aristotelian principle that in each kind there is some primary species that plays a role comparable to the role of unity in the domain of natural numbers: it is a sort of measure and basis of the identity and distinction

---

[9] See e.g. Kraus 1936 and Heider 2014, ch. 4.
[10] Scotus 1973, *Ord.*, *loc. cit.*, n. 175: "Ita concedo quod quidquid est in hoc lapide, est unum numero, – vel primo, vel per se, vel denominative".
[11] Scotus 1973, *Ord.*, *loc. cit.*, n. 172: "Concedo igitur quod unitas realis non est alicuius exsistentis in duobus individuis, sed in uno".
[12] Scotus 1973, *Ord.*, *loc. cit.*, n. 175.

of all the other species of that kind; in the domain of polygons such a primary species is the triangle, in the domain of metrical feet – *mora*. Now Scotus claims that the primary species is marked with some sort of unity or singleness that is real and is *not* individuality in the strong sense, since the sort of essential priority in question does not belong to individuals.[13]

The point of the argument seems to be that there is a common measure for all the species of the kind, for example, a common measure for iambus and dactyl or a common measure for square and pentagon; moreover, the species which is the common measure, as opposed to all the other species, is something *single*. By 'a *common* measure' which is something single, however, we do not mean any particular individual, but just some species. So, for example, triangle *as such* is here some single measure, and it is not any particular triangle that is such a single measure.

{ii} Then Scotus appeals to the notion of *comparability* in the sense of 'being more F than' or 'being less F than'. According to the VIIth book of Aristotle's *Physics*, such comparisons are possible when F is not only univocal, but is a *species infima*; so, for example, when you take a red thing and a blue one, one of them is not more *coloured* than the other, but if you take two red things one may be more or less *red* than the other. Aristotle himself explains the difference here by saying that the genus is not something one in the way in which the species is; in other words, colour lacks some sort of unity necessary for being the ground for comparison in question. Scotus maintains that the unity that we ascribe here to redness (as opposed to colour) must be real (because other sorts of unity do belong to colour), and that it must not be individuality in the strong sense.[14]

{iii} The third argument is based on the Aristotelian thesis that similarity, like equality and identity, is based on unity; so he claims that a real similarity must be based on a real unity, but this real unity cannot be individuality in a strong sense, because similarity occurs between distinct things.[15] The basic idea of the argument seems to be the following: if two things are coloured, that does not yet make them similar; but if both are white – that makes them similar. The source of the difference between being coloured and being white here is that being white is being something one, while being coloured is not; so, generally, two things are similar if they are both F and being F is being something one in a special weak

---

13 Scotus 1973, *Ord., loc. cit.*, n. 11–15; 1982, *Lect., loc. cit.*, n. 13–17. Scotus refers to *Met.* 1052b18 (for the notion of the ordered series of species see also Lloyd 1962).
14 Scotus 1973, *Ord., loc. cit.*, n. 16–17; 1982, *Lect., loc. cit.*, n. 18–20. Scotus refers to *Phys.* 249a3–8 and 22.
15 Scotus 1973, *Ord., loc. cit.*, n. 18; 1982, *Lect., loc. cit.*, n. 21. Scotus refers to *Phys.* 1021a9–12.

sense. (The arguments {ii} and {iii} might suggest that according to Scotus one and the same being F is realized in the two things that are comparable or similar; so it should be stressed again that Scotus does *not* claim this.)

{iv} The fourth argument is based on the notion of contrariety (*contrarietas*) as a sort of real opposition (*oppositio realis*). Scotus claims that each real opposition has two primary terms (*prima extrema*); they are real and they are, just as terms of an opposition, unities; but they are not individual in the strong sense. For example, the primary terms of the opposition of white and black are *not* particular patches of white and black; if they were, there would not be just one opposition of white and black, but as many oppositions as there are individuals of the opposite species.[16]

{v} The fifth argument appeals to a theory of perception; Scotus claims that the object of a single perception is something really single, but not single in a strong sense. He argues for the latter by noting that sense does not discern two objects of the same species (e.g. two red patches) unless there are some exterior signs of their distinction.[17] So, for example, what the sense grasps is not a particular redness as such, but rather redness in general; on the other hand Scotus would probably insist that the external sense as such grasps something that it just founds in extramental reality, so the weak unity of the proper object of perception is not a result of some abstraction procedure.

{vi} The sixth argument appeals to grades of difference. Scotus claims that if any real unity is just individuality in the strong sense, any real distinction will be a numerical distinction in the strong sense; but any numerical distinction as such is equal. So if any real unity were individuality in the strong sense, Socrates would not differ from a line *more* that he differs from Plato. So, for example, the difference between Socrates and Bucephalus is *another sort of difference* than the difference between Socrates and Plato; more precisely, the former is the difference of a living being, whereas the latter is the difference of a man.[18] Let us note in passing, that someone might think that the former sort of difference occurs *not* between Socrates and Bucephalus, but rather between *species* of man and horse. Scotus claims, however, that *this* sort of difference occurs between individuals as well: the difference between Socrates and Bucephalus is the difference between *species* of living beings. And the point of the argument is that if Socrates and Bucephalus do differ in that way – do differ as *species* of living beings – there must be something in Socrates which is *not* immediately individual.

---

16 Scotus 1973, *Ord.*, *loc. cit.*, n. 19; 1982, *Lect.*, *loc. cit.*, n. 22.
17 Scotus 1973, *Ord.*, *loc. cit.*, n. 20–22; 1982, *Lect.*, *loc. cit.*, n. 23–24.
18 Scotus 1973, *Ord.*, *loc. cit.*, n. 23–27; 1982, *Lect.*, *loc. cit.*, n. 26–27.

{vii} The seventh argument is based on the notion of *generatio univoca*, producing or giving birth within one and the same species. Scotus claims that there is some real unity between cause and effect here, although this unity is not individuality in the strong sense. The point of the argument seems to be that such a generation is a proliferation or preservation of the *species* which in a way *continues to exist* in the new individuals, although there may be nothing numerically common to all these individuals. The conclusion is again that there must be something in those individuals that has the unity weaker than individuality.[19] (Again one may be inclined to think that Scotus claims that there is some numerically one nature which is common to distinct individuals here, so again it should be stressed that Scotus explicitly rejects this idea.)

To sum up, the strategy of these seven arguments is the following. If we interpret "unity weaker than individuality" as singleness in a weak sense, we have some singleness in a weak sense wherever we count sorts of things. Now each of the arguments {i}–{vii} appeals to some context in which this kind of singleness plays an interesting role that is not reducible to the criteria of correctness of counting sorts of things; this role suggests that the unity in question is *real* in some special sense. Moreover, all the arguments suggest that in some cases to be F just *is* to be something one, so the unity, being an essential feature of the nature, may be ascribed to its instances, too, and, moreover, it belongs to them *immediately* and is appropriate to them.

The arguments {i}–{vii} are anti-nominalistic in the following sense: a nominalist might tend to claim that (*) 'to be cadmium red as such is to be something single' means just that each instance of cadmium red is immediately single in the strong sense; so for a nominalist (*) is just another formulation of the Strong Self-Individuation Thesis. Scotus, by contrast, tries to show in {i}–{vii} that what (*) is about is some sort of unity distinct from singleness in the strong sense – and henceforth singleness in the strong sense belongs to instances of cadmium red in some other way.

---

[19] Scotus 1973, *Ord.*, *loc. cit.*, n. 28; 1982, *Lect.*, *loc. cit.*, n. 25.

3.4 Avicenna on Instantiable Natures

Scotus supplements the arguments sketched above with the explanation of the weak unity belonging to instances of natures; the explanation is based on Avicenna's treatment of instantiable natures known as the theory of *triplex status naturae*.[20]

The basic idea is that of the definition of F (F being some general predicate like 'man', 'horse' or 'red') as the expression showing *what it is to be F* – in other words, showing the nature or the essence of F[21]. So, for example, the definition of horse shows what it is to be a horse or the nature or essence of horse; the definition of red shows what it is to be red or the nature of redness. Roughly speaking, the nature of F is what it is to be F.[22] In the Latin translation of Avicenna's text both the abstract nouns (like *'equinitas'*) and concrete ones (like *'equus'*) stand for natures in the sense sketched above; the phrase *'ipsum* F' ('F itself') is also used in the same role.

Avicenna's point of departure is that there is a variety of true statements with 'F' in the subject place in which we ascribe various features to the nature of F; some of these features are part of the nature of F, and some not. As for the former, it is part of the nature of horse to be a living being, and it is part of the nature of redness to be a colour. As for the latter, we may ascribe to the nature of F being in some number (that is, having some number of instances), being something common (to various instances) and being something specific (to a given particular instance), and being instantiated in the sensible reality as well as being instantiated in someone's cognitive powers (when someone is perceiving F, recalling F, imagining F or thinking of F). For the moment I leave aside here all the controversies concerning the logical form of such ascriptions with a general term in the subject position. I take it for granted that in some sense one might say that the nature of redness (that is: what it is to be red) is instantiated in a particular

---

20 Avicenna 1980, *Metaphysica*, vol. 2,227–238. For an outline of Avicenna's doctrine of *triplex status naturae* see e.g. Bäck 1996, Angelelli 1967, 143–145 and Geach 1961, 78–79.
21 Park claims surprisingly (1996, 282) that "the common nature is neither definable nor the subject of acquaintance by us"; it seems to me, however, that the whole *triplex status naturae* theory as well as its Scotistic interpretation assumes that we basically may *know* natures and give definitions of them.
22 This general description of the nature of F is close to Lowe's description of essence: "In short, the essence of something, X, is *what X is*, or *what it is to be X*" (Lowe 2013, 144–145). Lowe, Fine and Oderberg (2007) postulate a "serious essentialism" as opposed to, as Lowe calls it, *ersatz* essentialism treating essence as the set of necessary properties. Of course Avicennian nature of F is much closer to the essence of the contemporary serious essentialists than to its *Ersatz*.

red tomato, and in virtue of this instance some sort of unity or a number can be ascribed to the nature of redness; and if someone is thinking just of redness, the nature of redness is instantiated in his power of reason, making his thoughts thoughts *about* redness.

Now the basic claim of Avicenna is that

> **(The Instance Ascription Thesis)** Having (a given number or a given sort of) instances, and henceforth unity and plurality, can be truly ascribed to the nature of F, but are not part of the nature of F and do not belong to the nature of F as such.[23]

The fundamental intuition of the Instance Ascription Thesis is clear: the answer to the question how many horses (how many instances of the nature of the horse) are there, is not part of what it is to be a horse. Having a given number of instances, having or not having instances at all, do really belong to the nature of horse, but they are not part of it.[24] Using Frege's terminology we may say that for the *Begriff* horse these are all *Eigenschaften* as opposed to *Merkmale*.[25]

It is also clear that the Instance Ascription Thesis is basically an anti-Platonic thesis. It is namely the main idea of (at least some varieties of) Platonism that to be F *as such* is to be something "one over many" or something divided from its instances, or something universal. By contrast, according to the Instance Ascription Thesis neither oneness nor plurality belong to the nature of F as such, and it has no special mode of existence opposed to the various instances of F.[26]

It is worth noting in this context that the Instance Ascription Thesis does not pose the existence of *the nature of F in itself* as some special sort of entity. As Angelelli rightly says (1967, 144), "to inquire about the sort of existence or about the ontological status of essence taken in itself would be, in my view, to miss the real significance of the doctrine in question". It turns out, however, that there is a strong temptation to think of "the nature of F in itself" as some special sort of

---

[23] Avicenna 1980, vol. 2, 228,32–36: "ipsa equinitas non est aliquid nisi equinitas tantum; ipsa enim in se non est multa nec unum, nec est existens in his sensibilibus nec in anima, nec est aliquid horum potentia vel effectu, ita ut hoc contineatur intra essentiam equinitatis, et ex hoc quod est equinitas tantum. Unitas autem est proprietas quae, cum adiungitur equinitati, fit equinitas propter ipsam proprietatem unum. Similiter etiam equinitas habet praeter hanc multa alias proprietates accidentes sibi. Equinitas ergo, ex hoc quod in definitione eius conveniunt multa, et communis, sed ex hoc, quod accipitur cum proprietatibus et accidentibus signatis, est singularis. Equinitas ergo in se est equinitas tantum".
[24] For an excellent presentation of this see Geach 1961, 78–79 and Geach 1969a, 45–52.
[25] Frege 1987, §53. For some details of this analogy between Avicenna and Frege see Angelelli 1967, 138–145.
[26] See Geach 1961, 78–79 and Geach 1969a, 45–47.

entity, and this temptation is crucial for Scotus's thinking about individuation[27]; I will return to this issue in 3.4.1–3.4.3

Obviously the Instance Ascription Thesis is also an anti-nominalistic thesis, for it shows some sense in which unity or individuality belongs to something *not* in an immediate way; so in a way the Instance Ascription Thesis is incompatible with the Strong Self-Individuation Thesis as far as the latter states that anything that individuality can be truly ascribed to must be individual *just by itself*. From a general point of view, the Instance Ascription Thesis is one of the most important ways of rejecting the Strong Self-Individuation Thesis.

The Instance Ascription Thesis is in a way an anti-conceptualist thesis; it says that being F as such is *not* something inhering in a cognitive power (although being F happens to have some instances in various cognitive powers); in a way the Instance Ascription Thesis is comparable to Frege's claim that *Begriffe* are not a sort of psychological entities. But we have to remember that the point of the Instance Ascription Thesis is that denying that the nature of F is as such a sort of psychological entity does *not* amount to saying that the nature of F as such enjoys a sort of extramental reality.

Finally, it should be noted that the Instance Ascription Thesis concerns ascribing something to *natures* as opposed to ascribing something to their instances; so the Instance Ascription Thesis itself is *not* an argument for the Scotistic Weak Unity Thesis according to which individuality cannot be ascribed to an *instance* of the nature immediately (if I am right in my main claim that the three Scotistic theses focus on individual instances of natures and not on instantiable natures themselves).

Finally, it is worth noting here that the Instance Ascription Thesis offers a general framework for theories of universals; it claims that being a genus or a species, or being a universal in general, do *not* belong to natures expressed by general terms as such; for example, that it is not part of the nature of redness to be universal; this leaves the question open in what way universality *does* belong to natures expressed by general terms. The latter is just the main question of the theory of universals. One of the crucial issues to be considered here, I think, is the question whether it is part of the nature of e.g. redness to be instantiable; it seems that according to the Instance Ascription Thesis the answer should be negative, but, on the other hand, it seems that the nature in question is not instantiable in virtue of having instances or in virtue of being intellectually grasped. A

---

[27] It might seem that the claim of Park (1996, 282): "if there is no such thing as a common nature in itself, there would be no room for raising the problem of individuation" is another manifestation of this temptation.

similar problem concerns the way in which being unsaturated in the Fregean sense may be ascribed to a nature. So, in general, the question of individuation concerns the way in which individuality belongs to natures expressed by general terms, and the question of universals concerns the way in which universality and instantiability belong to them.

The problem is, however, that although these aspects of the Instance Ascription Thesis are pretty obvious, there remain many troublesome details to be worked out; they concern mainly the relationship between the nature of F and its instances. Avicenna considers these details in two steps; first he analyses some general principles of ascribing something to natures, and then he proceeds to the analysis of the very relationship between the nature of F and various individual instances of F. The point is that the conclusions reached by Avicenna at the latter stage seem to contradict immediately some basic intuitions expressed by the Instance Ascription Thesis, and it is just this fact that is fundamental to Scotus's interpretation of Avicenna.

3.4.1 Some Details of Instance Ascription

What Avicenna considers first is answering questions of the sort 'Is F as such (*ex hoc quod est* F) *a* or not?' in cases where *a* is not part of the nature of F; he begins with distinguishing between two kinds of these questions.

(i) On the one hand, there are questions to be resolved by one of *contradictory* answers: 'Is F as such *a* or is it not?' Here Avicenna states that in cases of *a* not being part of the essence of F the answer is always negative. He adds, however, that there is some ambiguity to be warned against here. Let us illustrate it first with a simple example. 'A philosopher as such is not bald' may be understood either as 'a philosopher, as far as he is a philosopher, is not bald' or as 'it is not true that a philosopher is bald *as* a philosopher'; the former implies that no philosopher is bald, while the latter denies only that a bald philosopher would be bald in virtue of being a philosopher. There is a somewhat similar ambiguity in 'being a horse as such is not single'; it may be taken to mean either 'being a horse, as far as it is being a horse, is not single' or 'it is not true that being a horse is single as such'. Avicenna opts for the latter sense: by giving the negative answer we mean just that it is not true that being a horse is single just in virtue of being a horse.[28]

---

28 Avicenna, *op. cit.*, 229,43–49: "Si quis autem interrogaverit nos de equinitate secundum contradictionem, scilicet an equinitas, ex hoc quod est equinitas, sit *a* vel non *a*, non erit responsio

(ii) On the other hand there are questions to be resolved with one of the *contrary* answers: 'Is F as such *a* or not-*a*?' (For example: is being a horse as such something one or something in a greater number?). Now in case of *such* questions, Avicenna says, both possible answers are to be rejected, if only *a* is not part of the essence of F; and the rejection of one of the answers does not imply the acceptance of the other.[29] By rejecting both answers we do not deny that some number in fact may be truly ascribed to being F; what we deny is that it may be truly ascribed to it just in virtue of being F.[30]

Now the key case considered by Avicenna himself is the question:

(*) Is the humanity which is in Plato (*humanitas quae est in Platone*) as such distinct from the humanity in Socrates?

Since we ask in (*) about being distinct in virtue of humanity, the answer is 'no'; it does not imply, however, that the humanity in Plato and the humanity in Socrates are one and the same humanity;[31] the answer to the question 'is the humanity which is in Plato as such identical with the humanity which is in Socrates?' is also 'no'. The humanity of Plato is distinct from the humanity of Socrates, but this distinction is not truly ascribed to humanity *as such*.[32]

---

nisi secundum negationem, quicquid illud fuerit, non autem negationem eius quod est, sed eius quod dicitur de ea, videlicet quoniam non debet dici equinitas ex hoc quod est equinitas non est *a*, sed, ex hoc quod est equinitas, non est equinitas *a* nec aliquid aliorum."; 232,97–99: "dicemus nos non respondisse quod ipsa, ex hoc quod est humanitas, non est ita, sed quod ipsa, non ex hoc quod et humanitas, est ita. Iam autem nota est in logica horum differentia."

29 *Ibidem*, 229,50–51: "Si autem partes quaestionis fuerint duae affirmativae immediate, tunc non erit necesse respondere aliquam illarum ullo modo"; 230,58–61: "Cum ergo subiectum quaestionis posita fuerit ipsa humanitas secundum quod est humanitas veluti aliquid unum, et interrogaverint nos secundum aliquod contrariorum dicentes quod aut est unum aut multa, tunc non erit necesse respondere aliquod illorum".

30 *Ibidem*, 230,63–70: "si proprietas eius est esse unum vel multa, sicut proprietas quae eam sequitur, tunc sine dubio appropriabitur per hoc, sed tamen ipsa non erit ipsum appropriatum, ex hoc quod est humanitas; ergo, ex hoc quod ipsa est humanitas, non est ipsum unum vel multum, sed est aliud quiddam cui illud accidit extrinsecus. Cum ergo ipsa consideratur secundum hoc quod est humanitas tantum, non erit necesse considerari cum hoc id quod accidit ei extrinsecus".

31 *Ibidem*, 231,74–77: "si quis interrogaverit an humanitas quae est in Platone, ex hoc quod est humanitas, sit alia ab illa quae est in Socrate et necessario dixerimus non, non oportebit conentire ei ut dicat: <ergo haec et illa sunt unum numero>".

32 *Ibidem*, 231,78–81: "intelleximus in ea [*scil.* negatione] quod illa humanitas, ex hoc quod est humanitas, est humanitas tantum, sed hoc quod ipsa est alia ab humanitate quae est in Socrate

The main problem of (*), however, concerns the role of the relative clause 'which is in Plato/Socrates' ('*quae est in Platone/Socrate*'). The semantics of relative clauses was extensively discussed in medieval logic[33], and Avicenna himself makes some brief remarks on the relative clause in question, concluding that either it makes the whole phrase intrinsically incoherent or it may be eliminated from the question without any change of sense.[34] The theory to which the brief remarks of Avicenna appeal must be a pretty complex one; but I think that we may grasp the sense of the remarks without dwelling on the details of the theory, using just the distinction of determinative and explicative relative clauses. Avicenna says namely that the role of 'instantiated in Plato/Socrates' in (*) may be twofold; either it is comparable to the role of 'as such' and consists in showing the respect (*positio respectus*) in which belonging an attribute to the subject should be considered (but it should be noted that these respects are mutually incompatible); or it is a relative clause. In the latter case, it is either an explicative relative clause, or a determinative one. If the former, it can be eliminated without much change of sense of the question; if the latter, it seems incompatible, on Avicenna's account, with the role of 'as such'.

On Avicenna's account the fact that in the case of questions (ii) (to be resolved with one of the *contrary* answers) neither answer is true is closely related to the fact that the general term in the subject position is not preceded by a determiner (*signum*). Were it preceded by a determiner, Avicenna says, one of the answers would have to be true. So, for example, in the case of the question 'Is man a mathematician or not?' neither of the contrary answers is true (as far as people are not mathematicians in virtue of being humans), but in case of 'Is that given man a mathematician or not?' one of them must be true. This shows, according to Avicenna, that the phrase 'as humanity' (or 'taken as humanity') does not play the role of the determiner or, as Avicenna says, is not part of the subject of the proposition (*pars subiecti*). In other words, we do not use the phrase 'as humanity' or 'taken as humanity' to single out 'humanity itself' as a distinct object ('humanity as humanity' or 'humanity taken as humanity'). But if we do make the error and treat '(taken) as humanity' as part of the subject of the sense we fall into the illusion of 'humanity (taken) as humanity' as some distinct object of a very

---

quiddam extrinsecum est. Ipse vero non interrogavit de humanitate nisi ex hoc quod est humanitas".
33 See, for example, Parsons 2014, 140–144 and 282–285.
34 Avicenna, *op. cit.*, 231, 80–232, 94.

special sort; and then we cannot maintain that neither of the contrary answers is true.[35]

So the phrase '(taken) as F' is one of phrases that are attached to determine the respect in which the nature or essence of F is to be considered and in which something can be (or cannot be) truly ascribed to it. Avicenna's doctrine of the *"triplex status naturae"* distinguishes three sorts of such respects: on the one hand the nature of F may be considered just as the nature of F; on the other hand it may be considered as instantiated in some domain – either as instantiated in the extramental sensible reality or as instantiated in the cognitive powers.[36] Then the doctrine asks what can be truly ascribed to the nature of F in each of these three respects.

3.4.2 Natures and Instances, Parts and Wholes

At the second stage Avicenna presents an analysis of the nature of F and its instances in terms of parts and wholes; it is at this stage than he comes to some conclusions incompatible with the Instance Ascription Thesis, which, on the other hand, are basic for Scotus's interpretation of Avicenna. He claims that the nature of F taken in itself without what is attached to it, is nothing else than the nature of F; but "universal F" or "individual F" or "F instantiated in the sensible extramental reality" and "F instantiated in a cognitive power" are, as he claims, "F together with something else". Henceforth he concludes that

> **(The Weak Instance Composition Thesis)** The nature of F is present in what is "F together with something else" (in particular: in an individual F) *as its part* and is prior to it (*praecedit*

---

35 *Ibidem*, 232,00–7: "Subiectum huiusmodi quaestionum plerumque videtur indefinite cum non determinatur signo, et tunc non fiet ad illam responsio nisi ponatur ipsa humanitas quasi aliqua designata absque omni multitudine, et tunc nostra dictio, scilicet *ex hoc quod ipsa est humanitas*, non est pars subiecti, eo quod <non> congrue dicitur *humanitas quae est ex hoc quod est humanitas*, alioquin, fieret indefinita. Si autem dicitur *ipsa humanitas quae est ex hoc quod est ipsa humanitas*, iam cecidit in eam designatio quae addita est supra humanitatem."; see also Anscombe 1981b, 208 for a similar point: "There aren't such objects as an A *qua* B, though an A may, *qua* B, receive such-and-such a salary, and, *qua* C, such-and-such a salary". It is precisely because of this fact that, as Angelelli says, inquiries concerning the ontological status of "the nature in itself" do miss the real significance of the Avicennian doctrine.
36 Avicenna, *op. cit.*, 230,71–231,73.

in esse) in the way in which something simple precedes the complex and a part precedes the whole it belongs to (*sicut simplex praecedit compositum et sicut pars totum*).[37]

So there is a peculiar sense of 'part' in the Weak Instance Composition Thesis, a sense in which horse is a part of this horse, and whiteness a part of this whiteness. Such a part, Avicenna claims, can exist (*esse*) only within such a whole, together with something else, but is distinct from the rest of such a whole.[38] Avicenna claims, moreover, that what exists is not just the whole, for example: a particular horse, but also its part, that is, the nature of horse.[39]

These ideas of parts and wholes seem to have the following source: it is clear that the expression 'F-ness' is a part of the expression 'this F-ness' or '*x*'s F-ness'. And because this kind of parts and composition has a fundamental *logical* significance (as opposed to a grammatical one) one may tend to think that it mirrors some metaphysical sort of composition occurring in the thing itself. And it is this metaphysical composition that Avicenna tries to analyse here.

In this context Avicenna recalls a popular but deceptive argument (which, as he says, led astray many authors who seemed to be wise) and shows what is incorrect about it; his remarks shed much light on his idea of the nature of F as part of its instances.

The argument is that being F as being F does not exist (*non habet esse*) in its instances, because what exists in them is just a particular F, and not F as such. If, the argument goes, being F as being F had existed in an individual F, it must have been either specific to it (*eius proprium*) or not. If the former, being F as being F would be distinct from it and would not exist in it, and henceforth there would be only some particular being F; if the latter, one and the same being F would exist in many distinct Fs, which is impossible. But being F as such does exist (*habet esse*); so it exists as distinct from its instances.[40] It is easy to trace many Platonic intuitions in this argument.[41]

---

[37] *Ibidem*, 233,29–35: "animal commune et animal individuum, et animal secundum respectum quo in petentia est commune vel proprium, et animal secundum respectum quo est in his sensibilibus vel intellectum in anima, et animal et aliud, non animal consideratum in se tantum. Manifestum est autem quod, cum fuerit animal et aliud quod non est animal, animal tunc erit in hoc quasi pars eius; similiter et homo."; and 234,42.
[38] *Ibidem*, 234,44–46.
[39] *Ibidem*, 234,50–57.
[40] *Ibidem*, 234,58–235,66.
[41] It seems that a somewhat similar line of argument is to be found in King (1992, 57) who asks about "the ontological status of the uncontracted nature" and claims that "the uncontracted nature, as such, necessarily does not exist" or that "it is necessarily non-existent as such" and comments on "the nature's inability to exist as such". Although King's conclusion is contrary to the

I think it is clear that what Avicenna said about answering various questions concerning natures (3.4.1) offers a good strategy of rejecting this Platonic line of argument. First, it enables one to say that (i) it is not true that being F as such exists in its instances, although (ii) being F does exist in its instances; then it is possible to reject (iii) being F as such does not exist in its instances and (iv) being F as such exists as distinct from its instances, and even (v) being F as such exists. It is important that (ii) and the fact that there is no contradiction between (i) and (ii) may suggest a weak interpretation of Avicenna's Weak Instance Composition Thesis characterising being F as part of its instances. Moreover, the way in which Avicenna treats the question (*) (3.4.1) could be used to show that there is no answer to the question 'Is being F in this particular instance, as being F, something specific to this instance, or instead something common to many instances?'.

As a matter of fact, the Avicennian answer to the Platonic line of argument does employ the ideas sketched above.[42] The point is, however, that it goes *much further* in a way which seems to contradict some crucial intuitions expressed in the Instance Ascription Thesis. Avicenna goes on to distinguish "being F as such and not as far as it is attached to something" (*animal ex hoc quod est animal per se, sine condicione alterius*) and "being F as such, as far as it is not attached to anything" (*animal, ex hoc quod est animal per se, cum condicione non rei alterius*).[43] Now appealing to this distinction Avicenna says at least three times that it is true that

(The Strong Instance Composition Thesis) Being F as such exists in the extramental sensible reality (*animal, ex hoc quod est animal, habet esse in sensibilibus*).[44]

The thesis is supposed to be a way of rejecting Platonism. The point is, however, that it plainly contradicts the Instance Ascription Thesis, according to which it is not true that being F *as such* exists in its instances in extramental sensible reality. (The contradiction is not so clear in the case of the Weak Instance Composition Thesis, so I distinguish between the Weak and the Strong Instance Composition Theses; but it is possible that for Avicenna there is no such difference).

Platonic one, the reasoning seems to involve some sort of reference to "the nature as such" that Avicenna and Angelelli warn us against.
42 Avicenna, *loc. cit.*, 235,74–77; 235,82–236,88; 236,92–98.
43 *Ibidem*, 236,98–1.
44 *Ibidem*, 236,5–237,11: "animal vero per se, non cum condicione rei alterius, habet esse in sensibilibus. Ipsum vero in se in veritate sua est sine condicione alterius rei, quamvis sit cum mille condicionibus quae adiunguntur ei extrinsecus. Animal ergo per se ex sua animalitate habet esse in istis sensibilibus".

The Strong Instance Composition Thesis is closely related to (ii), but the key difference is that in the Strong Instance Composition Thesis it is stated that the existence in extramental sensible reality belongs to being F as such in an extrinsic way (*accidit extrinsicus*). Against the Strong Instance Composition Thesis it may well be objected that it is not true that anything belongs to being F as such in an extrinsic way; 'as such' and 'in an extrinsic way' are just two *mutually exclusive* ways of considering being F; what belongs to being F *as such*, does not belong to it in an extrinsic way, and *vice versa*. To repeat: 'being F as such' does not refer to some special object to which something may belong in an extrinsic way, just because 'as such' is not "a part of the subject". So it seems that what Avicenna says in the Strong Instance Composition Thesis collapses in what Avicenna himself warns us against: in treating '(taken) as such' as a sort of determiner or part of the subject, and henceforth in thinking that "being F (taken) as such" is some special sort of object. Then to reject Platonism Avicenna claims that this object, "being F (taken) as such", does exist in its instances; but the right way of rejecting Platonism suggested earlier by Avicenna himself is not claiming something about the alleged object described as "being F (taken) as such", but instead claiming that "being F (taken) as such" is no more the designation of any special object whatsoever than, say "being a cat taken as an example of entity".

There is also another sort of contrast we may appeal to here. Geach suggests that expressions like 'the F-ness of *x*' (like 'the wisdom of Socrates') should be analysed as consisting of a function symbol 'the F-ness of _' (e.g. 'the wisdom of _') and the name of the argument, like in the case of 'the square root of 2'.[45] So being F would be a function whose arguments would be subjects of wisdom, and values – their instances of wisdom. On such a construal being F is *not* a part of its particular instance.[46] We do not have to think that just this sort of composition of

---

45 Geach 1961, 79-81 and Geach 1969a, 45–46 and 49–53; see also Frege 2008a and 2008b. It is precisely here that my comparison of Avicenna and Scotus with Frege depart from the picture sketched in Park 1990. In Park's picture the prominent role is played by Fregean concept correlates conceived as denotata of nominalized predicates like 'horseness' (1990, 260–262). Following Geach I assume that the predicate '_ is a horse' and 'the horseness of _' signify the same, although in different ways (Geach 1961, 78 and 1969a, 48–49), and I do not introduce concept correlates (being objects of special sort) into the picture.

46 Geach 1969a, 52: "if one designation is part of another, it does not follow that the things designated are respectively part and whole. 'The square root of 25' is a complex designation having as parts the designations 'the square root of' and '25'; but it does not follow (as Frege oddly inferred) that there is some sense of 'part' in which we may suitably say that the number 5, which is the square root of 25, has two heterogeneous parts – the square root function and the number 25".

expressions mirrors some metaphysical composition in the value of the function; the square root of 4 is *not* composed in any way of the square root function and 4. Accepting this sort of analogy we should not say that being F as such exists in its Socratic instance or in Socrates; and we would not be tempted to say that being F as such exists somewhere as divided from Socrates. Following Geach we might claim that being F (or the nature of F) is itself no kind of *Gegenstand*, is not anything one in the way comparable to the unity of Socrates or his instance of wisdom. Geach warns us, however, that the function analogy is itself not quite free from some dangers;[47] I will return to this analogy many times in due course.

3.4.3 The Scotistic Interpretation of Avicenna

Referring to the Avicennian analysis I have sketched above, Scotus makes three points.[48] First, he repeats that being F (or the nature of F) as being F is neither something individual nor something in a greater number, nor something universal; although these attributes do belong to the nature of F, they do not belong to it as such (but, we may add, in virtue of various sorts of instantiation).[49]

Then Scotus says that the nature of F exists (*habet esse*) both in the power of reason (*in intellectu*), and in its instances in extramental reality (*in particulari*). So in its particular instance the nature of F is something real and some real entity (*entitas*).[50] It seems that in this thesis Scotus says more than (ii) (see 3.4.2); and maybe what he wants to say is just the Avicennian Strong Instance Composition Thesis (see 3.4.2).

---

47 In Geach 1991, 254 he says: "I compared Aquinas's doctrine of the *modus significandi* of abstract nouns with dependent genitives to Frege's doctrine of the incompleteness of functional signs. I remain convinced that here I laid hold of an important clue; but with the passage of years I have come to think I did not get so far into the labyrinth as I once thought I had".

48 King (1992) says that Scotus "spells out his reading of this dark saying [*equinitas est tantum equinitas*]"; I try to show, however, that what the "dark saying" of Avicenna means is relatively clear, as opposed to the Scotistic interpretation of it.

49 Scotus 1973, *Ord.* II, d. 3, p. 1, q. 1, n. 31–32: "Intelligo: non est 'ex se una' unitate numerali, nec 'plures' pluralitate opposita tali unitati; nec 'universalis' actu est (eo modo scilicet quo aliquid est universale ut est obiectum intellectus), nec est 'particularis' de se. Licet enim numquam sit realiter sine aliquo istorum, de se tamen non est aliquod istorum, ed est prius naturaliter omnibus istis".

50 *Ibidem*, n. 34: "ita etiam in re extra, ubi natura est cum singularitate, non est illa natura de se determinata ad singularitatem, sed est prior naturaliter ipsa ratione contrahente ipsam ad singularitatem illam".

Finally, Scotus claims that unity of a weaker sort belongs to the nature of F in its particular instance.[51] It is hard to say what the relationship is between that thesis and the Avicennian Instance Ascription Thesis. Referring to the Instance Ascription Thesis Scotus admits that the weak sort of unity in question does *not* belong to the nature of F *as such*, being part of the essence of F (*ita quod sit intra rationem naturae*); nevertheless he claims that the unity in question *is* some sort of internal property (*propria passio*) of the nature of F.[52] It seems that it must be in some way internal or essential if it is to be ascribed to individual instances of natures as well.

So Scotus seems to claim that when we say that being F is something individual in the sense discussed in 3.3, the logical form of this statement is distinct from *both* kinds of ascription distinguished by Avicenna (3.4); using Frege's idiom Scotus might say that here we do not ascribe to a *Begriff* neither an *Eigenschaft* nor a *Merkmal*.

It seems that Scotus opts for a weak interpretation of the Avicennian Instance Ascription Thesis so that it does not challenge his Weak Unity Thesis ascribing a weak sort of unity to the (instances of) the nature of F. I think that what is closest to Scotus in Avicenna's considerations is just the Strong Instance Composition Thesis that, at least *prima facie*, plainly contradicts the main Avicennian Instance Ascription Thesis.

At any rate, the Scotistic Weak Unity Thesis ascribing a weak sort of unity to instances of the nature of F seems much stronger than the Avicennian Instance Ascription Thesis.

---

51 *Ibidem*, n. 34: "et licet non habeat eam [*scil.* istam unitatem] de se, ita quod sit intra rationem naturae (quia 'equinitas est tantum equinitas', secundum Avicennam V *Metaphysicae*), tamen illa unitas est propria passio naturae secundum entitatem suam primam, et per consequens neque est ex se 'haec' intranee, neque secundum entitatem propriam necessario inclusam in ipsa natura secundum primam entitatem eius".

52 *Ibidem*, n. 34. Joseph Owens (1967) claims that Aquinas and Scotus revised the Avicennian theory of natures in two distinct ways; the Scotistic way consists in ascribing some unity to natures that Avicenna did not ascribe to them, and the Thomistic one – in denying some sort of being that Avicenna did ascribe to them.

3.5 Can Things be Differentiated by What They Have in Common?

The second argument for the Distinction Thesis is that the distinction between the single Fs must be ultimately traced back to some entities in them that are primarily diverse; but the instances of the nature of F in Fs, the argument goes, are not primarily diverse entities, because they are rather what the Fs have in common than what distinguishes them; so, for example, Scotus would claim that Socrates cannot be distinguished from Plato by Socrates's humanity, because it is humanity that, in some sense, they have in common; the conclusion is that Plato's humanity is not something individual by itself.[53]

The strong version of the crucial premise of the argument would be that, in any relevant sense, Socrates and Plato do not differ by their humanities. This strong version of the premise, however, would be clearly false in the light of the Aristotelian notion of *diafora* (see 2.4.2); basically the difference between Socrates and Plato consists in the difference of their humanities: Socrates and Plato (as opposed, say, to two hands of Socrates), are two human beings. Anyway, there is no reason to think that Scotus does actually embrace this strong version of the premise.

In the weak sense, by contrast, the crucial premise states only that Socrates's humanity cannot be the *ultimate* ground of Socrates's difference from Plato, or that Socrates's humanity and Plato's humanity are not primarily diverse entities. In other words, it states that if x's humanity is distinct from y's humanity, there is some other ultimate ground of their distinction. Someone might claim in a similar way that the redness of a patch on a wallpaper and the whiteness of another patch on the same wallpaper are distinct instances of being a colour, but the ultimate ground of the distinction of the redness and the whiteness in question cannot be just their instances of being a colour; there must be something distinct from the redness's instance of being a colour in the red patch that makes these instances of being a colour distinct ones; so, one might conclude, the instance of

---

[53] Scotus 1973, *Ord.* II, d. 3, p.1, n. 170: "omnis differentia differentium reducitur ultimate ad aliqua primo diversa (alioquin non esset status in differentibus); sed individua proprie differunt, quia sunt 'diversa aliquid-idem entia'; ergo eorum differentia reducitur ad aliqua quae sunt primo diversa. Illa autem 'primo diversa' non sunt natura in isto et natura in illo, quia non est idem quo aliqua conveniunt formaliter et quo differunt realiter, licet idem possit esse distinctum realiter et conveniens realiter; multum enim refert aliquid esse distinctum et esse quo aliquid primo distinguitur. Ergo praeter naturam in hoc et in illo, sunt aliqua primo diversa, quibus hoc et illud differunt, hoc in isto et illud in illo".

being a colour in the red patch is not being redness immediately or by itself.[54] This involves the same pattern of argument as the Scotus's one, but it is applied to a distinction of species within one genus and not to the distinction of individuals within one species.

The claim that the uniformly red patch is not distinguished from the white one by its colour, however, is actually a strange claim. Why should we claim that the difference between being red and being white is constituted by something else than by their instances of being a colour? Why should we claim, more precisely, that it is not the colour of the red patch (that is, the instance of being a colour in the red patch) that makes the red patch distinct from the white one?[55] At any rate, the difference between the red patch and the white one is just a difference of colour, and it is just the colour of the red patch that is the ground of that difference. I do not claim that the genus and species case is strictly similar to the species and individual case, but I do claim that there are cases in which it would be quite reasonable to claim that things are distinguished just by (the instances of) what belongs to both.

The basic idea of the Scotistic argument is the following: the instance of being a colour in the red patch and the instance of being a colour in the white one are different; so there must be two distinct things in the red patch: on the one hand the instance of being a colour, on the other hand – its diversity or difference; it is the latter that makes the former distinct from the instance of being a colour in the other path. This idea is very closely related to the idea of Avicenna and Scotus that the nature of F is a part of its particular instance in an F; maybe there is a single intuition manifested in both cases. The problem is that, as I have shown, these intuitions prompt claims that do plainly contradict the Instance Ascription Thesis (see 3.4.2 in particular); in other words, there are strong reasons to reject these intuitions.

On the other hand the Instance Ascription Thesis itself entails that in some important sense being redness does not belong immediately to being a colour; or that being a colour as such is not being redness or whiteness, and it is only in virtue of some particular instance that being redness can be ascribed to it. Moreover, it entails also that the nature instantiated both in being redness and being

---

54 This is precisely what Scotus says about colour and whiteness in *Ord.* II, d. 3, p. 1, q. 6, n. 174: "Color igitur in albedine est unus specie, sed non est de se nec per se nec primo, sed tantum denominative; differentia autem specifica est una primo, quia sibi primo repugnat dividi in plura specie; albedo est una specie per se, sed non primo, quia per aliquid intrinsecum sibi (ut per illam differentiam)".
55 See e.g. Geach 1961, 81.

whiteness, namely being a colour, is in a way distinct from its instance in the red patch. Within the function analogy introduced by Geach, these claims are comparable to claiming distinctions between functions and between a function and its value. The point is that the Scotistic argument seems to include an incomparably stronger claim, namely that in a given red patch the instance of being a colour is distinct from the instance of being red; within Geach's function analogy this is comparable to claiming the distinction of function values. More precisely: it is comparable to claiming some special sort of distinction between, say, the square root of 1 and the power of 1.

3.6 The Scotistic Way of Rejecting Self-Individuation

Mastri and Belluto say in their *Cursus scotisticus* that anyone who is not a nominalist agrees that a principle of individuation is in some way distinct from what it is a principle of individuation of; what is debatable, however, is the kind of distinction between them.[56] There are various sorts of distinction, for example: the distinction between Socrates's humanity and Plato's humanity; the distinction between a rose and its redness; the distinction between the redness of the rose and a given degree of intensity it actually has; the distinction between the redness the rose and the colour of the same (uniformly coloured) rose, and many more other sorts of distinction. (The very idea that there are distinct sorts of distinction would be decidedly rejected by the nominalist; I think, however, that what I have said against nominalism in chapter 2 is enough to show that this nominalistic rejection is implausible.)

The disputes within the Scotistic school over varieties of distinctions are immensely sophisticated. Here I will confine myself to two points.

First, Scotus says clearly that the distinction between an instance of the nature of F and its individuality is not the sort of distinction that occurs between things (*res*), taking 'res' in such a general sense that also the matter and the form it is informed by are two distinct things (*res*); so, in particular, the instance of the nature of F is not distinct from its individuality in the way in which matter is distinct from its form or form from its matter.[57] Mastri and Belluto stress that it is quite impossible that the distinction between an instance of the nature and its individuality is a distinction between two *things*; in this way, we may add, they

---

56 Mastri and Belluto 1727, vol. 5, *Met.*, disp. 10, q. 2, n. 13.
57 Scotus 1973, *Ord.* II, d. 3, p. 1, q. 6, n. 189–190; 1982, *Lect.* II, d. 3, p. 1, q. 6, n. 178.

agree with a modified version of the Self-Individuation Thesis – like the nominalists they think that it is quite impossible to be individual in virtue of some *distinct thing*.[58] In this sense the Scotists embrace something that might be called the Weak Self-Individuation Thesis (by contrast, the Thomistic theory of individuation reject the Weak Self-Individuation Thesis; see 5.1).

Secondly, however, Scotus claims that the instance of the nature of F and its individuality are not identical;[59] we may grasp the sense of this claim by considering what it is intended to deny. Consider namely a uniformly red patch; one might claim that its redness and its colour are one and the same, although being red and being a colour are not one and the same (using Geach's function analogy again: one might claim the identity of function values for the argument in question, although the functions themselves are clearly not identical).[60] I think that such a claim would be quite plausible; and it is precisely the claim that Scotus intends to reject when he states the non-identity of the instance of the nature of F and its individuality (see 3.4.2 and 3.4.3). Here this tendency also has the following aspect. It would be natural to say that being red is some sort of realization of being a colour; and it is clear that here we ascribe something to the *nature* of being a colour. Now it seems that according to Scotus in 'being red is a sort of realization of being a colour' something is ascribed to the *particular instance* of the nature of being a colour; in other words, it seems that according to Scotus being a realization of something is also a relation between individual instances of natures; and there must be some special sort of weak distinction between an instance of the nature and the realization of this instance: a sort of distinction which proves very difficult to explicate.[61]

---

[58] Mastri and Belluto 1727, vol. 5, *Met.*, disp. 10, q. 2, n. 14: "Dico primo principium individuationis non essse quidpiam realiter, seu physice superadditum naturae, et ab ea eodem modo distinctum. Conclusio haec est communis in omni schola [...] Et ita in hoc sensu dici potest res omnes seipsis esse individuas, quatenus non individuantur per aliquid ab eis realiter distinctum".

[59] Scotus 1973, *Ord., loc. cit.*, n. 190: "neque entitas specifica includit per identitatem entitatem individualem, nec e converso, sed tantum aliquid tertium – cuius ambo ista sunt quasi per se partes – includit ambo ista per identitatem"; 1982, *Lect., loc. cit.*, n. 178.

[60] See Geach 1961, 121–122; Geach 1969a, 51–52.

[61] In general it seems that Scotus tends to assimilate 'redness is a realization of colour' to 'a form is a realization of matter' – so that his relation of realization between instances seems similar to the relation between form and matter, although he makes a proviso that these relations are by no means identical.

3.7 What Individuality is Not?

This leaves open the question what is the entity to which individuality (in the strong sense) belongs immediately and which makes an instance of the nature of F – for example, Socrates's humanity or a given rose's redness – individual? Answering this question Scotus appeals first to some sort of analogy between the entity in question and the entity corresponding to a specific difference; this analogy has three aspects.[62]

(i) The entity of a specific difference is incompatible with the division into many species; this incompatibility belongs to the entity of a specific difference immediately; in a similar way the entity of an individual difference is (immediately) incompatible with the division into many individuals of one and the same species.[63]

(ii) The entity of a specific difference is a sort of realization or actuality (*quasi actus*, as Scotus says) of the entity of the relevant genus; similarly, the entity of the individual difference is a sort of realization or actuality of the entity of the relevant species, although (unlike a specific difference) it does not add to the entity of the species any additional determination belonging to form (one might say: no new content), but only, as Scotus says, the *ultimate* realization or *ultimate* actuality (*ultima realitas*).[64] So, for example, what distinguishes redness from whiteness is some realization of being a colour, and what distinguishes Socrates from Plato is some realization of being a man. In the former case we have distinct kinds of realization and some new content specific to them; moreover, each of these realizations can have its realizations, and is not an *ultimate* realization. In the latter case, by contrast, we have just distinct realizations with no new content, and these realizations cannot have their realizations in turn; in this sense they are ultimate realizations. The ultimate realization, adding no new content, is *not* an instance of any nature.

The special sense of 'being a realization of' involved here, is, as I have suggested in 3.6, distinct from the usual sense in which we say that being red is a realization of being a colour; the Scotistic being a realization of something is a sort of relationship between particulars (typically – particular instances of natures, in the case of ultimate realization adding no new content – between an instance of the nature of *infima species* and something that is *not* an instance of any nature).

---

[62] Scotus 1973, *Ord.* II, d. 3, p. 1, q. 6, n. 176.
[63] *Ibidem*, n. 177.
[64] *Ibidem*, n. 179–180.

(iii) Entities of specific differences are primarily diverse (*primo diversa*); similarly the entities of individual differences are primarily diverse.⁶⁵ They are so partly because they are not instances of any natures.

It seems, however, that all this still leaves open the question what the entity of individual difference is; it presents rather some general conditions that this entity must meet, and we may well ask now what is the entity that meets them; for example, whether the matter of the individual, or its form, or something other meets the conditions explicated above.⁶⁶

Answering such a question Scotus claims that neither the matter of the individual nor its form are to be identified with the entity of individual difference, because individuality or singleness cannot be ascribed to them immediately. Both the matter and the form do have in them the instances of their specific natures as well as their entities of individual differences.⁶⁷ From a more general perspective, Scotistic *haecceitates* resemble Bergmann's bare particulars, although *haecceitates* are not subjects of properties, but rather ultimate realizations.⁶⁸

Here two important doubts may be raised against Scotus's treatment of matter and form.

First, the critics of Scotus had claimed that if the argument against matter and form is sound, it may be applied also against *haecceitates* themselves; one might namely argue that one can distinguish between a given *haecceitas*, say *Petreitas*, some other *haecceitas*, say *Paulitas*, and *haecceitas* as such; and that in the given *haecceitas*, say in *Petreitas*, there is, on the one hand, the instance of the nature of the *haecceitas* and, on the other hand, the entity of the individual difference specific to this *haecceitas* as opposed to any other; or that the *haecceitates* of Peter and Paul are not primarily diverse, because there is something

---

65 *Ibidem*, n. 183.
66 *Ibidem*, n. 187.
67 *Ibidem*, n. 187–188: "Omnis entitas quidditativa – sive sit partialis sive totalis – alicuius generis, est de se indifferens 'ut entitas quidditativa' ad hanc entitatem et illam, ita quod 'ut entitas quidditativa' est naturaliter prior ista entitate ut haec est, - et ut prior est naturaliter, sicut non convenit sibi esse hanc, ita non repugnat sibi ex ratione sua suum oppositum; et sicut compositum non includit suam entitatem (qua formaliter est 'hoc') in quantum natura, ita nec materia 'in quantum natura' includit suam entitatem (quae est 'haec materia'), nec forma 'in quantum natura' includit suam. Non est igitur 'ista entitas' materia vel forma vel compositum, in quantum quodlibet istorum est 'natura', – sed est ultima realitas entis quod est materia vel quod est forma vel quod est compositum". Similarly Fonseca 1615, *In Met.* V, c. 6, q. 5, sect. 1.
68 For comparisons between *haecceitas* and bare particular see Park 1990a and 1990b. For a detailed analysis of the individual difference in Scotus see e.g. King (1992) and King (2005). For some sort of disappointment this explanation of what thisness is see also Noone 2003, 120 and Pini 2005, 50–53.

in virtue of what both are *haecceitates* (instances of being a *haecceitas*), and something other that makes them two distinct *haecceitates*.[69]

It may well be replied in defence of Scotus that the objection rests on an unacceptable assimilation of 'this haecceitas' to 'this humanity', and the assimilation of *'haecceitas'* to an usual sortal term expressing some instantiable nature; it is the point of introducing *haecceitates* that such an assimilation cannot be made. The problem is that the same sort of defence would be relevant in the case of the Scotus' thesis against matter. One might well say that Scotus's argument rests on an unacceptable assimilation of 'this matter' to 'this humanity' and 'matter' to a usual sortal term; I return to the issue of this assimilation in 6.3.2. Perhaps a similar line of defence would be plausible in the case of Scotus's argument against form.

Secondly, Scotists usually claim that in Socrates, besides his own individuality (that is, the individuality of his own humanity), there are also the individualities of his matter and his form, and the individualities of the various parts he is composed of.[70] Now it seems that in some cases the distinction between these individualities might be controversial; and it seems that some of these individualities are in various ways dependent upon some other individualities within the same individual.

In summary, form and matter seem so deeply related to a thing's individuality (and its *haecceitas*, whatever it is) that in order to grasp the principle of individuation, it is necessary to understand this relationship; and it is a serious objection against Scotus that he does not offer any hint of such an analysis at all. Suárez says that according to Scotus the appeal to *haecceitates* should terminate the inquiry of principles of individuation (*suis haecceitatibus quaestionem hanc terminandam esse censuit*);[71] the point is, however, that the inquiry cannot be terminated in the way in which Scotus wanted it to be. So I think it is obviously true what the Carmelites of Alcala say about the proponents of *haecceitates* (Scotus and Fonseca) that neither of them, appealing just to thisness as the ultimate prin-

---

[69] See Henry of Lübeck 1975, 106,44–107,66, in particular 107,64–66: "cum haecceitas posset accipi in communi, ut iam assumptum, sicut etiam materia vel forma potest accipi in communi et ut huius non videtur esse aliqua ratio, quare haecceitas dicat signationem potius quam materia vel forma". For Scotistic considerations on this topic see e.g. Punch 1672, *Logica*, disp. 6, q. 2, n. 10–20.

[70] See e.g. Fonseca 1615, *In Met.* V, c. 6, q. 5, sect. 2 i 3.

[71] Suárez 1866, *Disp. met.* V, sect. 7, 1.

ciple of individuation, have even touched the heart of the problem (*punctum difficultatis, qui in tota hac disputatione a Doctoribus controvertitur, [non] attingerunt*).[72]

3.8 Scotism and Nominalism

The Scotists and the nominalists seem to be radical adversaries. According to the nominalists, only self-individuation in the strong sense is conceivable, according to the Scotists instances of the nature of F in particular Fs are not self-individuated in the strong sense (there is a distinction between what is individual and what makes it individual). On the one hand, the Scotists appeal to the Avicennian Instance Ascription Thesis (see 3.4), according to which individuality does not belong immediately to the nature or essence expressed by the predicate F. On the other hand, they add some very sophisticated considerations that are intended to show that individuality not only does not immediately belong to the nature or essence of F, but also to instances of the nature of F in the particular Fs; the fundamental idea here is that in some important sense of 'part' the nature of F is a part of its instances in particular Fs. Both strands of Scotistic thought are fundamentally incompatible with the nominalistic Strong Self-Individuation Thesis. The latter one is specific to the Scotistic way of rejecting self-individuation.

In spite of this fundamental incompatibility, however, there are at least five deep similarities between the nominalistic and the Scotistic standpoints.

(i) Both the nominalists and the Scotists assert that there are some entities which are individual by themselves, and that they are fundamental to understanding sources of individuality. According to the nominalistic standpoint all the individuals are individuals by themselves, according to the Scotist – only *haecceitates*.

(ii) The nominalists and the Scotists agree on some features of the entities that are individual by themselves. In particular, they think that the individuality that immediately belongs to those entities is not analysable or describable in general terms; in an important sense it is impossible to say what such an immediately individual entity is.[73] In particular, both the nominalists and the Scotists seem to think that self-individuated entities are *not* instances of any instantiable natures.

---

[72] Collegium Salamanticense Fratrum Discalceatorum B. Mariae de Monte Carmeli 1679, vol. 1, tract. 1, disp. 1, dub. 1, n. 2.
[73] See Pini (2005); Pini suggests that the Scotistic individual difference is just not a special sort of *thing*, and that is why the Scotistic account might seem mysterious; as a matter of fact it seems

(iii) The Scotists accept the Weak Self-Individuation Thesis: they think that an individual cannot be made individual by a *distinct thing*. In order to reject the Strong Self-Individuation Thesis, they postulate a very peculiar sort of distinction between what is individual and what makes it individual.

(iv) Both the nominalists and the Scotists reject the idea that form or matter, being important principles of beings in general, are also, in some important sense, principles or sources of individuality. The consequence is that considerations concerning individuality apply equally well to material beings, to matter and form, to immaterial substances or to accidents.

(v) Both the nominalists and the Scotists reject the idea that answers to questions about the source of individuality may vary from one kind of being to another; in other words, they reject the idea that there may be something peculiar about individuation in some kinds of beings – something peculiar about the way in which individuality belongs to beings of these kinds.

As far as the relationship of Scotism with non-nominalistic theories of individuation is concerned, I think that the distinction between the two strands of Scotistic thought on individuation plays a crucial role. On the one hand, there are some ideas expressed in the Avicennian Instance Ascription Thesis. On the other hand, there is an intuition that the nature of F must be a special sort of part of instances of this nature; in other words, that there is some sort of metaphysical composition corresponding to the logical composition of expressions like 'this humanity' or 'Socrates's humanity'; these intuitions, as I have shown in 3.4, ultimately lead to the rejection of the Instance Ascription Thesis both in Avicenna and in Scotus, and to an enormous complication of the Scotistic ontology of natures. The former strand, as I will show, is common to the Scotists and various Thomistic theories of individuation which offer a much better understanding of the Avicennian Instance Ascription Thesis; the latter strand, by contrast, is the main bone of contention between the Scotistic and the Thomistic standpoints: the Thomists seem to be totally immune to the idea that the nature of F must be a part of its instances.[74]

---

important that the nominalistic simple entities are a sort of fundamental *things* in the world, and Scotistic haecceities cannot be treated in that way.

[74] This is just some version of the general suggestion to be found in Owens 1967 that Scotism and Thomism offer two different developments of the Avicennian *triplex status naturae* theory.

4 Forms and Self-Individuation

4.1 Forms as Principles of Individuation: the Main Thesis and Standard Arguments

The view that

> (The Formal Individuation Thesis) For any particular F, its principle of individuation is its form of F (the formal cause of this F).

is embraced by Godfrey of Fontaines, Peter of Auvergne and John Baconthorpe.[1] The former two authors, unlike the latter one, do assign some role in individuation to extension or quantity; this sort of principle of individuation will be discussed in chapter 7. It seems that Aristotle asserts some version of the Formal Individuation Thesis when he says in *De anima* that it is the form of a being that makes it a *tode ti*.[2]

So, for example, what makes the Sigismund Bell a single bell, according to the Formal Individuation Thesis, is the very form of a bell, that is, the specific shape that makes a given piece of the stuff a bell; and what makes Socrates a single man, is his substantial form (his soul). It may be worth noting, however, that Baconthorpe restricts the scope of the Formal Individuation Thesis to the individuation of natural substances as opposed to artefacts.

Forms or formal causes of different sorts of being are deeply different themselves. The formal cause of a building is its structure, the formal cause of a piece of fabric is its weave, and the formal cause of a human being – the rational soul.[3] Each of these forms makes a subject, as long as it remains in it, a being of a given sort and is the source of activity specific to that sort of being. On the one hand what form makes a being of a given sort is some stuff or matter, on the other hand what it makes a being of that sort is some individual constituted by the stuff and the form; so there are two closely connected senses in which a form makes something a being of a given sort.

---

[1] Godfrey of Fontaines 1914, *Quodl.* 7, q. 5; Peter of Auvergne 1934, *Quodl.* 2, q. 5; John Baconthorpe 1526, *In Sent.* III, d. 11, q. 2; for a brief survey of this standpoint see Wippel 1994 and Wippel 1999, 349–370.

[2] Aristotle 1961, *De an.* 412a6–9. Suárez says that this passage of *De anima* is the main source of the Formal Individuation Thesis (1866, *Disp. met.* V, sect. 4, 1).

[3] For some general points concerning forms in the Aristotelian sense see Geach 1961, 74 and 82–83.

A form of F is basically something distinguishable from the particular instance of the nature of F in the F constituted by the form; so, for example, Socrates's rational soul (which is his form) is something distinguishable from Socrates' humanity; and the form of the Sigismund Bell is something distinguishable from the Bell's being a bell. Forms have a sort of *causal* role: so, for example, humanity is instantiated in some matter in virtue of (or *via*) the relevant form.

The main argument in favour of the Formal Individuation Thesis appeals – like the nominalistic arguments for the Strong Self-Individuation Thesis (see 2.2 and 2.3) and the Scotistic argument for the Distinction Thesis (see 3.2) – to the principle of convertibility of being and unity: what makes a thing something real or actual, makes it also something single. Godfrey, Peter and John say that what makes a thing something real or actual is its formal cause, and henceforth it is also what makes it something single.[4]

Peter of Auvergne adds the following line of reasoning; (*) what makes something an F, makes it a single or undivided F; so what makes someone a man, makes him an undivided or single man. But it is the form of man that makes a man a man.[5]

Both Peter and Godfrey also add the argument that the form is a principle of the individuation of immaterial substances (angels), so *pari ratione* it must also be a principle of the individuation of material substances.[6] The premise of the argument is a principle accepted by the nominalists as well as the Scotists that there is a uniform answer to the question of the principle of individuation for all kinds of beings. The rejection of this premise is specific for the Thomistic theories of individuation (as well as for Baconthorpe's proviso concerning natural substances as opposed to artefacts).

---

[4] Godfrey of Fontaines 1914, *Quodl.* 7, q. 5, 323–324; Peter of Auvergne 1934, *Quodl.* 2, q. 5, 374,50–375,63: "per illud, per quod aliquid est vel secundum quid vel simpliciter, est indivisum et unum simpliciter vel secundum quid; sicut per quod aliquid est album, puta per albedinem, per illud est indivisum in albedine; et sicut caliditate est calidum, ita in caliditate indivisum est; et per hoc quod aliquid est homo, est unum et indivisum in eo quod homo; et similiter se habet in aliis, quod etiam Boetius satis ostendit libro de unitate et uno. Sed substantia composita in actu extra animam per formam subsistit in esse, sicut ostensum est in quaestione praecedenti, quia esse in effectu convenit formaliter substantie per formam. Igitur per formam est indivisum in esse in plura eiusdem rationis: hoc autem est individuum in genere substantie. Igitur per se principium individuationis est forma in substantia composita". The argument is mentioned also by John of Naples 1951, *Quodl.* III, q. 5, 152,11–14; Henry of Lübeck 1975, 109,129–132; and Suárez 1866, *Disp. met.* V, sect. 4, 2).

[5] Peter of Auvergne 1934, *Quodl.* 2, q. 5, 374,50–375,55.

[6] Godfrey of Fontaines, *op. cit.*, 323; Peter of Auvergne, *op. cit.*, 376–377.

Here I present an analysis of the main argument for the Formal Individuation Thesis sketched above. I begin with showing the way the form is the principle of existence or actuality (4.2), and then I focus on the line of reasoning (*) added by Peter of Auvergne (4.3); in this context I distinguish between two fundamentally different senses of the Formal Individuation Thesis. Finally I compare the standpoint of Godfrey and Peter with Scotism (4.4).

4.2 Effects of Formal Causes

The formal cause of a thing is the source or principle of many traits related immediately to the unity of that thing. (i) The form of a given thing makes it a thing of a given kind. (ii) The form makes that thing something actually existing; it is the principle of its existence. (iii) The form is the principle of that thing's identity over time; it is obvious especially in the case of beings that thanks to their forms do retain their identity in material change, like living beings undergoing metabolism. (iv) The form also makes all the parts of the thing parts of one and the same whole of a given sort (that is why, in Aristotle's view, forms cannot have parts: otherwise they require other forms to make their parts parts of one and the same whole[7]). (v) Finally, it is the distinction of similar forms that explains why parts of distinct wholes do not compose one and the same being – for example, that parts of two organisms of the same species taken together do not make up one and the same organism.

There are three conclusions to be drawn here. The first is that, *pace* nominalism, some traits closely related to unity and identity do not belong to the stuff or matter immediately, but only in virtue of the form. Moreover, in a way these traits do not belong to the material individual immediately, but only in virtue of its form which is distinct from it. These traits seem to belong to the form itself in a more immediate way. The second conclusion is that, *pace* Scotism (see 3.7) form and matter are not on a par as far as traits related to unity and identity are concerned: in a way these traits belong primarily to form as opposed to matter. Finally, the third conclusion is that these considerations may well make it plausible that singleness or individuality, being one of these traits, does immediately belong to the form, and that it belongs to the matter or to the material individual just in virtue of its form.

In the light of (*) these intuitions may be given a more precise form in the following way. A form making something an F also makes it an actually existing

---

7 Aristotle 1953, *Met.* 1041b12–25.

F, an F retaining its identity over time, a whole of the kind F, and an F distinct from other Fs; so the very same form bestows a thing with being an F, identity over time, internal unity and distinction from others. For example, the form that makes something a house makes it a distinct whole from other houses (in the way specific to houses) and a whole retaining its identity over time (in the way specific to houses). This strongly suggests that a form making something an F makes it also an individual or single F.

Let us note in passing that these intuitions could be premises of an argument for the thesis that there cannot be anything non-individual in the world; such an argument would be significantly different from the nominalistic one presented in 2.5, and in a way different from the rival line of reasoning sketched in 2.5.

4.3 Formal Causes, Kinds, and Singleness

The main argument for the Formal Individuation Thesis is supplemented by Peter with some additional explanations showing the connection between the form and various sorts of undividedness. To begin with, the form is responsible for generic undividedness and makes the thing it informs belong to a single genus; then the form is responsible for specific undividedness and makes the thing it informs belong to a single species; finally, Peter claims, it is responsible for undividedness in the sense of being single and individual, and it makes the thing it informs something individual.[8] So, for example, one and the same form of bell makes the Sigismund Bell a bell in general, and a bell of the sort it is; and, Peter would claim, it also makes the Sigismund Bell an *individual* bell. Similarly one and the same human rational soul makes a man a living being and a human being, and Peter claims that it also makes a man an individual man.

To grasp the meaning of Peter's explanation let us make two points concerning belonging to a given genus and species. (i) It is a fundamental thesis of Peter's metaphysics of formal causes that in one and the same being there is one and the same form that makes it belong both to its genus G and to its species S. So there is one and the same form that is both a form of G and a form of S; for example, there is one and the same form in Socrates, namely his rational soul, that makes

---

[8] Peter of Auvergne, *op. cit.* 376,77–377,97: "in substantiis materialibus, sicut forma est principium essendi, similiter ita est principium indivisionis per se. Est enim indivisa secundum rationem suam in diversas formas genere, et sic ab ipsa sumitur ratio unitatis generis; est etiam ex se indivisa in diversas formas secundum speciem, et sic ab ipsa sumitur ratio unius secundum speciem; est et indivisa secundum se in plura eiusdem rationis et ab ipsa secundum quod huiusmodi sumitur ratio individui in substantia materiali in actu".

him belong both to the genus of living being and to the human species; that form is both a form of living being and a form of human being. (ii) A form of G and S is a form of G and S immediately and of itself – as opposed to the individual S which is S and G not by itself, but just in virtue of its form (which is distinct from it). So we can ask what makes the Sigismund Bell a bell, and the answer is that it is its form of bell. But if we were to ask what makes that form a form of bell (as opposed to a form of house or of human being), the answer would be that the form in question is the form of bell just by itself and not in virtue of anything distinct from it.

The point is that Peter claims that something very similar can be said about the form being the form of an individual bell (and perhaps even about the form being the form of the Sigismund Bell). Peter suggests namely that the form of bell in the Sigismund Bell is the form of an individual bell (and perhaps even the form of the Sigismund Bell) in an equally immediate way in which it is the form of bell in general.

In the light of this claim of Peter's we should distinguish between the strong and weak version of the Formal Individuation thesis.

The Strong Formal Individuation Thesis says that the Sigismund Bell is something individual because its form is the form of an individual bell (and perhaps of the Sigismund Bell) in the same equally immediate way in which it is the form of bell; there is nothing distinct from that form that makes it the form of bell, and there is nothing distinct from that form that makes it the form of an individual bell (and perhaps the form of the Sigismund Bell). Note that by 'the form of the Sigismund Bell' I do not mean here just the form that inheres in the Sigismund Bell, but the form that makes some stuff just the Sigismund Bell. In general the claim is that a form is the form of an individual immediately and by itself; this claim might be called the *Strong Formal Individuation Thesis*.[9] For an argument against the Strong Formal Individuation Thesis see 5.5.

By contrast, the weak version of the Formal Individuation Thesis says that what makes The Sigismund Bell a single bell is its form which is both a form of bell and the form of this bell, but although this form is the form of bell just by itself, it is not necessarily the form of this bell (and of a single bell) just by itself. Admittedly the form of bell in the Sigismund Bell is the form of the Sigismund Bell in the sense that is not reducible just to its inherence in the Sigismund Bell, but it is not the form of the Sigismund Bell in the way in which it is a form of bell.

---

9 The Strong Formal Individuation Thesis is to be distinguished from the claim that *besides* the form of species there is in the individual another form which is (just by itself) the form of that individual. The latter claim implies that there are distinct forms in one and the same individual that correspond to its genus and to its species – whereas Peter claims the unity of form.

It is a form of bell immediately, but it is not the form of the Sigismund Bell immediately. This might be called the *Weak Formal Individuation Thesis*. As I am going to show in chapter 6, Aquinas himself and many Thomists do embrace the Weak Formal Individuation Thesis, although they reject the Strong Formal Individuation Thesis. Godfrey and Peter, by contrast, do embrace the Strong Formal Individuation Thesis.

Note finally that since natures are instantiated in matter *in virtue of* the relevant forms being received in matter, we should distinguish instantiation of natures and reception of forms, the latter being the cause of the former. In general, however, I decide to speak here about *instantiation* of forms in matter and I do not introduce systematically the distinction between the instantiation (reception) of forms and the instantiation of natures; for some details of the theory, however, the distinction may prove indispensable (see also 5.2.1, 6.2 and 6.3.2).

4.4 Formal Causes and Self-Individuation

Finally I would like to compare the way in which, according to both formal individuation theses, individuality belongs to the matter of the individual in virtue of something distinct from matter itself, and the way in which, according to the Scotistic Distinction Thesis and the Weak Unity Thesis, individuality belongs to a given instance of the nature in virtue of some entity distinct from that instance. Both Scotus and Peter of Auvergne assert that there is something really individual which, however, is individual only in virtue of something distinct from it; but there are two important differences between Scotus and Peter.

(i) On Peter's account there is a stronger kind of distinction between what is individual and what makes it individual than in Scotus's theory of individuation; in particular, matter can lose the form that actually makes it individual.

(ii) The distinction Peter is appealing to is relatively easy to grasp in the broader context of Aristotelian metaphysics, unlike the peculiar sort of difference between an instance of nature and its individuality on Scotus's account. The composition of matter and form is different from the sort of composition that the Instance Composition Thesis appeals to.

There are two other ways of being individual in virtue of something else connected with the formal individuation theses. First, a material individual is individual in virtue of its formal cause. Secondly, if one accepts the Weak Formal Individuation Thesis, one thinks that the very form of that individual is the form *of* that individual not just by itself (although it is a form of a given species by itself), but in virtue of something else; I will say more about the latter sort of being individual in virtue of something else in 5.2 and in 7.8.

5 Subjects as Principles of the Individuation of Their Accidents

5.1 Aquinas's Main Thesis Concerning the Individuation of Accidents

What is peculiar about Thomistic theories of individuation is the view that there is no uniform answer to the question of a principle of individuation for all sorts of entities; there are instead various answers for various sorts of being. In particular, the answer concerning the individuation of *accidents* is different from the answer concerning the individuation of *substances*; moreover, there are different answers for different kinds of accidents and different answers for different kinds of substances (for example, the material and immaterial ones). This peculiarity sets the Thomistic theories of individuation apart from both the nominalistic and the Scotistic ones.

The main thesis of Aquinas concerning the individuation of accidents is that

(The Subject-Individuation Thesis) What makes accidents individual is their subject.[1]

The thesis is embraced by a great number of later prominent Thomists like Capreolus, cardinal Cajetan, and John of St. Thomas.[2]

For some reasons discussed below the Subject-Individuation Thesis does not apply equally to all sorts of accidents; in particular, geometrical attributes or extension require distinct treatment in this context (see 7.2–7.5). Anyway, the standard example that illustrates the Subject-Individuation Thesis is whiteness (*albedo*). So Aquinas says that something is *this* whiteness insofar it is in *this* subject (*dicitur enim haec albedo, inquantum est in hoc subiecto*); he also says that this whiteness is distinct from that whiteness only due to being the whiteness of this or that subject (*haec albedo non differt ab illa nisi per hoc, quod est huius vel illius*), or that this whiteness is distinct from that one only due to being in this or that subject (*haec albedo non differt ab illa nisi per hoc quod est in hoc vel in illo subiecto*); he also says that instances of whiteness are in some number only insofar as they are in substances that are in some number (*albedines non sunt plures nisi*

---

[1] See Aquinas 1980, *S. th.* I, q. 29, art. 1, corp; *S. th.* I, q. 39, art. 3, corp; *S. th.* III, q. 77, art. 1, corp; *Quodl.* 3, q. 1, art. 2.
[2] See Capreolus 1902, *Defensiones* I, d. 54, art. 2, concl. 2; Cajetan 1888, *In Summam* I, q. 29, art. 1, 5–8; John of St. Thomas 1933, *Phil. nat.* p. 2, q. 9, art. 5.

secundum quod sunt in pluribus substantiis); finally, he says that it is impossible to conceive of a plurality of instances of whiteness not conceiving just the instantiation of whiteness in a plurality of subjects (*non possunt apprehendi multae albedines nisi secundum quod sunt in diversis subiectis*).³

To avoid some misunderstanding concerning the Subject-Individuation Thesis it should be stressed that according to it the whiteness of a given square on a chessboard *is* something individual and really distinct from the whiteness of another square on the chessboard, so that you can count instances of whiteness on the chessboard. The point is that according to the Subject-Individuation Thesis the whiteness of a square is individual in virtue of the individuality of the square it is the whiteness of, the distinction between instances of whiteness is derivative from the distinction of the squares, and counting instances of whiteness is derivative from counting the squares.

There are some clarifications to be made here as far as the notion of a subject (*subiectum*) is concerned. In the example sketched above the subject of whiteness is, on the one hand, the wood of the chessboard, on the other hand – some piece of its surface, and it is the latter subject that, according to the Subject-Individuation Thesis, is a principle of the individuation of whiteness and the source of the distinction between its instances. More generally, the Subject-Individuation Thesis is not the claim that anything that is a subject of a given accident in some otherwise important sense is a principle of the individuation of that accident; and the task of finding the *relevant* subject is usually far from being trivial.

In the context of nominalism and Scotism it is worth noticing that according to the Subject-Individuation Thesis there is a strong kind of distinction between what is individual and what makes it individual; the kind of distinction is far stronger than the Scotistic distinction between an instance of a nature and its individuality. So the Subject-Individuation Thesis allows that individuality can belong to something not immediately, and even in virtue of some entity belonging to another Aristotelian *category*. So while the Scotists embrace the Weak Self-Individuation Thesis, the Thomists reject it. And the Scotists side with the nominalists taking the Subject individuation Thesis to be just inconceivable.⁴

---

3 See respectively: Aquinas 1980, *S. th.* I, q. 29, art.1, corp. *S. th.* I, q. 75, art. 7, corp.; *De spiritualibus creaturis*, q. 8, corp.; *S.th.* I, q. 50, art. 4, corp.; *Contra gent.*, IV, 65, 5.
4 For the nominalistic criticism of the Subject-Individuation Thesis see e.g. Suárez 1866, *Disp. met.* V, sect. 7, 3: "subiectum non potest dici principium intrinsecum individuationis accidentis, tamquam intrinsece et per se componens accidens, quia nunc non agimus de composito ex subiecto et accidente, sed de ipsa accidentali forma, quam constat non componi ex ipso subiecto, nec subiectum hoc modo esse principium intrinsecum eius". For the Scotistic criticism see Mastri

It is worth noticing, moreover, that while Aquinas says that an instance of an accident is individual in virtue of something distinct from it, he does *not* say that the instance enjoys some sort of unity weaker than individuality in the strong sense (*unitas minor unitate numerali*). I return to this issue in 5.2.2.

The argument in favour of the Subject-Individuation Thesis in Aquinas is the following: {*} since accidents do *exist in* their subjects, they owe to their subjects not only their existence, but also their unity or plurality (*sicut esse habent in subiecto, ita ex subiecto suscipiunt unitatem et multitudinem*).[5] In other words: the singleness of a given accident depends on the subject of that accident in a way strictly parallel to the way in which the existence of that accident depends on the subject. The existence of the accident does obviously depend on various factors in various ways, but there is a special sort of dependence in the case of the subject in which the nature of the accident is instantiated.

It is an important feature of this general formulation {*} that it suggests that while various sorts of accidents may depend on their subject in *various* ways, individuality of those sorts of accidents also depends on their subjects in *various* ways.

Aquinas himself and later Thomists do offer some more general formulation of the argument for the Subject-Individuation Thesis: {**} something that can be instantiated *in the subject*, is not single or individual by itself, but in virtue of the subject it is instantiated in.[6]

It seems that {*} and {**} are just sketches of the arguments; to go into some details of them I present the connection between an accident's being instantiated in the subject and the individuality of that accident and distinguish two different senses of the Subject-Individuation Thesis (5.2). Then I offer an analysis of one philosophically significant example of the individuation of accidents, namely the case of the individuation of human virtues (5.3). Next I sketch various sorts of an accident's dependence on the subject and various sorts of subjects of accidents, and henceforth various sorts of extrinsic individuation (5.4). Finally I compare the Subject-Individuation Thesis with the strong and weak versions of the Formal Individuation Thesis (5.5).

---

and Belluto 1727, *Met.*, disp.10, q. 7, n. 112: "nullum ens est singulare formaliter per aliquod alterius generis [...] differentia individualis debet esse intrinseca individuo, imo ei realiter identificata".

5 Aquinas 1980, *S. th.* I, q.39, art. 3, corp.; Suárez analyses the argument in 1866, *Disp. met.* V, sect. 7, 2.

6 See Aquinas 1980, *S. th.* III, q. 77, art. 2, corp.

5.2 Being in a Subject and Singleness

5.2.1 Various Senses of 'Being in a Subject'

In light of the Avicennian Instance Ascription Thesis, which Aquinas himself embraces in *De ente et essentia* (c. 2), saying that whiteness is instantiated in a subject (say, in a given square on a chessboard) – can be understood in two fundamentally different ways.

(i) In the first sense being instantiated in the square is ascribed to the instantiable nature of whiteness (or to some sort of form which is the form of whiteness). According to the Avicennian Instance Ascription Thesis being instantiated in the square is something that is not part of the nature of whiteness but just happens to it. I think it is just *this* sense that is intended by Aquinas in the formulation of {*} quoted above; he says there that accidents owe their "unity and plurality" to their subject (*ex subiecto suscipiunt unitatem et multitudinem*)[7]; now plurality obviously cannot be ascribed to a particular instance of whiteness, but just to the instantiable nature of whiteness actually having a number of instances.

(ii) In the other sense being instantiated in the square is ascribed *not* to the nature of whiteness, but rather to the particular instance of whiteness in that square, or to a particular form of whiteness received in a given subject (in Geach's function analogy: to the value of the function and not to the function itself). Here being instantiated in the square certainly does *not* just *happen* to that instance; being instantiated in the square is instead an *intrinsic* characteristic of that particular instance of whiteness. I think that this sense should also be taken into consideration; in some discussions about the Subject Individuation Thesis there are some hints concerning some special sort of relationship to the subject belonging to the particular instance of nature in this subject.[8] I return to this issue later.

There are two important specifications to be added here.

---

7 Aquinas 1980, *S. th.* I, q. 39, art. 3, corp.
8 See e.g. John of St. Thomas 1933, *Phil. nat.*, p. 2, q. 9, art. 5: "quia autem [forma] receptibilis est in alio, ordinem dicit, et habitudinem ad illud, in quo semel recepta forma non potest transire ad aliud neque fieri communis multis, ergo inde ut ex principio, vel per ordinem ad illud habet incommunicabilitatem, et consequenter individuationem"; Collegium Complutense 1693, *De generatione et corruptione*, lib. 2, disp. 14, q. 4, n. 40: "et per praedictum respectum sit *hoc* accidens numero positive; quin hic respectus etiam per divinam potentiam auferri valeat"; Collegium Salamanticense 1679, tract. 1, disp. 2, dub. 1, n. 12: "[accidentia] individuantur ex eo, quod respiciunt hoc numero subiectum formaliter sumptum, non vero aliud; et hic respectus non distinguitur realiter a sua entitate".

As far as (i) is concerned, we should discern being instantiated in a subject (e.g. being instantiated in a square on a chessboard) and being instantiated in an instance of the nature in question. It is clearly the latter, as opposed to the former, that both Avicenna and Scotus focus on. Their reason for not focusing on being instantiated *in a subject* might be that the subject of instance is just a more or less extrinsic *circumstance of instantiation*. You obviously have such an extrinsic circumstance of instantiation when you say that whiteness is instantiated in a busy street or in Cracow in February; a Thomist might well argue, however, that 'in the square', unlike 'in a busy street', 'in Cracow' or 'in February', does not express just an extrinsic circumstance of instantiation of the nature of whiteness, but instead some intrinsic trait of the instantiation. The reason is that the very instantiation of, say, whiteness in the case in question, does *consist* in the square becoming white, and nothing similar holds in the case of a busy street, Cracow or February. This roughly corresponds to the fact that we speak of the whiteness *of* the square in the sense in which we obviously do *not* speak of the whiteness *of* Cracow or *of* February. We may add that the contrast between the *subject* of instantiation and the *extrinsic circumstances* of instantiation may be stronger or weaker for various sorts of subjects and various kinds of dependence of an accident on the subject (some authors, for example Pasqualigo, restrict the Subject Individuation thesis to the cases where the dependence and the contrast itself are *strong*).

What I call here being instantiated in a subject is not being *exemplified by* a subject in the sense of Lowe's ontological square. What the Thomistic theory analyses here is just the relationship of *instantiation* in the case of accidents, and the point is that in the case of accidents the subject itself must be taken into account to grasp the very nature of instantiation. So the Thomistic theory focuses here on instantiation in a subject instead of instantiation in general; I will return to some key issues related to that important shift in 6.3.2.

As far as (ii) is concerned, we may again discern two senses of being instantiated in a subject ascribed to particular instances. On the one hand we may mean that some particular instance of whiteness *is actually present* in a given square. On the other hand, we may mean that a particular instance of whiteness is the whiteness *of* that square. (In terms of Lowe's ontological square there are two senses of characterisation of a subject by a mode.) These two senses might well seem indiscernible. Consider, however, the question of whether the whiteness of the square might continue to exist actually being no longer present in that square. My point is that if this question can reasonably be asked, there is a distinction to be made between being the whiteness *of* the square and being actually present in the square. I think the question is a serious one and far from being trivial, so I've introduced this distinction.[9] I return to some applications of this distinction in 7.8, and here I will focus on the latter of the senses of being instantiated in the subject.

5.2.2 Being in a Subject, Parts, and Wholes

As I have shown in 3.4.2, Avicenna claims (in the Weak Instance Composition Thesis) that in the case of a particular instance of whiteness, (the nature of) whiteness is a special *part* of its particular instance. The Scotistic theory of the unity specific to the instance of the nature seems to be an attempt to develop this intuition. Both the intuition itself and its Scotistic development are hardly compatible with the main Avicennian Instance Ascription Thesis. Within Geach's function analogy a counterpart of this intuition would be the idea that the division of a designation into a function symbol and a symbol of its argument corresponds to some metaphysical division of a value of the function into the function itself and the argument. Part of this story is a special sort of distinction between the part of the value which is the function itself, and the other part of the value which is the argument; the study of this sort of distinction is one of the most specific Scotistic topics, and it is crucial for the Weak Self-Individuation Thesis.

Geach, as mentioned above (3.4.2), rejects this idea of a metaphysical composition corresponding to the composition of the designation, as well as the idea that the function is, in some important sense, a part of its value. It seems to me that Aquinas would also reject this Avicennian and Scotistic idea.

Employing the function analogy in the case of the Thomistic theory of the individuation of accidents makes it easier to see why the Scotistic idea leads us astray. Within this analogy the whiteness of a given square on a chessboard is something like the value of the function (the whiteness of _), and the relevant argument is just the square. Now if the composition of the designation mirrored a metaphysical composition of the function value containing in a way both the function and the argument, we should say that the square is in some important sense a part of the whiteness of the square – but it is obviously not a part of its whiteness. The name of the square B5 is a part of 'the whiteness of the square B5',

---

9 For some contexts in Aquinas that make the question a serious one see Brower 2014, 250–254.

but this does not mean that the square B5 is a part of the whiteness of the square B5.[10]

Anyway there is something convincing in the intuition of Avicenna and Scotus. Within the function analogy we could grasp this in the following way: for a given value of the function it should something *intrinsic* that it is the value of the function for such and such an argument. And it is something intrinsic and essential for a given instance of whiteness that it an instance of something instantiable *in a certain subject*. It seems that it is just this idea that is an important source of Avicenna's thesis that the nature is a part of its instance.

On the one hand, it is a deeply anti-nominalistic idea; it is against nominalism to think that it is something *intrinsic* for a given instance of whiteness that it is an instance of something instantiable. On the other hand, as Avicenna's considerations show (see 3.4.2), it is also an anti-platonic idea; Avicenna's aim is to ensure that whiteness does not exists besides its instances.

Now the point is that this idea may be saved without thinking of the instantiable nature as a *part* of its instance. We may say, namely, that it is essential for a particular instance that it is *an instance of some nature in a certain subject*, so that there is a sort of intrinsic relationship of that instance to its subject; we express this relationship by saying that, for example, a given instance of whiteness is the whiteness *of the square B5*. By contrast: when we say of an instance of whiteness that it is remembered or discussed by someone, we express some sort of relationship of this instance to the person in question, but this relationship is an *extrinsic* one. Being the whiteness *of something* is a deep and intrinsic trait of the very entity of that instance of whiteness. As the Scholastics say, it is a sort of transcendental relationship (*relatio transcendentalis*); transcendental relationships may be real without being distinct from the entity of what is related to something; a transcendental relation *pervades* the whole entity that is related to something in this way[11]. The point is that the transcendental relationship to the subject involves in a way the relevant instantiable nature.

---

10 A Scotist would probably respond that within the function analogy we *have* to treat the argument as a part of the value, and precisely this shows that the square which is not a part of its whiteness, is not so essential for the individuality of the whiteness as it seems.

11 John of St. Thomas 1933, *Logica*, p. II, q. 17, art. 2: "relatio transcendentalis non est forma adveniens subiecto, seu rei absolutae, sed ei imbibita"; art. 4: "[relationes] transcendentales non sunt aliquid distinctum a re absoluta [...] neque enim habent specjale praedicamentum, sed per omnia vagantur, et sic ex sua transcendentia habent imbibi in re absoluta, non distingui"; John of St. Thomas 1884, Ia, q. 49, disp. 18, art. 2, n. 20: "relatio transcendentalis est intima, et imbibita ipsi entitati, nec superadditur substantiae rei, sed est ipsamet substantia ut ordinata per se ad alterum".

5.2.3 Being in a Subject and Individuality

Now we can return to Aquinas's argument {*} sketched in 5.1. It seems natural to construe the argument as being about the way in which individuality belongs to *natures* of accidents rather than to their instances). So the argument would be that as far as the subject is essential for the realization of the nature of F, it is also essential for the individuation of nature of F (for the individuality ascribed to the nature of F). So we ascribe singleness to whiteness as far as we ascribe to it being instantiated in a single square; we ascribe distinction to the nature as far as we ascribe to it being instantiated in a distinct square; and we ascribe plurality to whiteness as far as we ascribe to it being instantiated in a plurality of squares. So singleness or individuality, distinction and number are ascribed to the nature of whiteness as far as instantiation in a subject is ascribed to that nature.

It is also possible, however, to construe the argument {*} as being about *instances* of the nature of F (and not about the nature of F). So the argument would be that if something is an instance of the nature of whiteness in a given square of a chessboard, it has some intrinsic transcendental relationship to that square: it is *its* whiteness; and individuality that belongs to that instance of whiteness consists also in the transcendental relationship to the square. The whiteness of the square B5 is a single whiteness, because it is the whiteness of a *single* square.

As far as the more general argument {**} is concerned, it should be construed in the following way; if something is instantiable in something else – in the sense in which the nature of whiteness is instantiable in squares on a chessboard – it is multiply instantiable. So if singleness is ascribed to it, it is ascribed in virtue of its being instantiated in a single subject. We may also ascribe individuality to some instance of whiteness in an individual subject, but here we cannot ascribe plurality. I return to some aspects of this line of argument in chapters 6 and 8.

Let us note that the fundamental dependence on the subject (in which the nature of a given accident is instantiable) shows some sense in which accidents are not individual *by themselves*. This sense of not being self-individuated, on the one hand, is considerably stronger than the one involved in the Avicennian Instance Ascription Thesis that individuality is something that *happens* to the nature of F or does not belong to it *as such*. Now according to the Subject-Individuation Thesis individuality happens to the nature of F, but, moreover, it happens to it in virtue of being realized *in a subject*; moreover, the individuality of *any particular instance* of the nature of that accident in a subject does depend in a way on the subject.

On the other hand, this Thomistic sense of not being self-individuated is clearly different from the Scotistic one involved in the Weak Unity Thesis or the

Instance Composition Thesis, because the Thomists do not say that a part of an instance of the nature of accident F is immediately marked with some sort of unity weaker than individuality.

To repeat, the accident's dependence on the subject of instantiation can be stronger or weaker; in cases in which it is very strong the sense in which the accident is not self-individuated is very strong, too; I return to this issue in 5.4.

Another problem faced by the Subject-Individuation Thesis is that there may be a plurality of accidents of the same species occurring *successively* in one and the same subject; I return to this problem in 5.5.

5.2.4 The Two Senses of the Subject-Individuation Thesis

To sum up: there are two senses of the Subject-Individuation Thesis. I would argue that it is true in both senses.

So on the one hand the Subject-Individuation Thesis may be construed as being about the way in which individuality belongs to *instantiable natures* of accidents in the sense of the Avicennian Instance Ascription Thesis. In this construal the thesis is that

> **(The Nature Subject-Individuation Thesis)** As far as natures are instantiated in subjects, individuality belongs to them in virtue of their subjects.

On the other hand the Subject-Individuation Thesis may be construed as being about the way in which individuality belongs to particular *instances* of natures of accidents. In this construal the thesis is that

> **(The Instance Subject-Individuation Thesis)** Any particular instance of a nature of an accident is marked by a transcendental relationship to its subject of instantiation, and individuality belongs to that instance in virtue of that transcendental relationship.

The Instance Subject-Individuation Thesis is compatible with saying (that we find, for example, in *Cursus philosophicus* of the Salamanca Carmelites) that accidents are individual in virtue of their own entities (*accidentia individuari proxime per suas entitates*), because they are individual in virtue of their relationship to their subjects, and that relationship, being a transcendental one, is not something distinct from the entity of the accident itself (*hic respectus non distinguitur realiter a sua entitate*).[12] So the accidents' being individuated immediately by their own entities is compatible with their being individuated by their relationship to their subjects.

There are two important differences between the two construals of the Subject-Individuation Thesis. The first is that the Nature Subject-Individuation Thesis is about the way individuality belongs to the nature of a given sort of accident, while the Instance Subject-Individuation Thesis – about the way in which individuality belongs to particular instances of that nature. The other difference is that the Nature Subject-Individuation Thesis is about individuality and *plurality* or *number*, while the Instance Subject-Individuation Thesis is about individuality and *distinction* from other instances of the nature of F. What we ascribe to the nature of F is plurality or number, but not distinction from other realizations;[13] and what we ascribe to a particular instance of the nature of F is distinction from other instances, but not plurality or number.

5.3 The Individuation of Human Virtues

The whiteness of something like a square on a chessboard is a standard scholastic example of an accident, but it may invite various doubts; to reject all of them we should engage in an advanced study of the metaphysics of colours and visual perception. So I think it may be helpful to add one more example of the individuation of an accident of another sort, namely a human moral virtue like justice, courage, temperance or patience. The nature of these accidents is the object of some scholastic debates that shed much light both on the Thomistic standpoint concerning the individuation of accidents and on the nature of accidents in general; so I briefly sketch one of these debates.

The problem I focus on here is the growth of intensity (*intensio*) of virtue that one already has, without any change of its scope. A man undergoing this kind of

---

[12] Collegium Salamanticense 1679, tract. 1, disp.1, dub. 2, n. 12: "patet ex dictis disputatione praecedenti, quomodo ad summum probet, accidentia individuari proxime per suas entitates, ut sunt *haec*: quia individuantur ex eo, quod respiciunt hoc numero subiectum formaliter sumptum, non vero aliud; et hic respectus non distinguitur realiter a sua entitate; non tamen individuari a seipsis, ut a primo, et radicali principio: quin potius ex eo quod subiectum sit *hoc*, provenit accidentia esse *haec*, et ex eo quod praedicta accidentia sint talia numero, et numerice solummodo distincta, ex habitudine praedicta, optime sequitur, subiectum esse primam radicem talis individuationis et distinctionis".
[13] Aquinas ascribes to natures individuation and plurification (*individuatio et multiplicatio*); see e.g. 1980, *De unitate intellectus*, c. 5.

change becomes *more* just or courageous than he used to be; there are no new objects in the scope of his virtue, but his resolution and facility in doing good are greater than they used to be. Now the question that arises in such cases is whether, in such a change, there remains one and the same (trope of the) virtue that in some way becomes greater or more intense, or rather the change in question consists in the former (trope of the) virtue being replaced by a new and greater one. Most of the scholastic authors writing on the subject opt for the former solution in the case of human moral virtues.

It should be noted, however, that there are cases when some subject becomes more and more F and it does not seem plausible to think of one and the same instance of F retaining its identity in the change and just becoming greater. Consider water that becomes hotter and hotter; it does not seem *prima facie* natural to think that there is one and the same heat in the water that retains its identity in the change in question and just becomes greater. There is at least one author, namely Durand of Saint-Pourçain, who thinks that the case of virtue growth is similar to the case of the growth of heat; he offers some arguments to the effect that it is just impossible to have one and the same virtue retaining its identity and becoming greater.[14]

The nominalists, the Scotists as well as the Thomists all agree that Durand's standpoint in the case of virtue growth should be rejected, and that there is one and the same instance of the virtue in the virtue growth that becomes greater. Scotus offers a series of arguments for this identity, and, interestingly, Ockham approves some of them. Two of the arguments are especially interesting.

The first is that when someone becomes more and more just, the change occurs thanks to his action in which he *makes use* of the virtue he already has; it is the very use of the virtue one has that makes one still more virtuous, and that at least suggests the identity of growing virtue.[15] We may add, by contrast, that if someone becomes dirtier and dirtier or more and more tired, the change does not occur thanks to his *making use* of the instances of the accidents he already has; so in the case of becoming dirtier and dirtier or more and more tired there is no such reason to admit the identity of accident instance in the change.

The other argument is that if one performs an unjust action that makes his virtue of justice lesser than it used to be, it does not seem that in the change the former greater virtue of justice is replaced by a new lesser one; otherwise we had to admit that the unjust action not only destroyed the former virtue of justice, but

---

14 Durand 1537, I, d. 17, q. 7, n. 9–15, 26–30, 31–35. I have discussed the details of the debate in the context of individuation in Głowala 2013.
15 Scotus 1959, *Ord.* I, d. 17, p. 2, q. 1, n. 205. Ockham 1977, *In Sent.* I, d. 17, q. 5, 490,7–12.

also produced a new one of a lower degree; but it seems impossible that the unjust action could produce any virtue of justice, be it more or less intense.[16]

So the Thomists, the Scotists and the nominalists all agree that when someone becomes more and more patient, one and the same trope of the virtue of patience, namely *his* patience, retains its identity and becomes greater.[17] Here, however, one may ask what kind of individual this trope is and what does its identity consist in; and the answers given by the Scotists and the Nominalists on the one hand and the Thomists on the other are radically different.

Scotus and Ockham (disregarding for the moment all the important differences between them) agree that the trope of virtue in question is some whole composed of parts acquired successively in the course of the change; any time someone becomes more virtuous, he acquires a new part or degree of the virtue. Ockham claims even that it is, in principle, possible to identify, for a given period of growth, the part that was acquired during that period[18] (they are, one may think, something like the growth rings of a tree).

The point is that both Aquinas and many of the subsequent Thomists, from Cardinal Cajetan to John of St. Thomas, unanimously reject this account of trope identity in the change as simply inconceivable. On the one hand, they reject the idea of identifying the part of the trope acquired during a given period of growth; on the other hand, they think that even if such distinct parts of the trope could be identified, it would have been impossible to explain the way they are united in one and the same trope.

From a Thomistic perspective the standpoint of Scotus and Ockham just ignores both the kind of individual someone's virtue is and the nature of its dependence on the subject the relevant nature is instantiated in (as well as the nature of its transcendental relationships to the subject).

The point of the Thomistic standpoint is the following idea: the growth of someone's justice consists precisely in the fact that the virtue inheres more deeply in its subject or pervades it more fully, thereby leaving less room for the opposite vice; what changes in the change in question is precisely *the way in which the trope inheres in its subject*. In other words, someone's virtue of justice becomes greater precisely by changing its way of inherence in the subject: by inhering more *deeply* in its subject. Moreover, as John of St. Thomas makes clear,

---

16 Scotus 1959, *Ord.*, *loc. cit.*, n. 212. Ockham 1977, *loc. cit.*, 490,18–491,2.
17 Let us note in passing that even for the Thomists accepting Subject-Individuation Thesis the very identity of the subject is *not* any argument for the identity of the trope; I return to this issue in 5.5.
18 Ockham 1977, *In Sent.* I, d. 17, q. 6, 509,10–511,13.

we should not think that the way of inhering in the subject is determined by the degree of the trope of the virtue itself, so that the trope of virtue inheres deeply in its subject *because* the trope itself has the relevant degree; having some degree just *is* nothing else than inhering in some way, so that the change of degree just *is* the change of the way of inhering in the subject.[19]

So when we ascribe to the nature of the virtue being instantiated in some subject, we ascribe to it a given degree of pervading that subject (each time the virtue is instantiated in some subject, it is instantiated *to some extent*); this degree is to be *identified* with the degree of the instantiation of the virtue in the subject itself. The degree of intensity of a given trope is just a sort of its transcendental relationship to the subject, and it is the transcendental relationship to the subject that changes in the intensive change of the virtue. So the degree of intensity, on the one hand, can be ascribed to the nature of the virtue (in the sense of the Avicennian Instance Ascription Thesis) as some trait of the way in which it is instantiated in a given subject; on the other hand, it can be ascribed, as some transcendental relationship to the subject, to the particular instance of that nature in the subject.

To sum up let us make three points related to the arguments {*} and {**} discussed above.

(i) The nature of a given virtue is realized in a given subject as far as it pervades that subject, and (in the case of intensive magnitudes) it can pervade the subject more or less; the degree to which it pervades the subject is the intrinsic transcendental trait of the instance of that nature. This sheds some light on the idea sketched above (see 5.1) that the subject of instantiation is something essential to the instantiation and not just some external circumstance of it.

(ii) The actual degree of a given instance of the nature of virtue is an intrinsic feature of the instance, although it consists in some relationship to the subject of that instance; this shows that some intrinsic features of the instances of accidents do consist in some transcendental relationships to the subjects of those instances.

(iii) There is, however, a fundamental difference between the degree of an instance of the virtue that consists in the (changeable) way of inhering in the subject and can change while the instance retains its identity, and individuality of the instances that consists in some relationship to the subject, but cannot change in that way.

---

[19] John of St. Thomas 1949, I–II, *De habitibus*, disp. 13, art. 6, 13, n. 774, 777; and n. 16–18, n. 787–799. John of St. Thomas 1933, *Phil. nat.*, p. 2, q. 4, art. 2, 604.

5.4 Subjects of Accidents and the Thomistic Way of Rejecting Self-Individuation

Finally, there are some points concerning subjects of accidents that should be made to complete the picture of the Thomistic theory of the individuation of accidents; in general they show some complexity of the general concept of a subject used in the Subject-Individuation Thesis and a variety of relationships between accidents and their subjects. This in turn shows some key aspect of the Thomistic rejection of self-individuation.

(i) In scholasticism, there is a widely accepted distinction between *subiectum praedicationis* (the subject, in the sense of something that the accident is *ascribed to* or *predicated of*), and *subiectum inhaesionis* (the subject, in the sense of something that the accident is instantiated in, or something in which the accident inheres). What is the subject of an accident in the former sense does not have to be its subject in the latter. A much discussed scholastic example from the metaphysics of sound could serve to illustrate the distinction. Suppose that the Sigismund Bell is ringing; the *subiectum praedicationis* of ringing is the bell itself, because it is the bell that ringing is predicated of. The issue of *subiectum inhaesionis* of ringing – of the thing in which ringing is instantiated or inheres – is far from being trivial and much disputed in the scholastic *De anima* commentaries; is it, for example, the bell itself, the air or maybe someone's hearing? More generally, this shows that the issue of *subiectum inhaesionis* is much more difficult than the issue of *subiectum praedicationis*. It is clear that what is crucial for the individuality of accidents is their *subiectum inhaesionis* rather than *subiectum praedicationis*.

(ii) On the one hand, a particular instance of the nature of some accident may be considered both as the *subiectum praedicationis* and the *subiectum inhaesionis* of the nature of that accident; being that accident may be predicated of it *in abstracto*, as when we say that the whiteness of the square B5 is whiteness, and it is true that whiteness is instantiated in a particular instance of whiteness. On the other hand, it is the subject that the accident is predicated in *concreto* (when we say e.g. that square B5 is white) that may be considered as a subject both in the sense of *subiectum praedicationis* and in the sense of *subiectum inhaesionis*. The Thomists, as I have remarked in 5.2, focus on the latter sense as opposed to the former one.

(iii) As remarked above, not everything that in some sense is a *subiectum inhaesionis* of the accident is the source of its individuality in the sense of the Subject-Individuation Thesis. For example, there are many instances of whiteness on one and the same chessboard; what grounds their distinction is not the distinction of chessboards, but the distinction of squares. It is because the proper subject (*subiectum adaequatum*) or the immediate subject (*subiectum immediatum*) of being white is the (piece of) surface and not the chessboard; as Aquinas says, the prime subject (*subiectum primum*) of colour is surface.[20]

In general, the proper subject of instantiation of a given kind of accident is something that is immediately engaged in the instantiation of that kind of accident. So the proper subject of colour is the surface it inheres in, the proper subject of a virtue is a power of the soul it pervades (and it may be discussed which power is relevant for a given sort of virtue). The question what is the immediate or proper subject of a given sort of accident is far from being trivial; for various sorts of accidents there are various sorts of proper subjects. (Note that in the case of a black and white *pattern* on the chessboard, as opposed to the case of colour, the proper subject is not a square, but rather some plurality of squares, because the pattern is realized immediately not in squares, but rather in manifolds of squares.)

(iv) The connection between an accident and *its proper* subject may be stronger or weaker for various sorts of accidents; accident in general is something that should inhere in the subject, but there are various sorts of accidents according to various sorts of inherence. The differences between them are so deep that there is not just a single sort of dependence on the subject that is specific for accidents *in general*. Aristotelian theories of categories provide some introductory typology of various sorts of dependence of an accident on its subject. For example, a decision as some sort of accident of the agent inheres in its subject (and immediately in his power of will) in a different way than the cubic shape inheres in some cubic piece of clay.

Accidents may be divided in another way, too, in order to restrict the Subject-Individuation Thesis to some kinds of accidents that are dependent on their subjects in a very strong sense. So, for example, Pasqualigo distinguishes on the one hand accidents that have some entity (*entitas*) distinct from the entity of their subjects (he thinks that heat and light belong to this type), and, on the other hand, accidents that do not have distinct entity of their own, but are some beings only in virtue of the entity of their subject (*sunt entia entitate subjecti*). Pasqualigo's example of the latter sort is sitting (*sessio*), that is, some position of the body, and modal accidents (*accidentia modalia*) in general (a given degree of intensity is a modal accident of someone's virtue). Obviously there is a very strong sort of dependence on the subject in case of such accidents.[21] Now

---

20 Aquinas 1980, *S. th.* IIIa, q. 77, art. 2, corp.
21 Pasqualigo 1636, disp. 42, sect. 2, n. 1.

Pasqualigo, at least according to some authors commenting on them, restricts the validity of the Subject-Individuation Thesis to modal accidents and only a few of the other kinds of accidents.[22]

5.5 The Subject-Individuation Thesis and the Formal Individuation Thesis

It is worthwhile to focus on the relationship between the Subject-Individuation Thesis and the Formal Individuation Thesis, especially in its strong version (see 4.3). According to the Formal Individuation Thesis, the whiteness of a given square on a chessboard (this particular instance of whiteness) makes (in the sense of formal causality) the square something uniformly coloured, something uniformly white, and, finally, a *single* case of something white. According to the strong version of the Formal Individuation Thesis the form of whiteness inhering in the square is as such and by itself a form of colour and a form of whiteness, and it is the form of an individual instance of white *just by itself*, too. I think that the Subject-Individuation Thesis is incompatible with the last claim; according to the Subject-Individuation Thesis the form in question is the form of a colour and a form of whiteness *just by itself*, but it is not a form of *an individual whiteness* by itself, but in virtue of something else. More precisely, when we consider (in the context of the Nature Subject-Individuation Thesis, see 5.2.4) being a form of whiteness as such, being a form of whiteness and being a form of colour do belong to it just by itself; by contrast, being the form of a given instance of whiteness belongs to it in virtue of its instantiation in a given subject. On the other hand, when we consider (in context of the Instance Subject Individuation Thesis, see 5.2.4) an instance of the form of whiteness, it is a form of *this* whiteness in virtue of some internal transcendental relationship to its subject (for example, a given square on the chessboard). So both senses of the Subject-Individuation Thesis (distinguished in 5.2.4) are incompatible with the strong version of Formal Individuation Thesis as far as accidental forms are concerned.

There is much more to be said, however, about the relationship between the Subject-Individuation Thesis and the Formal Individuation Thesis. To see an important aspect of it consider a sort of accidental form which is the structure of a building; such a form is something that makes a number of pieces of the building a single whole; it is a sort of unifying factor. Now one of the reasons for accepting the Formal Individuation Thesis is the idea that all the parts of a single building

---

[22] Pasqualigo 1636, *Disp. met.* 42, sect. 2; Mastri and Belluto 1727, *Met.*, disp. 10, q. 7, n. 111.

are (or constitute) a *single* building, because there is a *single* instance of such a unifying factor, and the unity of the unifying factor is, in a way, primitive: there is nothing that unifies that factor in the way in which it unifies the building. Forms are *simple* entities. These considerations might offer a reason for accepting the Formal Individuation Thesis at least in its weak form.

On the other hand, there are some considerations concerning the unifying factor that may speak in favour of the Subject-Individuation Thesis. It is possible that there is just one instance of the unifying factor, but it is also possible (in spite of its simplicity) that there are many instances of it; if the latter is the case – there are many instances of the unifying factor in some pieces – these pieces do *not* constitute a single building, but a number of buildings. The simplicity of the unifying factor itself does not, pace the Strong Formal Individuation Thesis, account for singleness.

Here we may ask how does the unity or plurality of instances belong to a given kind of unifying factor. The Nature Subject-Individuation Thesis provides an answer to that question: the unity or plurality of instances belong to a given kind of unifying factor in virtue of what is united – in virtue of its *proper* subject.

We may also ask, speaking not about kinds of unifying factors, but rather about their particular instances, what makes such an instance distinct from other instances of the same sort of unifying principle. The Instance Subject-Individuation Thesis provides an answer to that question: any such instance is distinct from others in virtue of its internal transcendental relationship to its subject; in other words, it is distinct from others in virtue of its being a unifying principle of *a certain manifold of parts*.

Here we encounter a well-known objection against the Subject-Individuation Thesis. Consider an amount of stuff that had been unified by some form (and had been, say, a building), then broken into pieces, and after some time has been unified again by the same sort of unifying principle. It seems obvious that the present instance of the unifying principle is distinct from the past one, unless there is some special factor that warrants their identity; the point of the objection is that *this* distinction of instances of the unifying principle does not occur in virtue of the distinction of subjects, for both times the form is realized in one and the same subject. Similarly, when one and the same square on a chessboard had been white, then changed its colour, and then has become white again, the past and the present instances of whiteness in the square seem distinct, although they are *not* instances of whiteness in distinct squares.

This might suggest that, *pace* the Subject-Individuation Thesis, the distinction of proper subjects is not even a necessary condition of having a plurality of instances or of being a distinct instance; and that the identity of the subject is not enough for the identity of the instances of accidents in that subject.[23]

It is improbable that the adherents of the Subject-Individuation Thesis just have not noticed this problem; and the very debate over the identity of virtue tropes in intensity changes (see 5.3) shows that they do not think that the identity of the subject is a sufficient condition for the identity of an instance of its accident. When the Thomists say that *one and the same* instance of the virtue inheres in its subject, they do *not* think that the identity of the subject is any reason to be in favour of the identity of a virtue instance in the intensity change: instead they offer much more sophisticated arguments.

I think there are at least three ways of rejecting this sort objection; they are not necessarily mutually exclusive ways, and it is not quite clear how far they differ. I hope, however, that they will shed some important light on two versions of the Formal Individuation Thesis and the two versions of the Subject-Individuation Thesis.

(i) The answer sketched by the Carmelites of *Collegium Complutense* and *Collegium Salamanticense* is that in the cases in question there is one and the same thing (e.g. one and the same square) that is the subject of whiteness both times, but this does not necessarily mean that there is also the same *being a subject* or the same *subject* of both instances.[24] This, I think, might be compared to claiming that if one and the same piece of stone was used twice as a column to support a vault, it does not necessarily mean that it was twice *one and the same column*, for it is perfectly possible that one and the same piece of stone might be two distinct columns supporting the vault. Similarly, one might argue, if one and the same square was twice a subject of whiteness, it does not follow that it was twice *the same subject* of whiteness. As the Carmelites say, the square remains the same as a thing, *in esse rei* (so, in our example, it remains the same square); but it does not remain the same as the subject, *in esse subiecti* (so, in our example, it does not remain the same subject). The reason for the lack of the identity of the subject,

---

[23] For considerations concerning this objection see e.g. Collegium Complutense 1693, disp. 14, q. 4. n. 38; Collegium Salamanticense 1679, tract. 1, disp. 2, dub. 1, n. 16; Mastri and Belluto 1727, *Met.*, disp. 10, q. 8, n. 114.

[24] Collegium Complutense 1693, disp. 14, q. 4. n. 39: "ut subiectum conferat unitatem numericam oportet, quod fit unum formaliter in esse subiecti; ad quod praeter eius entitatem, quae materialiter semper est eadem, requiritur inter alia, circumstantia eiusdem temporis. Unde eadem entitas materialis subiecti connotans diversa tempora, sit multiplex numero in munere subiecti, et potest subinde diversam unitatem numericam accidentibus impertiri"; Collegium Salamanticense 1679, tract. 1, disp. 2, dub. 1, n. 15–16. For a criticism of this sort of solution see e.g. John of St. Thomas 1933, *Phil. nat.*, p. 2, q. 9, art. 5.

they explain, is that time (*circumstantia temporis*) is essential for being the subject of an accident. So there is, the argument might go, the distinction between subjects required by the Instance Subject-Individuation Thesis. On the other hand, there might be the identity of subject without the identity of the thing that is the subject: in a way, this seems to be the case with metabolism. (I do *not* claim that there is such a similarity between being a column supporting a vault and being a subject of instantiation of whiteness; but I do claim that the question whether there is any similarity is an important question that sheds some light on the issue.) Anyway, there is another problem with this solution: it seems namely to imply that when a formerly white square becomes black there is *not* one and the same subject of both colours, but only one and the same thing that is the subject of colour instance in both cases; this sounds at the very least strange. Perhaps one might reply in favour of this line of argument that the very concept of a subject is so equivocal, that it is not strange at all that in the sense of '*subiectum*' relevant for the Subject-Individuation Thesis such special criteria of the subject identity should be employed (although they should not be employed when we discuss subjects of change). It is clear, however, that much more should be said if this strategy of defence of the Subject-Individuation Thesis is to be accepted.

(ii) Anscombe and Geach suggest that the issue of a principle of individuation in general is the issue of the source of distinction of *co-existing* individuals, and not of any sort of distinction within one and the same species; and that the issue of a principle of individuation is to be carefully distinguished from the issue of identity over time which has its source in the formal cause.[25] A somewhat similar strategy may be found in John of St. Thomas: he says that in cases of plurality of *successive* instances there is no *actual plurification* of forms, and each time there is actually only one form.[26] One might say in a similar vein that there is no *actual distinction* between particular instances in such a case. Here, as in the case of the solution (i), much more is to be said if we were to accept this line of defence of the Subject-Individuation Thesis. In particular, it should be shown why the "actual" distinction of co-existing instances is to be explained in an utterly different way than a "non-actual" distinction of successive instances in one and the same subject. At any rate in both cases of distinction we ascribe number to instantiable natures of accidents.

---

25 Anscombe 1981a, 64; Geach 1961, 55–56 and 72–73.
26 John of St. Thomas 1933, *Phil. nat.*, p. 2, q. 9, art. 5: "In casu successionis formarum eiusdem speciei, non est necesse subiectum entitative dividi in actu, quia non datur multiplicatio formarum in actu, sed una tantum est in actu, alia vero praeteriit, et in actu non est".

(iii) One might also say that the internal transcendental relationship of a given instance of an accident to its subject includes some temporal aspect. Then in the case of successive instances in one and the same subject it would be true that the distinction between the instances consists in their relationships to their subjects; these relationships would then be different in virtue of the very difference of time, but they would not necessarily be relationships to different subjects. This solution clearly requires a better explanation of why the temporal aspect enters the very internal transcendental relationship of an instance to its subject.

These three possible solutions, I think, suggest some general lessons to be learned concerning the Subject-Individuation Thesis.

On the one hand, according to the Nature Subject-Individuation Thesis the unity and plurality of instances of *the instantiable nature of* a given accident are in some way grounded in the unity and plurality of the subjects of instantiation of these natures. The point is that *the way in which* they are grounded should be described more precisely for various kinds of accidents; such a more precise description should take into account both the circumstances sketched in 5.4 and some problems concerning identity over time, "actual distinction", and so on.

On the other hand, according to the Instance Subject-Individuation Thesis individuality of a particular instance and its distinction from other instances are grounded in some internal transcendental relationship of an instance to its subject. The point is that *the relevant sort of transcendental relationship* should be precisely described for various sorts of accidents; and the circumstances and problems which must be taken into account in this description are similar to the ones referred to in the last paragraph. I return to this issue in 7.6–7.8.

At any rate, the following seems crucial: on the one hand, *pace* the Strong Formal Individuation Thesis, the transcendental relationship of a form to the subject it is instantiated in is essential for the individuality of the form and for its being the form of a *single* F. Forms are simple unifying principles, but their simplicity itself does not account for singleness; what accounts for it is rather the transcendental relationship. On the other hand, the transcendental relationship to the subject consists just in the fact that a given form is an instance of some instantiable nature *in this subject* (within the function analogy it is comparable to the relationship between a value of the function *for a certain argument* and that argument); the point is that this relationship involves in a way the instantiable nature itself, but, *pace* the Instance Composition Thesis, this does not mean that the instantiable nature is a special sort of part of its instance.

6 Matter: Noninstantiability and Self-Individuation

6.1 Matter and Individuality: Aquinas's Main Thesis

The Matter-Individuation Thesis that

> **(The Matter-Individuation Thesis)** The matter in which a substantial form is instantiated is a principle of individuation of the form.

is to be found in Aquinas and a great number of Thomists: Capreolus, Cajetan, Soncinas, Ferrara, Javelli, Dominic of Flandria and John of St. Thomas (it is also usually ascribed to Aristotle, but this may be doubtful as we find no systematic treatment of the question of individuation in him). Most authors that embrace the Matter Individuation Thesis think that it stands in need of various qualifications, especially as far as a parallel role of extension or quantity is concerned; the details of these qualifications, however, are a very contentious issue, and Suárez says ironically that there is a surprising divergence in the ways in which the Thomistic thesis is explicated by its defenders.[1] I return to this troublesome topic (concerning the so-called *materia signata*) in 7.5–7.6. Here, by contrast, I focus on those of Aquinas's intuitions that concern the connection between matter and individuality and constitute the common core of the Thomistic individuation doctrine and the point of departure for further debates.

Leaving aside for the moment the issue of various qualifications of the Matter-Individuation Thesis we have to make two general points concerning its general sense.

(i) The Matter-Individuation Thesis designates a principle of the individuation of *material substances* as opposed both to immaterial substances and to accidents. The authors who embrace the Matter-Individuation Thesis typically think that there is no *uniform* answer to the question of individuation for various kinds of beings. (ii) The Matter-Individuation Thesis does not claim that the matter of a thing is *the* principle of the individuation of that thing; it claims instead that it is *a* principle of individuation, having some irreducible role in individuation. The authors who embrace the Matter-Individuation Thesis typically think that there is no such thing as *the* principle of individuation in a given case; there

---

[1] Suárez 1866, *Disp. met.* V, sect. 3, 8.

is instead a number of principles (including also the form and extension or quantity) responsible for various aspects of individuality. So, for example, Capreolus says that in material substances their matter is their principle of individuation *in one way*, while the quantity is their principle of individuation *in another way*.² So the most important thing to be understood in the case of the Matter-Individuation Thesis is the supposed *way in which* matter is a principle of individuation; or, in other words, the way in which matter is supposed to be responsible for the individuality of a material substance.

It is precisely this issue that Aquinas focuses on in his mature treatment of individuation in the third part of the *Summa*. He considers and wants to distinguish the roles of both matter and quantity; he says

> it is of the very notion of an individual that it cannot be in several [*non possit in pluribus esse*]; and this happens in two ways. First, because it is not natural to it to be in any one [*non est natum in aliquo esse*]; and in this way immaterial separated forms, subsisting of themselves, are also individuals of themselves [*per seipsas individuae*]. Secondly, because a form, be it substantial or accidental, is naturally in someone indeed, not in several [*est nata in aliquo esse, non tamen in pluribus*], as this whiteness, which is in this body. As to the first, matter is the principle of individuation of all inherent forms, because, since these forms, considered in themselves, are naturally in something as in a subject [*sint natae in aliquo esse sicut in subiecto*], from the very fact that one of them is received in matter, which is not in another [*recipitur in materia quae non est in alio*], it follows that neither can the form itself thus existing be in another [*iam nec ipsa forma sic existens potest in alio esse*]. As to the second, it must be maintained that the principle of individuation is dimensive quantity.³

---

2 Capreolus 1902, lib. II, d. 3, q. 1, concl. 2: "In substantiis materialibus et corporeis, principium individuationis est materia, uno modo; et quantitas, alio modo". Similarly, in the question whether matter is a sufficient principle of individuation Dominic of Flandria (1621, *In Met*. VII, q. 22, art. 1) says that matter is a principle of individuation, but it is not sufficient principle "materia est bene principium individuationis [...] non tamen est sufficiens principium individuationis".
3 Aquinas 1947, *S. th*. III, q. 77, art. 2, corp. (trans. by Fathers of the English Dominican Province). The Latin text (Aquinas 1980): "Est enim de ratione individui quod non possit in pluribus esse. Quod quidem contingit dupliciter. Uno modo, quia non est natum in aliquo esse, et hoc modo formae immateriales separatae, per se subsistentes, sunt etiam per seipsas individuae. Alio modo, ex eo quod forma substantialis vel accidentalis est quidem nata in aliquo esse, non tamen in pluribus, sicut haec albedo, quae est in hoc corpore. Quantum igitur ad primum, materia est individuationis principium omnibus formis inhaerentibus, quia, cum huiusmodi formae, quantum est de se, sint natae in aliquo esse sicut in subiecto, ex quo aliqua earum recipitur in materia, quae non est in alio, iam nec ipsa forma sic existens potest in alio esse. Quantum autem ad secundum, dicendum est quod individuationis principium est quantitas dimensiva".

I focus primarily on this text for two reasons. The first is that it tries to assign the roles of matter and quantity in individuation, and that, I will argue, is the key to understanding the troublesome issue of *materia signata*. The other is that it is a mature text of Aquinas which employs many of his earlier thoughts on the topic and combines them into an ordered whole. It seems that Aquinas's views on individuation changed in some respects during his career; here, however, I do not focus on these supposed changes at all, but instead consider the mature and comprehensive treatment coming from the last part of the *Summa*.

Let us begin with noting two things. (i) Aquinas is talking about the individuality of substantial and accidental *forms*, and about a principle of the individuation of *forms*. Many passages in Aquinas show that he accepts the Weak Formal Individuation Thesis (see 4.3); he claims that the form of an individual is a principle of individuality of what it is a form of.[4] So according to the Matter-Individuation Thesis matter is a principle of the individuation of *forms*. (ii) Aquinas points out two ways in which individuality is related to being instantiated in a subject. On the one hand, individuality belongs to what is instantiated in a subject in the sense in which whiteness is instantiated in a square on a chessboard (see 5.2 and 5.4); now here (according to the Nature Subject-Individuation Thesis) individuality belongs to something insofar as it is instantiated in a single subject. On the other hand, there is a sense in which what is individual is not instantiable at all; anything that is instantiable at all is multiply instantiable (that is the fundamental idea of the argument {**} for the Subject-Individuation Thesis, see 5.1).

Now the point of the quoted passage on individuation in the third part of the *Summa* is that matter is responsible for the latter aspect of individuality (and quantity or extension – for the former one). I discuss the issue of the relationship between these two aspects of individuality in 7.6, and in this chapter I focus on the connection between matter and the latter aspect of individuality.

So the main argument for the Matter-Individuation Thesis is the following. What is instantiable in a subject may have many instances; so what is a source of noninstantiability is a source of individuality. It is matter, however, that in some important sense is not instantiable in any subject. So it is matter that is a source

---

4 See especially Aquinas 1980, *De spiritualibus creaturis* q.3, corp.: "cum unitas rei sequatur formam, sicut et esse, oportet quod illa sunt unum numero quorum est forma numero una"; *S. th.* I, q.76, art.3, corp. "nihil est enim sipliciter unum nisi per formam unam, per quam res habet esse, ab eodem enim habet res quod sit ens et quod sit una"; *Contra gent.* II, 73, 5: "ab eodem habet aliquid esse et unitatem: unum enim et ens se consequuntur. Sed unumquodque habet esse per suam formam. Ergo et unitas rei sequitur unitatem formae. Impossibile est igitur diversorum individuorum esse formam unam".

of individuality of the form that is instantiated in it. In some sense it is matter that makes forms noninstantiable and hence individual.[5]

This intuition might be conveniently expressed within Geach's function analogy. Natures expressed by general terms are instantiable in subjects (or may have values *for* arguments) in virtue of their *unsaturatedness*; uninstantiability corresponds to saturatedness specific for objects as opposed to functions.[6] So individuality is connected to saturatedness, and a source of saturatedness is a source of individuality.

To go into the details of this general argument for the Matter-Individuation Thesis I will first make some points concerning subjects of substantial forms (6.2) and the noninstantiability of matter (or its being a prime subject) (6.3). Finally I sketch the way in which matter makes a form which is instantiated in it noninstantiable (6.4).

6.2 Subjects of Substantial Forms: Matter

Various things may be said to be a subject in which a given substantial form is instantiated. Take for example a sort of substantial form which is the human soul. Now it is instantiated, in different (although obviously interconnected) senses, (i) in the human body; (ii) in various parts of the organism, for example in the heart or the right hand; (iii) in the totality of stuff that (at a given time) constitutes the human body (although after some time *it* will not constitute the body due to the metabolism of the organism); (iv) in a part of this stuff; (v) in a particular person whose soul it is, for example in Socrates. This list is by no means exhaustive; its aim is only to show that there are various things that may truly be said to be a subject in which a substantial form is instantiated. A general theory of substantial

---

5 For a similar argument see Aquinas 1980, *S. th.* I, q. 3, art. 2, ad 3: "formae quae sunt receptibiles in materia individuantur per materiam, quae non potest esse in alio, cum sit primum subiectum substans"; *De spiritualibus creaturis*, art. 5, ad 8: "materia est individuationis principium, in quantum non est nata in alio recipi"; *De unitate intellectus*, c. 5: "non enim materia est principium individuationis in rebus materialibus, nisi in quantum materia non est participabilis a pluribus, cum sit primum subiectum non existens in alio". See also Ferrara (1898), I, c. 21; Dominic of Flandria 1621, *In Met.* VII, q. 22, art. 1, corp.; Soncinas 1588, *Quaestiones metaphysicales acutissimae*, VII, q. 23, corp.; Capreolus 1902, II, d. 3, q. 1, concl. 2. The argument is referred to also by John of Paris (Quidort) (1974), Peter of Auvergne (1934, *Quodl.* II, q. 5, 370,14–15), and Suárez (1866, *Disp. met.* V, sect. 3, 6). By contrast, it seems to be ignored in Brower 2012, where the discussion of the role of matter in individuation is focused on material difference (which I discuss in ch. 7 in the context of the role of quantity).
6 See Frege 2008a and 2008b.

forms should show various connections between the senses in which something is a subject of a substantial form.

There are, moreover, two important differences between subjects of accidents and subjects of *substantial* forms. The first difference is that an accidental form and its subject belong to distinct categories and taken together are something one only in a weak sense which in Aristotelian metaphysics is usually referred to as accidental unity, *unum per accidens* (see also 8.4). A substantial form, by contrast, together with its subject (at least in some important senses of 'its subject') composes something one in a strong sense, *unum per se*. The other difference is that the subject of an accident is what it is independently of its accidental form; such a form bestows only some accidental feature on it, but does not make it what it is and does not make it actually exist. It is just the substantial form, by contrast, that makes its subject what it is, and makes it actually exist. I leave aside here the details of these two differences.

As for the very concept of matter used in the Matter-Individuation Thesis, there are two contexts crucial for its use. The first is the re-identification of matter in various changes; we say that it is *the same matter* that used to be one sort of thing and is now some other, for example – that it is the same matter that used to constitute the food and now constitutes some organism; we may also ask where is now the matter that used to constitute the snow on some roof on a January day in 1930. It is matter that we re-identify here and it is matter identity that we are referring to.

The other crucial context is *material change*, a change in which something, retaining its identity, exchanges its matter with its environment; metabolism and water exchange in rivers or seas are the most obvious examples of material changes, already discussed in the oldest Greek philosophy. It is matter, to sum up, that is exchanged or replaced in this kind of change.[7]

So these two contexts and these two ways of referring to the (non-)identity of matter are the most fundamental for the very concept of matter that is used to describe some important kind of subject of substantial forms and that is used in

---

[7] For brief remarks on the concept of (prime) matter see especially Geach 1961, 69–73. Another text that focuses on re-identification as a key to understanding the scholastic concept of *materia prima* is Brower 2014, 113–115. Another important thing about matter according to Brower is that it is something that can be compounded and divided (2014, 115–119). It seems to me, however, that there is some contrast between the issue of re-identification of the same matter and composition or division of matter, because in Aquinas the latter, as opposed to the former, belongs to matter only in virtue of something else (see 7.2 for more details).

the Matter-Individuation Thesis. To have a better grasp of what matter is, it is necessary to have a better grasp of these contexts.

6.3 Prime Subjects and Noninstantiability

6.3.1 Matter as a Prime Subject

The key concept used in the argument for the Matter-Individuation Thesis is the concept of a prime subject (*subiectum primum*). A *prime* subject may be defined as something that is not instantiable in some other subject (in the sense sketched in 5.2, 5.4 and 6.2), and, it seems, is not itself an instance (in some subject) of something instantiable. By contrast: whiteness or a building structure are not prime subjects because they do have instances and may be instantiated in various subjects. Particular instances of them are not prime subjects (at least in the narrow sense which I'm focusing on here) because, although they cannot have instances themselves, they *are* instances of their natures in some subjects.

Suppose that the alloy a cannon was originally made of is now being used to cast a big bell. We re-identify the matter that had been a cannon and now is a bell. Being a cannon (or a form of a cannon) used to be instantiated in that matter, and what is instantiated in it now is being a bell (or a form of bell). Moreover, before the alloy was produced, its components had already existed; so being the alloy (or a form of the alloy) that is now instantiated in the matter, was not instantiated in it before. The point is that although being a cannon, being a bell and being the alloy (and the relevant forms) are instantiated in the matter, there is nothing in which being *matter* is instantiated, and there is no form that makes some subject *matter*. It is precisely in this sense that matter is *prime* subject, and that the Scholastics talk about *prime* matter; being prime in the case of prime matter consists just in its not having any subject in which it is instantiated. By contrast, *kinds* of stuff, like the alloy, are to be distinguished from prime matter, and as far as they are distinct from it, they are not *prime* subjects, because in a sense they do have instances in subjects and are instantiable.

As Anscombe and Geach warned long ago, it is a mistake to think that prime mater is a mysterious *sort* of matter which we may come to discover or postulate in some analyses of changes in the world – a special sort of *component* of the cannon, the bell or the alloy.[8] When we talk about the prime matter *in* the bell or

---

[8] For a discussion of other contemporary misunderstandings related to prime matter as "pure potentiality" see Brower 2014, 119–129. Brower suggests that it is precisely the contemporary

in the alloy we are not referring to some special sort of component of these things, but about the matter that now *is* the alloy and the bell, although there used to be times when it was neither of them. We know that there is something that is now the alloy, although it was not the alloy before; and this knowledge is not based on any specific philosophical discovery: it is just common knowledge about the ways in which humans produce alloys and bells; within such common knowledge we identify not only the same piece of alloy, but also the same piece of stuff that wasn't the alloy before. One should also remember that there are also well-known cases of change that do *not* meet the identity of matter condition; these are changes that do consist in the very exchange of matter.

So the question: 'What is being a bell (or being the alloy) instantiated in?' is a legitimate one, and one of true answers to it refers to some *prime* matter and to the identification of prime matter sketched above. By contrast, the question: 'What is being matter instantiated in?' is misguided. Talking about matter we refer to something that is just a *prime* subject.

Predicates expressing instantiable natures typically occur in contexts like '_ becomes F'[9]; for example, something may become the alloy or a bell. The point is that the concept of matter cannot be used in this way: something may become the alloy, but nothing can become matter, and it is a logical or metaphysical rather than physical impossibility. This impossibility is another aspect of matter's being a prime subject.

Prime matter actually exists only insofar as there is actually something instantiated in it – in particular, some form that actually makes it a being of some kind. Aquinas says that the very claim that matter actually exists having no form is inconsistent. In other words, prime matter may actually exist only in virtue of something else being actually instantiated in it. This shows, *inter alia*, that actual existence belongs to matter in an utterly different way than it belongs to what is instantiated in matter.

Moreover, one and the same matter can be a thing of one kind for some time, and then a thing of quite a distinct kind; it is quite impossible in the case of a bell or a man. Man's or bell's identity over time consists in the fact that something continues to be one and the same man or bell (and if we take material change into account it is possible that something – some matter – that is the same man now was *not* that man before); by contrast, in the case of matter, as Geach says, "it is not that something continues to be the same matter, but that the same matter

---

concept of stuff that is most helpful for good understanding of the concept of prime matter in Aquinas (Brower 2014, 125–129).
9 See also Geach 1961, 77.

continues or begins or ceases to be a thing of a given kind" (1961, 92). This shows in general that identity over time belongs to matter in an utterly different way than it belongs to what is instantiated in matter.

Finally: one and the same matter can be something single – for example, a single bell – and then cease to be anything single and become, for example, a number of bells, or a part of some bell. This shows that individuality or singleness do *not* belong to prime matter in the way they belong to what is realized in matter. Anscombe and Geach claim that according to Aristotle and Aquinas (bits of) matter may cease to be even theoretically identifiable and it is possible that one and the same matter ceases to be the piece of matter it used to be for some time.[10] Henceforth it is also possible that a distinction between parts or pieces of matter that occurs for some time may then cease to exist.

To sum up: actual existence, identity over time, individuality and distinction belong to matter in ways which are utterly different from the ways in which they belong to instantiable natures or their instances. This, I think, is enough to show that saying 'this matter is an instance of matter (in a subject)' would at best be misleading and at worst simply false, were it to express something similar to what 'this whiteness is an instance of whiteness (in a subject)' expresses.

Matter does not have instances at all – instead it exists only as far as something else is instantiated in it. It is of course true that the Sigismund Bell is a realization of matter in the sense that it is an actuality of some power specific for mater; that, however, is not comparable to 'the Sigismund Bell is an instance of being a bell' or 'this whiteness is an instance of whiteness'. So, in particular, matter cannot have *many* instances. Various parcels of the alloy are various instances of being the alloy, but not various instances of being matter.

These metaphysical features related to instantiation in a subject are mirrored in the logic of the concept of matter. Geach says (1961, 92) that "'matter' [...] is not a general term predicable of pieces of matter".

Returning to Geach's function analogy: being a bell may be treated as a function whose argument is matter in which being a bell is instantiated, and the value for this argument is a particular instance of being a bell, or, in other words, being a bell of some matter. Being matter, by contrast, is not like a function: it has neither arguments (subjects of instantiation) nor values (instances in subjects).

In this respect matter is comparable to Scotistic *haecceitates*: neither of them is an instance of something instantiable (see 3.7).

---

[10] Anscombe 1961, 48: "it does not follow that a once identifiable bit of matter must remain (theoretically) identifiable".

6.3.2 An Old Objection and Various Responses to It

There is an old objection against the thesis of the noninstantiability of matter; the objection is to be found both in the nominalistic and the Scotistic texts. The ways of rejecting this objection shed much light on the very Matter-Individuation Thesis. So I present the objection itself and three possible responses to it: the first two of them I take to be insufficient, but the third one, I would argue, is the right one.

There are two main versions of the objection. The first is that being a form (of a given species) is truly predicated of various forms of that species, and, in a similar way, being matter is truly predicated of various matters.[11] Scotus argues, for example, that matter cannot be an individuation principle, because what is common to many things cannot be a cause of determination, and you have to look for a principle of the singleness of matter (*individuatio et singularitas materiae*) just as we look for a principle of individuality or singleness of other things.[12] As already noted (3.7) the idea that matter needs a distinct principle of individuality is one of Scotus's premises for his theses about *haecceitas*. Even Oderberg claims in his interpretation of the Thomistic doctrine of individuation that matter is not a principle of individuation because "it is common, i.e. multiply instantiable" (2002, 126).

The other version of the objection appeals to the distinction of *subiectum praedicationis* and *subiectum inhaesionis* (for the details of the distinction see 5.4 (i)). The objection (to be found, for example, in Suárez and Pasqualigo) is that noninstantiability in general is something specific for *subiectum praedicationis*, whereas matter is a prime subject in the sense of *subiectum inhaesionis*, and not in the sense of *subiectum praedicationis*; so, the objection goes, there is a plain equivocation in the traditional argument for the Matter-Individuation Thesis.[13] A

---

11 For example, Soncinas (1588, *In Met.* VII, q. 23) says that according to this objection (which he is going to answer to) "sicut forma praedicatur de distinctis formis, ita materia praedicatur de diversis materiis".

12 Scotus 1982, *Lect.* II, d. 3, p. 1, q. 6, n. 133: "ergo oportet quod materia possit abstrahi a ab hac materia et illa, sicut forma aut compositum. Ergo materia non potest esse causa individuationis, quia universaliter illud quod est indifferens ad plura eiusdem rationis, non potest esse causa determinationis. Unde convenit quaerere de causa individuationis et singularitatis materiae, sicut compositi".

13 Suárez 1866, *Disp. met.* V, sect. 3, 6: "si quis recte consideret, aperta aequivocatio in eo discursu committitur; cum enim dicitur materiam esse principium incommunicabilitatis individui, eo quod ipsa sit primum subiectum, de se maxime incommunicabile, aut illa vox *incommunicabile* aequivoce sumitur aut falsum in probatione assumitur. Multis enim modis intelligi potest materiam esse incommunicabilem: primo, quod sit incommunicabilis alicui ut subiecto physico

slightly modified version of the objection would be the following: noninstantiability (and being a prime subject in the sense of *subiectum praedicationis*) is specific to nameable individuals and is something utterly different from the features of matter which is a prime subject in the sense of *subiectum inhaesionis*; so the association of matter's being a prime subject and noninstantiability (which is crucial for the Matter-Individuation Thesis) leads us astray. *Subiectum inhaesionis* in general is irrelevant for accounting for (non)instantiability. In general, the objection suggests that the Thomistic shift (see 5.2.1) from considering instantiation in general to considering instantiation in a subject (in the sense of *subiectum inhaesionis*) is a mistake.

What must be taken seriously in the case of these objections is the following; we do appeal to the distinction of *this* matter and *that* matter, whereas in the case of, say, the Sigismund Bell there is no distinction of "*this* Sigismund Bell" and "*that* Sigismund Bell". In this respect the concept of matter is obviously closer to sortal terms than to proper names. In metaphysics one might claim that although matter does have some interesting features as a prime subject in the sense of *subiectum inhaesionis*, these features are not so closely related to individuality as the traditional argument for the Matter-Individuation Thesis seems to suppose.

There are two ways of responding to such an objection to be found in the old Thomists, and I will focus on them in turn.

(i) The first is to be found in Cardinal Cajetan, Dominic of Flandria, and in Chrysostom Javelli. The basic idea is that noninstantiability does not belong to *matter* in general, but rather to *this* matter which is distinct from some other matter; as they say, "matter is not a sufficient principle of noninstantiability [*incommunicabilitas*] unless it is *this* matter distinct from another part of matter".[14] At the same time this sort of response admits that the distinction in question belongs to matter only in virtue of something distinct from the matter itself; so this sort of

---

quod informet vel cui inhaereat, et hic sensus est verissimus, et recte ex eo probatur quod materia est primum subiectum; hoc tamen est impertinens ad rem de qua agimus"; *ibidem*, 7: "Atque ex his constat tertiam coniecturam nullam habere efficaciam, quia est longe diversa ratio de subiecto inhaesionis et de subiecto praedicationis; quamvis enim excogitari possit quaedam proportio inter haec duo subiecta, nam superius comparatur ad inferius sibi subiectum ut forma dans esse, tamen simpliciter non sunt eiusdem rationis, neque unum fundatur in alio; unde in simplicibus substantiis est subiectio seu subordinatio inferiorum ad superiora, sine subiecto inhaesionis seu informationis". Similarly Pasqualigo 1636, *Disp. met.* 37, sect. 1, 7; sect. 2, 3.

14 Dominic of Flandria 1621, *In Met.* VII, q. 22, art. 1, ad 3: "dicendum, quod materia, non est sufficiens principium incommunicabilitatis, nisi sit haec materia divisa, ab alia parte materiae, quod non sit nisi per quantitatem"; in a similar vein Cajetan 1907, q. 5, 55 and Javelli 1676, *In Met.* V, q. 15.

response admits that matter as such is not a sufficient principle of noninstantiability. (It is clear that it is not a sufficient principle of individuality; here, however, one admits that it is not a sufficient principle of noninstantiability, too.)

(ii) There is also a quite different sort of response to be found in Paulus Soncinas. He says that matter can be considered in two ways. On the one hand in abstraction from any actuality, and in this way it cannot be conceived in any general concept (*conceptus communis*). He claims that matter considered in this way cannot be plurified, is noninstantiable and is individual, "a this", by itself (*est de se haec*). It is matter in *that* respect that is a principle of individuation responsible for noninstantiability. It is impossible for us, however, to conceive of matter in this way, in abstraction from *any* actuality. On the other hand, matter can be considered in connection with some form or actuality; we can think of matter in this way, but if we consider it this way, we cannot ascribe noninstantiability to it and it is not a principle of individuation.[15] In short, while the first sort of response admits that matter in itself is not noninstantiable, the basic idea of the other one is that noninstantiability belongs to matter just in virtue of being matter itself, but the point is that matter in itself is in a sense inconceivable for us. To sum up, both sorts of response weaken in a considerable way the traditional argument for the Matter-Individuation Thesis.

Here I would like to present another kind of response to the objection that enables the defence of the traditional argument for the Matter-Individuation Thesis. Rejecting some ideas of (i) I would like to show that noninstantiability belongs to matter *as such* and not in virtue of some actuality or in virtue of some sort of division; and rejecting some ideas of (ii) I am going to show that matter is something that we can conceive of (and do in fact conceive of) in abstraction from any actuality; moreover, I claim that although matter is as such noninstantiable, it is not as such individual or single, "a this".

Let us note first that *this* matter distinct from other matter, is *not*, in some important sense, a prime subject – at least if you agree with Anscombe and Geach

---

15 Soncinas 1588, *In Met.* VII, q. 33, ad 2: "materia potest dupliciter accipi. Uno modo secundum se praescindendo eam ab omni actualitate quaecumque sit: et sic non potest concipi conceptu communi. Cuius ratio est, qua ut sic, est tantum una et nullo modo plurificata: licet impossibile sit quod a nobis hoc modo concipiatur: et hoc modo materia individuat: quia ei ut sic, convenit incommunicabilitas [...] Unde hoc modo est de se haec, id est, incommunicabilis. Alio modo accipitur: ut cadit in conceptu intellectus nostri: et quia nos non apprehendimus materiam nisi per analogiam ad formam [...] forma autem potest concipi conceptu communi cum de se sit communicabilis: ideo materia ut sic, concipitur conceptu communi: sed ex hoc non habet quod sit principium individuationis".

that one and the same matter may cease to be *this* matter distinct from other matter (see 6.3.1); being a distinct identifiable *piece* of matter is something *instantiated* in matter for some time. Being a prime subject may be ascribed to the matter that may cease to be *this* distinct matter, and not to this distinct matter itself. This does not exclude, of course, that there is some aspect of individuality that belongs to matter just in virtue of its actually being some *piece* of matter; what we are interested in here, however, is just being a prime subject and noninstantiability, and they belong to matter as such and not in virtue of being some *piece* of matter.

Now, returning to the main idea of the objection, we may note that the very fact that we talk about *this* and *other* matter does not necessarily mean that matter has many instances in the way in which being a bell or being white may have many instances; it may be just some superficial grammatical similarity. In fact, there is some reason to think that it *is* just some superficial grammatical similarity. A distinct whiteness is just a distinct instance of whiteness; distinct matter, by contrast, is matter that happens to be actualized as distinct. So it seems plausible that there is no serious *metaphysical* similarity here.

We may note then that, *pace* Soncinas, this sort of grasp of prime matter in abstraction from any actuality or form is not something that our reason cannot perform; it is something we do every day when we re-identify matter (see 6.2 and 6.3.1) without recourse to identity criteria of any particular *kind* of substance. Moreover, we have the relevant sort of grasp of prime matter when we see that nothing can *become* matter (and that this is not just a physical impossibility), although something can *become* a given sort of alloy. Finally, we have the relevant sort of grasp when we see that having an instance that is ascribed to a nature is something utterly distinct from being actualized in some way that is ascribed to matter. In a sense there is nothing more to be grasped in prime matter than that. Admittedly it is difficult to have a good *theory* of matter that explains the details of the identity of matter; but I think it is unquestionable that we do have some preliminary understanding of prime matter, especially in the contexts sketched above, and this is a good point of departure for construction of difficult theories.

It is important to note here, however, that the condition of noninstantiability is *negative* and various things may fall under it for *various* reasons. Both material individuals and prime matter are noninstantiable; Aquinas claims that immaterial separate forms are also noninstantiable, as opposed to forms instantiable in matter; for Scotus, *haecceitates* are clearly noninstantiable; finally, in a sense actual existence is also something noninstantiable (I return to this issue in 8.3.2). As far as the first cases are concerned, it seems obvious that they are noninstantiable for various reasons; the identity of matter is *not*, for the various reasons suggested above, identity of *an individual*. So I think that, *pace* Soncinas, the fact that matter is noninstantiable does not imply that it is individual or single, "a this". In short: Soncinas's response suggests that prime matter is some individual that our reason is not able to conceive of; by contrast, my claim is that the noninstantiability of prime matter is relatively clear for us, but prime matter is *not* a nameable individual. We are acquainted with prime matter quite well, but it is *not* an acquaintance with some nameable individual.[16] So I claim that the noninstantiability of matter is not its individuality, although I do think that the noninstantiability of form *is* its individuality: a noninstantiable form is an individual form.

This may make us also guess that, according to what Aquinas himself claims, the way in which noninstantiability as well as being a prime subject belong to immaterial substances or separated forms is utterly different from the way in which it belongs to forms having instances in matter. The noninstantiablility of separated forms is their individuality, and in this respect they are unlike matter; on the other hand, these forms are noninstantiable *by themselves* and are themselves prime subjects, so in this respect they are like matter and unlike forms having their instances in matter.

Returning to the function analogy: this also shows some important feature of Aristotelian metaphysics that perhaps distinguishes it from a Fregean metaphysics. According to the Aristotelian view sketched here there are various sorts of *saturatedness*; for example, prime matter is something saturated; but in some crucial respects it is also quite unlike a Fregean *Gegenstand*.

To sum up, I think that there is a good response to the old objection against the noninstantiability of matter. If this response is sound, it shows moreover that Thomists are right in focusing on *instantiation in a subject* as opposed to *instantiation in general*. I would also claim that we have a better grasp of the fact that matter is not an instance of anything, than of the alleged fact that a Scotistic *haecceitas* is not an instance of anything.

6.4 Matter and Noninstantiability of Forms

Now it is time to return to the main question: in what way does prime matter *make* the instances of forms noninstantiable? What I have said so far may show that matter is a prime subject and is noninstantiable. The Matter-Individuation The-

---

16 Non-individuality of prime matter is stressed also by Brower (2014, 119–129).

sis, however, says much more: it says that prime matter, being itself noninstantiable, makes the very instances of instantiable forms noninstantiable. So the main question is just *how* it makes them noninstantiable.

Let us begin by noting some contrast. In some cases we say that a form is instantiated in something that is *not* a prime subject; for example, we say that a building structure is instantiated in wood or stone, or that the form of a bell is instantiated in a given sort of alloy (when we say so we do not mean only that it is instantiated in something that otherwise happens to be that sort of alloy; being that sort of alloy is much more important for the instantiation, so we mean instead that it is instantiated in something *as far as it is* that sort of alloy). Now in such cases being wood or stone and being the given sort of alloy are themselves instantiable and instantiated in some subject. Now in some sense we may claim that a *building structure instantiated in wood* and *the form of a bell instantiated in such-and such an alloy* are themselves instantiable in some subject; another example would be *the human soul instantiated in the human body*. This kind of talk about kinds of subjects is quite widespread; it is quite natural, for example, to say that surface is a subject in which colour is instantiated, but here again surface is something instantiable. In general, in some contexts we refer to *kinds* of matter as subjects of form (and to kinds of subjects in general), and such a subject is *not* something that makes an instance of the form noninstantiable.

A form instantiated in a subject in this sense is itself instantiable, just because of the instantiability of the subject in question. By contrast, when we consider an instance of a form in prime matter, the subject in question is itself *noninstantiable*; and there is a sense in which a form instantiated in *prime* matter, that is: an instance of the form in prime matter, is noninstantiable, just because of the noninstantiability of matter. And a *noninstantiable* form is an *individual* form; so in this way prime matter, thanks to its noninstantiability, is a principle of the form's individuality. Finally, the individual instance of form is (according to the Weak Formal Individuation Thesis) a principle of the individuality of the material individual. *This* individuality may in turn be ascribed to prime matter (when we say, for example, that for some time it is an individual bell). Unlike noninstantiability, however, this individuality does not belong to matter just *qua* matter, but only in virtue of the form instantiated in it.

To return again to the function analogy: unsaturatedness is a feature of *both* functions and function symbols; now when we attach the symbol of the argument/subject to the symbol of the function, and the subject is not a prime subject, the whole remains an unsaturated function symbol; by contrast, when the subject in question is a prime subject, we get a saturated symbol of some object, namely of the value of the function for the given subject. Here one might say that the symbol of a prime subject saturates the function symbol. It might be tempting to say also that something parallel must hold for the unsaturated *function* itself and for a prime subject: that a prime subject saturates the function itself; one might think also that the unsaturated function is a special sort of part of its saturated value for a given argument, and that the instantiable nature is a special sort of part of its noninstantiable instance. This, however, might be an illusion, for, as I have claimed against Scotus (see 3.4.2 and 5.2.2) what is true of symbols does not necessarily exactly mirror the truth about things, and functions are not parts of their values.

We may also, however, explain the way in which a prime subject makes the instance of the form noninstantiable by the following: there is, as I have said, a transcendental internal relationship of an instance to its subject; the point of the Matter-Individuation Thesis is that this relationship makes the instance noninstantiable *as far as* it is a relationship to a prime subject (as opposed, say, to the *kind of matter* the form is instantiated in). That is the most obvious sense of the Matter-Individuation Thesis, and I would claim that in this sense the thesis is true.

Let us note finally that both the Scotistic theory of *haecceitas* and the Matter Individuation Thesis agree that a source of individuality is something that is not an instance of any instantiable nature. So, on the one hand, a *hacceitas* is not an instance of any instantiable nature, and, on the other hand, prime matter is not an instance of anything. There are, however, two crucial differences between these two strategies of recourse to something which is not an instance of anything. The first is that the relevant properties of matter may be established also outside the context of individuality. The other important difference is that within the Thomistic theory matter is just one of the sources of individuality: there are other sources of individuality of material substances, and the individuality of immaterial substances does not depend on matter at all.

7 Quantity and Self-Individuation

7.1 Quantity and the Individuality of Substances: Aquinas's Main Thesis

Pointing at matter or a prime subject as one of the principles of the individuation of material substances Aquinas says that the other principle of individuation which is responsible for the other aspect of individuality is quantity *(quantitas dimensiva)*. It is a principle of the individuation of material substance as far as it is responsible for the distinction of pieces of matter, and this distinction in turn is in some way responsible for the distinction of forms of the same species:

> It is of the very notion of an individual that it cannot be in several [*non possit in pluribus esse*]; and this happens in two ways. First, because it is not natural to it to be in any one [*non est natum in aliquo esse*]; and in this way immaterial separated forms, subsisting of themselves, are also individuals of themselves. Secondly, because a form, be it substantial or accidental, is naturally in someone indeed, not in several [*est nata in aliquo esse, non tamen in pluribus*], as this whiteness, which is in this body. As to the first, matter is the principle of individuation of all inherent forms, because, since these forms, considered in themselves, are naturally in something as in a subject [*sint natae in aliquo esse sicut in subiecto*], from the very fact that one of them is received in matter, which is not in another [*recipitur in materia quae non est in alio*], it follows that neither can the form itself thus existing be in another [*iam nec ipsa forma sic existens potest in alio esse*]. As to the second, it must be maintained that the principle of individuation is dimensive quantity [*quantitas dimensiva*]. For that something is naturally in another one solely [*aliquid est natum esse in uno solo*], is due to the fact that that other is undivided in itself, and distinct from all others. But it is on account of quantity that substance can be divided [*divisio accidit substantiae ratione quantitatis*], as is said in *Phys.* I. And therefore dimensive quantity itself is a particular principle of individuation [*quoddam individuationis principium*] in forms of this kind, namely, inasmuch as forms numerically distinct are in different parts of the matter. Hence also dimensive quantity has of itself a kind of individuation [*secundum se habet quandam individuationem*], so that we can imagine several lines of the same species, differing in position [*plures lineas eiusdem speciei differentes positione*], which is included in the notion of this quantity [*cadit in ratione quantitatis huius*]; for it belongs to dimension for it to be "quantity having position" (Aristotle, Categor. iv).[1]

---

1 Aquinas 1947, *S. Th.* III, q. 77, art. 2, corp (trans. Fathers of the English Dominican Province). The Latin text (Aquinas 1980): "Est enim de ratione individui quod non possit in pluribus esse. Quod quidem contingit dupliciter. Uno modo, quia non est natum in aliquo esse, et hoc modo formae immateriales separatae, per se subsistentes, sunt etiam per seipsas individuae. Alio modo, ex eo quod forma substantialis vel accidentalis est quidem nata in aliquo esse, non tamen in pluribus, sicut haec albedo, quae est in hoc corpore. Quantum igitur ad primum, materia est

So the Quantity-Individuation Thesis claims that

> **(The Quantity-Individuation Thesis)** Quantity is a principle of individuation of substantial forms instantiated in matter.

The Quantity-Individuation Thesis, in various formulations, is embraced by a great number of Thomists, for example by Henry of Lübeck, Ferrara, Capreolus, Cajetan and John of St. Thomas.

The very notion of dimensive quantity stands in need of some preliminary clarification. It is a sort of accident comprehending various geometrical attributes of material substances, for example: the sphericity of an ivory ball, a solid of timber, a given edge of a table, a square on a chessboard, its edge or its vertex. So the kind of accidents comprehends on the one hand solids, and, on the other hand, various sorts of *boundaries* of other objects of this sort: surfaces being boundaries of solids, lines being boundaries of surfaces, and finally points being boundaries of lines. Objects of this sort pose a great number of interesting philosophical questions disputed in scholasticism.[2] It is worthwhile to hint at at least two of them. On the one hand we could ask about the distinction of the instances of these accidents from the substances that are their subjects; for example, about the way in which a solid of timber is distinct from that timber. On the other hand we could ask about the distinction between objects belonging to that sort of accidents; for example, about the way in which the solid of timber is distinct from its surface and from its edge. The early modern discussions about the relationship between substances and extension seem to echo (usually in a limited and distorted way) these older scholastic debates. Here, however, I leave aside all the questions concerning the very nature of *quantitas dimensiva* and focus only on

---

individuationis principium omnibus formis inhaerentibus, quia, cum huiusmodi formae, quantum est de se, sint natae in aliquo esse sicut in subiecto, ex quo aliqua earum recipitur in materia, quae non est in alio, iam nec ipsa forma sic existens potest in alio esse. Quantum autem ad secundum, dicendum est quod individuationis principium est quantitas dimensiva. Ex hoc enim aliquid est natum esse in un solo, quod illud est in se indivisum et divisum ab omnibus aliis. Divisio autem accidit substantiae ratione quantitatis, ut dicitur in I *Physicorum*. Et ideo ipsa quantitas dimensiva est quoddam individuationi principium huiusmodi formis, inquantum scilicet diversae formae numero sunt in diversis partibus materiae. Unde ipsa quantitas dimensiva secundum se habet quandam individuationem, ita quod possumus imaginari plures lineas eiusdem speciei differentes positione, quae cadit in ratione quantitatis huius; convenit enim dimensioni quod sit quantitas positionem habens".

2 See e.g. Pasnau 2011, 53–76 and 277–398; for some connections between the scholastic and contemporary discussions see e.g. Chisholm 1989.

the issues that are immediately related to arguments for the Quantity-Individuation Thesis.

A traditional line of argument in favour of the Quantity-Individuation Thesis is the following: the ground of distinction of individuals of the same species is a *material difference*, being composed of distinct pieces of matter (more precisely, the immediate ground of distinction of individuals of the same species is the distinction of their forms, and the ground of the distinction of the forms is the distinction of matter, the fact that the forms are instantiated in distinct parts or pieces of matter). But the ground of distinction of parts or pieces of matter is just *quantitas dimensiva*, because it is this sort of accident that division into pieces in general belongs immediately and primarily to; this is closely related to the fact that position *(positio, situs)* belongs immediately and primarily to quantity. So, for some special reasons, dimensive quantity is a kind of being that in some sense is self-individuated *(individuatur per seipsam)*. So it is quantity that is responsible for the second of the two aspects of individuality that are ascribed to forms.[3]

So, for example, the ground of distinction of two co-existing ivory balls is the fact that their forms are instantiated in two pieces of ivory or in two pieces of prime matter that is ivory; and the ground of the distinction of pieces of ivory (or matter that is ivory) is the distinction of the geometrical attributes of the balls (say, of their sphericities); this distinction belongs immediately to the geometrical attributes of these balls, that is, in some sense they are distinct *by themselves*, because they are differentiated by their position and their position belongs to them immediately.

We should distinguish two senses of the Quantity-Individuation Thesis; they are parallel to the two senses of the Subject-Individuation Thesis (see 5.2). On the one hand we have a thesis concerning the way individuality and plurality belong to *natures*:

(The Nature Quantity-Individuation Thesis) Individuality and plurality belong to the instantiable nature of F in virtue of the division of matter (in which the nature is instantiated) into pieces, and that division in turn belongs to matter in virtue of quantity.

---

3 See e.g. Aquinas 1980, *Contra gent.* III, 49, 3: "Principium diversitatis individuorum eiusdem speciei est divisio materiae secundum quantitatem: forma enim huius ignis a forma illius ignis non differt nisi per hoc quod est in diversis partibus in quas materia dividitur, – nec aliter quam divisione quantitatis, sine qua substantia est indivisibilis"; Scotus gives a brief summary of this line of reasoning in 1973, *Ord.*, dist. 3, p. 1, q. 4, n. 73: "'hic ignis' non differt ab illo igne nisi quia forma differt a forma, nec forma differt a forma nisi quia recipitur in alia et alia parte materiae, nec pars materiae ab alia parte materiae nisi quia est sub alia parte quantitatis".

And on the other hand we have a thesis concerning the way in which individuality belongs to particular instances of (forms of) a given nature:

> **(The Instance Quantity-Individuation Thesis)** individuality and distinction from other forms of the same species belong to an individual form of a given nature in virtue of some internal transcendental relationship of the individual form to the division of matter into pieces that is based on quantity.

To shed more light on the issue I will proceed in the following way. I begin with some clarifications concerning material difference (7.2) and the sense in which it belongs primarily to dimensive quantity. Then I focus on some features of quantity closely related to the division into pieces, position and individuality, and the sense in which quantity is self-individuated (7.3). Next I proceed to the issue of the way in which geometrical attributes are responsible for the individuality of forms instantiated in matter (7.4) and for the individuality of parts of material substances (7.5). Finally I focus on the way in which, according to the Matter-Individuation Thesis and Quantity-Individuation Thesis, individuality belongs to the immortal souls of human beings (7.6).

7.2 Material Difference, Matter, and Extension

Material difference or *material distinction* may well be thought to constitute a primitive sort of difference and distinction; it occurs between co-existing *pieces* or *lumps* of some stuff, for example between two pieces of gold or two marble blocks. This type of difference may be an effect of the actual division of something that used to be continuous and one; for example, of an actual division of a single marble block. But it may well occur also in cases with no previous continuity or unity. Moreover, it occurs between parts of a continuous whole even without their actual division, as far as these parts might in principle be actually divided and made discontinuous. There are some features of material distinction that are relatively simply to grasp and that are discussed in scholastic metaphysics; a systematic development of the elementary intuitions (i)–(x) is what I present in 7.3 and 7.4.

(i) Material difference might be contrasted with specific difference that occurs, for example, between a piece of gold and a piece of marble; or, more generally, with a difference that is expressed in general terms. A material difference alone occurs when we have distinct pieces of *one and the same* (either one and the same individual or one and the same sort of substance). It is worth noting, however, that there are some distinctions that are neither material differences nor differences expressed in general terms; the distinction between successive strikes of a bell would be an interesting example.

(ii) The first two sorts of difference sketched above may be associated with various sorts of *division* or even with various senses in which something can be *divided*. So, on the one hand, one may divide the genus of colours into its species, on the other hand something may be divided into pieces.[4]

(iii) Material distinction – the distinction of the pieces of one and the same – is closely related to *extension*; the latter itself may be characterised as *being composed of pieces* or *being composed of parts differentiated by their position*; something is extended as far as it is composed of pieces, that is: parts differentiated by their position.

(iv) There are various sorts of entities to which, for *various* reasons, division into pieces or extension cannot be ascribed: entities that do not have pieces at all. So, for example, (*a*) points are unextended and have no pieces, but they belong to the sort of entities for which division into pieces is essential: they are boundaries of extended objects (namely lines), which in turn are boundaries of other extended objects (namely surfaces); (*b*) a particular instance of a building structure (that is, the individual form of a given building) is not, unlike the building itself, divisible into pieces (see 4.2 (iv)), but it is an internal principle of the building that does have pieces; by contrast, the whiteness of a square on a chessboard and the gold instantiated in a piece of gold was said to *have* pieces in some sense in scholastic metaphysics. (*c*) A particular thought instantiated in someone's mind is not divisible into pieces (as opposed to its expression on a piece of paper), although one who thinks may well be divisible into pieces.

(v) On the other hand, various entities that do have pieces may differ in the very way in which divisibility into pieces belongs to them; in other words, the genitive 'a piece of _' has various senses. For example, when we divide a piece of gold into two pieces, the division itself belongs to the divided piece in one way, and it belongs to the individual form of gold in another way; it belongs also, in still another way, to the matter that used to be in one piece and is now in two pieces. More generally, divisibility into pieces belongs to homogeneous stuffs like gold in an obviously different way than it belongs to organisms, especially those of a highly complicated organic structure.

(vi) According to the main tradition of scholastic metaphysics divisibility into pieces belongs to objects like solids, surfaces or lines; this does not mean, however, that a material difference occurs between them; material difference occurs

---

[4] For the distinction of these two types of division see Aristotle 1953, *Met.* 999a2–3 and *Met.* 1053a18–20. In Aquinas see 1980, *S. th.* I, q. 30, art. 3, corp.

only between pieces *of matter*, that is, only when division into pieces belongs to matter with its specific identity criteria (see 6.2), and the concept of the identity of matter is not a geometrical concept.

(vii) According to the main tradition of scholastic metaphysics divisibility into pieces does *not* belong to substances *immediately* (for some details of the concept of immediacy employed here see 2.4.1); more precisely, divisibility into pieces belongs immediately neither to *matter*, nor to a particular instance of substantial *form;* and it does not belong immediately to their sum which is material substance.[5] So in the case of matter we have the following contrast; on the one hand identity of matter in the sense sketched in 6.2 belongs to matter *immediately* and independently of forms instantiated in it, but division of pieces of matter does not belong to it immediately, but only in virtue of something else (this is closely related to the thesis (see 6.3.1) that the distinction of parts of matter may disappear while matter preserves its identity). As the scholastics say: *ablata quantitate substantia remanet indivisibilis*, without quantity substance remains indivisible. In this sense the scholastic metaphysics of material beings is an anti-Cartesian one.

(viii) Another important point is, however, that according to the main tradition of scholastic metaphysics divisibility into pieces *does* really belong to matter and to material substances, although it does not belong to them immediately. So there are really *pieces* of substance and *pieces* of matter, and substances really do have dimensions. In this aspect the scholastic metaphysics of material substances is an anti-Leibnizian one. Material substances are not indivisible *living points*; they are rather, so to say, *living solids* – although this phrase stands in need of various further specifications.

(ix) The division of matter into pieces is connected with some special type of entity that was singled out within the category of quantity and called number (*numerus*) in some special narrow sense. The examples of this sort of entity are, for example, four horses in a team, eleven football players on a pitch or six cups in a coffee set. More generally, objects of this sort are groups or manifolds of co-existing objects between which material difference occurs. Numbers in this special sense were distinguished from numbers being *transcendentals* in the scholastic sense – terms expressing some features that are not confined to a single kind or domain of reality, but do transcend borders between various sorts of reality. Now we can ask about the number of things of various sorts of things, ma-

---

5 See e.g. Aquinas 1980, *In De Trinitate*, II, q. 4. art. 2, 6.

terial and immaterial, sensible and not sensible, and the answers to such questions employ numerals expressing some transcendental features of beings. By contrast, a number in the special narrow sense considered here, being some sort of entity as opposed to a transcendental feature of entities, is something, as the scholastics used to say, caused by the division of something continuous (*numerus quod causatur ex divisione continui*), or more precisely, by the division of matter into pieces.[6]

(x) Material difference occurs between *co-existing* things; it requires the *actual* distinction in the sense indicated in 5.5.

7.3 Division into Pieces, Position, and Individuality

Aquinas several times makes some detailed remarks concerning the way in which divisibility into pieces belongs to dimensive quantity. They seem to focus on the four following points.

(i) A given pattern of relative position (*positio, situs*) of parts is essential for the objects that belong to the category of quantity; in other words, it is part of the essence of a given object of this sort, for example, of a sphere or cube, to have parts situated in such and such a way; to be a sphere or a cube just *is* to have parts situated in this way. So it is also part of the essence of objects of this sort to have parts differentiated by their situation. Objects of this sort are, as Aquinas says, essentially divisible (divisible *ex ipsa natura sui generis*). Since *pieces* are just parts differentiated by their position, it is part of the essence of this sort of objects to have pieces. By contrast: although a lump of gold does have pieces, to be gold does not necessariy consist in having (a given pattern of) pieces, and it is not part of the essence of gold to have parts differentiated just by their relative position.

(ii) Something similar should be said about the very parts of objects of this sort; they belong to the category of dimensive quantity, too. So, more precisely, the difference or distinction of position (*diversitas situs*) (as well as the situation

---

[6] For a distinction of these two senses of 'number' see e.g. Aquinas 1980, *S. th.* I, q. 30, art. 3, corp.: "omnis pluralitas consequitur aliquam divisionem. Est autem duplex division. Una materialis, quae fit secundum divisionem continui, et hanc consequitur numerus qui est species quantitates. Unde talis numerus non est nisi in rebus materialibus habentibus quantitatem. Alia est divisio formalis, quae fit per oppositas vel diversas formas, et hanc divisionem sequitur multitude quae non est in aliquot genere, sed est de transcendentibus, secundum quod ens dividitur per unum et multa". Aquinas clearly states that there is some sort of *transcendennal* number: *multitudo quae non est in aliquo genere, sed est de transcendentibus*. Similarly Godfrey of Fontaines 1914, *Quodl.* 6, q. 16. See also Geach 1961, 73–74.

itself) is some internal feature of parts of the objects belonging to *quantitas dimensiva*, for example parts of a sphere or of a cube. By contrast: situation and the difference of situation do belong, for example, to whiteness, but they are not part of what it is to be white.[7]

(iii) The connection between the diversity of objects belonging to the category of *quantitas dimensiva* and the diversity of their position is so strong that Aquinas thinks it is quite impossible that there are two distinct, although exactly similar, objects of this sort that were not differentiated by their site. For example, it is impossible that there are two distinct, although exactly similar, triangles or circles that were *not* differentiated by their position; that is to say, it is impossible that there are really distinct exactly similar triangles or circles exactly in the same place. By contrast, he maintains that it is not quite impossible that there are two distinct material substances of one and the same species *in one and the same place*. The source of the contrast is that in the case of the exactly similar geometrical figures they cannot be differentiated by anything other than their position (*nulla alia ratio distinctionis potest intelligi nisi ex situ*), and in the case of material substances or, more generally, objects that not only have geometrical features there can be some other grounds for their distinction (*alia ratio distinctionis*).[8]

(iv) Aquinas also remarks that while it is impossible to conceive of a plurality of instances of whiteness unless they are conceived of as instances of whiteness in distinct subjects, it is possible to conceive of a plurality of lines without conceiving of them as instances of being a line in distinct subjects: the difference of position is enough for the distinction of lines, and it belongs to them immediately and not in virtue of something else.[9]

---

7 Compare Geach 1961, 74: "Two instances e.g. of the same colour differ only in that there are (otherwise) different things that are coloured; but two instances of the same geometrical attributes – e.g. two circles of equal size – may differ is a strictly geometrical way (viz. in relative position)".

8 Aquinas 1980, *Quodl.* 1, q. 10, art. 2, ad 2: "duas lineas rectas mathematicas esse infra duo puncta, est impossibile, quia in eis nulla alia ratio distinctionis potest intelligi nisi ex situ; sed duas lineas naturales esse intra duo puncta est impossibile quidam per naturam, sed possibile per miraculum: quia remanet alia ratio distinctionis in lineis duabus ex diversitate corprum subiectorum, quae conservatur virtute divina, etiam remota diversitate situs"; similarly *In De Trinitate* II, q. 4, art. 3; *In Phys.* IV, l. 13, n. 1.

9 Aquinas 1980, *Contra gent.* IV, c. 65, n .5: "non possunt apprehendi multae albedines nisi secundum quod sint in diversis subiectis. Possunt autem apprehendi multae lineae, etiam si secundum se considerantur: diversus enim situs, qui per se lineae inest, ad pluralitatem linearum sufficiens est"; *Quodl.* 7, q. 4, art. 3, corp.: "possibile est imaginari duas lineas separatas eiusdem speciei, numero diversas secundum diversum situm [...] plures autem albedines sine subiecto imaginari est impossibile"; similarly *S. th.* III, q. 77, art. 2, corp.

7.4 Aquinas on the Self-Individuation of Quantity

Considering the points (i)–(iv) sketched above Aquinas says that the dimensive quantity, unlike other sorts of accidents, is in a way self-individuating (*ipsa secundum se individuatur*), or that in a way it has some sort of individuality just by itself (*secundum se habet quandam individuationem*). Each time he states this his reason is that division into pieces and position belong to the dimensive quantity just in virtue of its very nature.[10]

Recalling again the difference between the two senses of the Subject-Individuation Thesis (see 5.2.4) we can distinguish between the two senses in which dimensive quantity may be said to be self-individuated. On the one hand, one may focus on the way in which individuality and plurification belong to the instantiable nature of a given object of the species of dimensive quantity, for example, about the way they belong to being a sphere or a cube. On the other hand, one may focus on the way in which individuality and distinction belong to particular instances of these natures, for example, to some particular sphere.

If we take the self-individuation of dimensive quantity in the former sense (concerning instantiable natures), an argument for it would be the following; plurification belongs to a nature of this sort in virtue of the difference of position; but position is not something extrinsic for the nature in question in the way in which the subject of instantiation of an accident is extrinsic for the nature of that accident. So, for example, plurification belongs to being a square as such, because squares are differentiated by their position, and some pattern of the relative position of parts is part of what it is to be a square. Note that claiming this sort of self-individuation seems to be compatible with the Avicennian Instance Ascription Thesis. In other words, Aquinas could still claim that having instances at all, as well as any given number of instances, do not belong to the nature of square *as such*.

If we take the self-individuation of dimensive quantity in the latter sense (concerning instances), an argument for it would be the following; distinction from other squares is an intrinsic feature of a given instance of being a square; the ground of the difference is the difference of position, and position itself is essential for this particular instance of being a square. By contrast: in the case of particular instances of other sorts of accidents the ground of the distinction is the transcendental relationship to something distinct from the very instance in question, namely to its subject which belongs to a distinct category. In this sense a

---

[10] Aquinas 1980, *Contra gent.* IV, c. 65, 5; *S. th.* III, q. 77, art. 2, corp.; similarly *In De Trinitate* q. 4, art. 2, ad 3.

square on a chessboard is distinct from another exactly similar square just by itself (*seipso*), because it is distinct in virtue of its position on the chessboard, and in some sense its position is not something distinct from it (although the position of a piece of gold is something distinct from the very particular instance of being gold).

Now it is worthwhile to compare the sense in which Aquinas could say that squares on a chessboard are distinct by themselves (*seipsis*) or are individual by themselves, with the sense in which according to the Strong Self-Individuation Thesis anything is distinct from anything else by itself (*seipso*), and the sense in which the Scotists maintain that only *haecceitates* are individual by themselves. Five points deserve closer consideration: the first concerns the way in which individuality belongs to particular *instances*, and the rest of them – the way in which individuality belongs to the natures of objects of *quantitas dimensiva*.

(i) Aquinas thinks that a square on a chessboard is distinct from another square just *by itself*, because it is distinct from it *by its position*, and position is not something distinct from it. So in the case of entities that are distinct by themselves in Aquinas's sense it is possible to say, using some general term, how they are distinct. It is not possible in the case of nominalism and Scotism: there being distinct by itself is, in some way, something primitive and inexplicable in general terms.[11] Similarly, Aquinas says that there cannot be distinct, although exactly similar, geometrical figures in the same place, because there were nothing that they were distinguished by (that is, their distinction could not be accounted for in general terms). Now if one had objected against this (in a nominalistic or Scotistic vein) that these figures had been distinct just by themselves,[12] Aquinas could have replied that *in this case* being distinct by itself should have been being distinct by position; and there is no other meaning of being distinct by or of itself applicable in the case of objects of geometry considered as such. In general, what is self-individuated here is itself *an instance* of some instantiable nature – as opposed, say, to *haecceitates* which are not instances of anything.

---

[11] It is worth noting that Suárez explicitly rejects the Thomistic idea that objects belonging to *quantitas dimensiva* are distinct *by their position*; he says that their position is different because they are distinct in themselves: "Et in eodem sensu videtur intelligendum quantitates ipsas distingui numero ex sitibus; est enim id verum quoad nos; ideo enim illas sensibiliter distinguimus et numeramus, quia eas in diversis sitibus conspicimus; non tamen est verum secundum se; nam potius occupant quantitates diversos situs quia in se distinctae sunt" (Suárez 1866, *Disp. met.* V, s. 3, 33).

[12] As a matter of fact Suárez tends to suppose (following Ockham) that it is possible to have two distinct objects belonging to *quantitas dimensiva* without any difference of position (1866, *Disp. met.* V, s. 8, 24).

(ii) The nominalist could not say that plurification belongs to some instantiable nature as such, because he would reject the claim that plurification really belongs to anything at all; so he could not grasp the contrast between the ways in which plurification belongs to, say, being white and to being a square.

(iii) The Scotist, on the other hand, for several reasons would not agree that plurification or individuality could belong to *any* nature *as such*. The first reason is that according to Scotism plurification or individuality do not belong to *any* nature as such (in any sense that is considered by Scotists). The other reason is that according to Scotism plurification and individuality cannot belong to anything *in virtue of something else* in the sense in which, according to the Subject-Individuation Thesis, they belong to natures of accidents in virtue of their subjects. For both reasons there is no contrast between quantity and other sorts of accidents in Scotism. On the other hand, if the Scotist admitted that there was something like *haecceitas* in general – such a *sort* of entity (see 3.7), he could admit also that plurification and individuality belong to being a haecceity in general *immediately* in the sense comparable to the one employed in the Thomistic theses about dimensive quantity.

(iv) Even in the latter case, however, there would be a significant difference between the Scotist and Aquinas. Aquinas appeals to some features of quantity that are not defined in terms of individuality and can be analysed apart from the context of individuation. By contrast, Scotistic haecceities are defined just in terms of individuality (in particular, the very concept of an ultimate actuality is defined in terms of individuality).

(v) More generally, both in nominalism and in Scotism self-individuation is not treated as something specific to some instantiable natures that can be discovered in the investigation of these natures. It seems, however, that some intuitions concerning self-individuation to which both standpoints appeal do have their roots in some pictures of objects of dimensive quantity. So I think it is worth considering whether at least some versions of nominalist and Scotist standpoints concerning individuation stem from a generalization of some peculiar properties of dimensive quantity (that, after such a generalization, ceases to seem a very peculiar sort of being). It is worth noting that according to the definition of *entitas* given by Eustachius a S. Paulo *entitas* is *quasi entis quantitas*.[13]

The final question to be asked here concerns the relationship between the alleged self-individuation of quantity and the Subject-Individuation Thesis in both its versions; more precisely: does individuality belong to dimensive quantity

---

13 See Angelelli 1994, 537.

not only in virtue of the nature of quantity and position itself, but in virtue of its substantial subject, too? Consider, for example, two exactly similar wooden chessboards. According to the Quantity-Individuation Thesis a ground of the distinction between the chessboards is the distinction between the pieces of wood they are made of, and a ground for the latter distinction is the distinction of them *as solids*; this last distinction is primitive in the sense sketched above (its ground is the distinction of their position, and their position is not anything distinct from them). Now, do the Subject-Individuation Thesis hold for the geometrical attributes of the chessboards? Does the distinction of *solids* in some way depend on the distinction of their subjects, that is, the chessboards or pieces of wood? From a general perspective, this is a question concerning the way in which dimensive quantity is *self*-individuated.

Answering the latter question Aquinas says that his argument for the Quantity-Individuation Thesis does *not* exclude that the Subject-Individuation Thesis holds also in the case of quantity. So the solids of the chessboards are distinct by themselves, because they are distinct in virtue of their position, but they are *also* distinct in virtue of their subjects. Here Aquinas wants to distinguish in some way between the quantity the distinction of which is, in a way, prior to the distinction of substance, and the quantity the distinction of which is derivative from the distinction of substance.[14] Moreover, we should remember that according to Aquinas it is impossible that two distinct, although exactly similar, solids are not differentiated by their position, but it is *not* impossible that two substances are equal solids that are *not* differentiated by their position; it seems natural that in such a case the solids would be differentiated by their substantial subjects. I am not able now to go into the details of the solution Aquinas offers or at least suggests here (that would probably involve a theory of the distinction between *dimensiones interminatae* and *dimensiones terminatae*)[15]; but two points are clear enough to be made here.

(i) According to Aquinas it is quite possible that two squares are distinct both *by their position*, that is: *by themselves*, and by their subjects, that is, by their internal transcendental relations to their subjects. (ii) In the case discussed above the distinction of solids is derivative from the distinction of chessboards as far as solids are instantiated *in the chessboards*; and the distinction of solids is prior to the distinction of chessboards as far as the solids are instantiated *in matter*. And

---

14 Aquinas 1980, *In De Trin.* q. 4, art. 2, ad 3; for some remarks see also Brower 2012, 98–99.
15 For a survey of Aquinas's discussions concerning *dimensiones terminatae* and *dimensiones interminatae* see Wippel 2000, 356–371.

it is clear that the solids are instantiated *both* in the chessboards and in the matter, in different senses of 'being instantiated *in* something'. This perhaps suggests some way of squaring the Quantity-Individuation Thesis with the application of the Subject-Individuation Thesis to the case of dimensive quantity.

7.5 Matter and Quantity. What is *Materia Signata*?

It was a typical objection against the Quantity-Individuation Thesis that it makes some *accident* a principle of the individuation of *substance*, and this may well seem at least controversial for at least two reasons.[16] The first and more general one is that it makes a principle of the individuation of some entity of a given category something that belongs to a *distinct* category;[17] the rejection of transcategorial individuation is the source of the Scotistic rejection of both the Subject-Individuation Thesis and the Quantity-Individuation Thesis (one might add that by the rejection of transcategorial individuation Scotism is much more nominalistic than Thomism). The other, less general (and far more serious as well) reason is that making an accident a principle of the individuation of a substance severely undermines the priority of the substance.[18] To grasp the details of the objections one obviously has to grasp the details of the role ascribed in the Thomistic theory of individuation to quantity as opposed to matter.

The two objections gave rise to two important discussions in scholastic metaphysics. On the one hand, one may investigate in general what the relationship is between matter, its division into pieces or extension, dimensive quantity, and, finally, substantial forms instantiated in matter.[19] On the other hand, one may investigate more closely the roles in the individuation of (the forms of) material substances ascribed in the Matter-Individuation Thesis and the Quantity-Individuation Thesis to matter and quantity.

As for the former problem, the main question of the debate is whether the division of matter into pieces is in some way prior to the instantiation of substantial forms in matter; in other words: is the substantial form preceded by quantity, or is quantity preceded by form? The Thomistic metaphysics opts for the priority of substantial forms rather than quantity, but this leaves many details (of the way

---

[16] For a presentation of these objections see e.g. Scotus 1982, *Lect*. II, d. 3, p. 1, q. 4, n. 71–106; 1973, *Ord*. II, d. 3, p. 1, q. 4, n. 75–110.
[17] See e.g. Scotus 1982, *Lect*. II, d. 3, p. 1, q. 4, n. 91–94; 1973, *Ord*. II, d. 3, p. 1, q. 4, n. 89–98.
[18] See e.g. Scotus 1982, *Lect*. II, d. 3, p. 1, q. 4, n. 79–90; 1973, *Ord*. II, d. 3, p. 1, q. 4, n. 82–88.
[19] See e.g. Maier 1955, Donati 1998, Pasnau 2011, 53–76.

in which the divisibility into pieces belongs to material substances and in which it belongs to matter itself) in need of further investigation.

As for the problem of roles ascribed to matter and dimensive quantity, it proves notoriously difficult for at least four reasons. (i) The general issue of the relationship between matter and extension is a troublesome one. (ii) It is not easy to see the relationship between the two aspects of individuality distinguished by Aquinas in *S. th.* III, q. 77 (see 6.1 and 7.1) for which matter and quantity are responsible. (iii) Apart from the late fragment of *S. th.* III, q. 77 there is a series of earlier fragments in Aquinas in which he says that a (the?) principle of the individuation of material substances is *materia signata quantitate*, that is to say, matter marked with quantity, or, in other words, matter *divided into pieces*. Now the very discussions within Thomism show that it is not easy to fully grasp the notion of *materia signata*. As Oderberg says, "the unpacking of this concept is tricky, and here Thomists of good will differ".[20] (iv) Finally it is not quite clear what the relationship of the doctrine of the two aspects of individuality in q. 77 to the earlier fragments appealing to *materia signata* is.

Here I would like to sketch four solutions that are to be found in old Thomists, as well as a solution that seems to me a most plausible one in light of what I have already said. The four solutions with which I begin are not necessarily mutually exclusive; but I think it is convenient to distinguish between them.

(i) *Cajetan. Materia signata* which is said to be a principle of the individuation of material substances is matter having some relationship to a given dimensive quantity. We find two versions of this view in Cajetan. In his commentary on *De ente et essentia* he says that *materia signata* is matter having the capacity for a given dimensive quantity (as opposed to any other dimensive quantity), and that this capacity itself is not anything distinct from the matter it belongs to. In this way Cajetan wants to secure that *materia signata* is not a transcategorial complex (*aggregatum*) of matter and quantity, and that the role of quantity itself is reduced to the role of the capacity being part of the nature of matter.[21] In his later commentary on the *Summa* Cajetan wants to secure the same, but thinks that the way suggested in the earlier text is not enough, because the capacity in question belongs to the category of its object: it is an accidental capacity and henceforth it cannot be identified with matter. Instead of the capacity Cajetan wants to introduce a sort of internal relationship to quantity, and he admits that the very distinction within matter (divisibility into pieces) is prior to its extension: *materia in*

---

[20] Oderberg 2002, 130. For a sketch of the Thomistic discussions see e.g. Peterson 1994, Beuchot 1994, and Gracia and Kronen 1994.
[21] Cajetan 1907, q. 5.

se est prius sic distincta quam quanta.[22] A similar solution is to be found in Javelli.[23] Admittedly on this construal *materia signata* is not a transcategorial complex and quantity is not immediately a principle of individuation; but the price that is paid for this is admitting that some kind of divisibility of matter into pieces is basically independent from quantity.

(ii) *Capreol and Ferrara*. Another solution is suggested by Capreol and Ferrara; they claim, in light of the question 77 of the third part of the *Summa*, that both matter (as a prime subject) and dimensive quantity (as the source of the division of matter into pieces) are principles of individuation, and that they are responsible for various aspects of individuality or singleness. It is sometimes said that on this solution *materia signata* is a compound (*aggregatum*) of matter and a dimensive quantity. It seems, however, that in this solution we need not treat matter and quantity as items *composing* any single principle of individuation in any way; it is enough to say that they are two distinct principles corresponding to two distinct aspects of individuality. The relationship between these aspects and their principles obviously needs further investigation. The problem with this solution, however, is that it seems to make substance dependent in some controversial way on one of its accidents.

(iii) To avoid this sort of dependence one may also try to weaken the role of quantity in some other way. One of the most interesting ways of doing it is the following: one may say that a single material substance is usually a part of a manifold or *number* of coexisting substances – taking 'number' not in the transcendental sense, but as some sort of accident (see 7.2 (ix)). So, for example, a single man may be a part of a group of men sitting on a bank. Now being a part of a number *in this sense* is obviously accidental for a substance (although it is an accident very closely connected with individuality of substance) and it is possible to maintain that it is precisely this sort of accidental aspect that quantity is responsible for, whereas matter is responsible for noninstantiability and individuality of form. This sort of solution is to be found in Henry of Lübeck.[24] Essentially the same strategy is adopted by Anscombe and Geach who maintain that the Thomistic theses concerning *materia signata* as the principle of individuation concern the material difference of *co-existing* individuals of the same species (see also 5.5).

(iv) Still another way of weakening the role of quantity is to maintain that dimensive quantity is responsible for the way in which we single out material

---

[22] Cajetan 1888, I, q. 29, art. 1, n. 9.
[23] Javelli 1676, V, q. 15.
[24] Henry of Lübeck 1975, 108,85–101 and 110,165–113,258.

substances using some circumstances of time and space; in other words, it amounts to saying that quantity is a principle of individuation in the epistemic rather than metaphysical sense of 'individuation' or 'principle'. This strategy is adopted in the treatise *De principio individuationis* as well as in Dominic of Flandria.[25]

I think the key to this issue is the distinction between the two aspects of individuality for which matter and quantity are responsible; and I think it is hard to overestimate here the role of Aquinas's mature treatment of the problem of individuation in question 77 of the third part of the *Summa*. The first conclusion to be drawn from this text, I think, is that there is no reason to suppose that matter and quantity in any way *compose* a single principle of individuation; they seem instead to be two distinct principles responsible for two aspects of one and the same thing. So I think that it is the strategy of Capreolus and Ferrara that is most promising here. And it depends on the details of this distinction whether there is something controversial in assigning a role in the individuation of substances to an accident, and whether we need any weakening of this role along the lines of Henry of Lübeck or of Dominic of Flandria. So next I'll just focus on the distinction between these two aspects of individuality.

7.6 The Two Aspects of Individuality

I think the core idea of the distinction between the two aspects of individuality in question 77 may be sketched out in the following way. On the one hand, individuality or singleness may be opposed to instantiability (within the function analogy: to unsaturatedness or having values for arguments); in this respect individuality or singleness is just noninstantiability of forms. Matter as a prime subject is responsible for this aspect of singleness. On the other hand, individuality or singleness may be opposed to being in some greater number or being a manifold; quantity is responsible for this aspect of individuality. More generally: an individual instance of some nature may be contrasted on the one hand with what it is an instance of; and on the other hand an individual instance of some nature may be contrasted with a plurality or manifold of instances of that nature.

We may add that the latter contrast is something that we encounter in any case of counting or plurality – also in the case of the pluralities of *kinds*; it is the contrast between *numerical unity* and *plurality* in the broad sense. So there is

---

[25] Dominic of Flandria 1621, *In Met.* VII, q. 22, art. 4.

something more about individuality or numerical unity in the *narrow* sense (particular to individuals as opposed to kinds). And the former contrast is precisely the contrast between numerical unity in the broad sense and numerical unity in the narrow sense. This shows that there are two mutually irreducible aspects essential for individuality. In particular, when we start with numerical unity, we have to remember that not only individuals can be counted, and we need another aspect of individuality, namely noninstantiability.

From another point of view we should note that *manifolds* of coexisting individual instances of some nature are not *individuals* or *single* instances of the nature; these manifolds, however, are *noninstantiable* and do instantiate the nature in question. This shows again that there are two irreducible essential aspects of individuality: numerical unity has to be added to noninstantiability to distinguish noninstantiable manifolds from noninstantiable individuals.[26]

So, to begin with an example of an accidental form, the whiteness of a given square on a chessboard (that is: a single or individual whiteness) may be contrasted, on the one hand, with the nature of whiteness which is instantiable, because a single whiteness is a *noninstantiable* whiteness. On the other hand, a single whiteness on a chessboard may be contrasted with manifolds of instances of whiteness on the chessboard (in particular, with the manifold of the thirty-two instances of whiteness on the chessboard), because a single whiteness is *just one* whiteness; these manifolds are *noninstantiable*, and do instantiate whiteness, but they may obviously be contrasted with a single or individual whiteness.

In the case of substantial forms instantiated in matter, it is prime matter as a prime subject that is responsible for the noninstantiability of instances of forms. On the other hand, the unity and plurality of prime matter are responsible for the unity and plurality of instances, and dimensive quantity is responsible for the relevant sort of unity and distinction of prime matter.

From this point of view one of the aspects of individuality is the contrast between an individual and a manifold of coexisting individuals; and according to the Quantity-Individuation Thesis quantity is responsible just for this aspect. (To repeat, it is not immediately responsible for each type of distinction between individuals of the same species.) It seems to me that this role of quantity in individuation does not undermine the primacy of substance, so there is a good response to one of the most serious arguments against the Quantity-Individuation Thesis.

---

26 In a way this (as well as the fact that matter is as such noninstantiable, although not individual) might be an argument against Gracia's claim that "noninstantiability is both a necessary and sufficient condition of individuality" (Gracia 1988, 27).

7.7 Quantity and the Individuation of Parts of Substances

Aquinas also says that quantity as a principle of individuation also accounts for the individuation of parts of one and the same substance – for example of hands or eyes of one living being; the same point is made clearly by Geach.[27] This corresponds to the intuition that the peculiar nature of dimensive quantity is manifested both in the distinction between, say, distinct squares, and in the distinction between parts of one and the same square. In general, the issue of the individuation of parts of one substance is distinct both from the issue of the individuation of substances and from the issue of the individuation of accidents. So it is worthwhile to focus on the issue itself as well as on the question of to what extent various principles of individuation of substances and accidents can account for the individuation of parts of substances.

To begin with, we should distinguish between two senses of the question of principles of the individuation of the parts of substance – corresponding to the two senses of the Subject-Individuation Thesis (see 5.2). On the one hand we may ask about the way in which individuality belongs to a particular part of a given sort, for example to a hand or an eye, and about the source of its distinction from another part of the same sort within the same substance, for example the other hand or eye. On the other hand we may ask instead about the way in which individuality and plurification belong to the *natures* of parts of a given sort, for example to being a hand or being an eye. As far as the latter sense is concerned, it should be noted that we talk about the *natures* of parts of substances in a special sense; hand and eye are, as such, parts of living beings, and to be an eye or a hand is to be a given sort of part of a living being. So being a hand and being an eye are not just two distinct natures, but rather the natures of two parts of something having one nature, or even, in some sense, parts of one nature. What precisely the close relationship between being an eye and being a living being of a given sort is, is a question that belongs to the theory of parts and wholes that I cannot dwell on here; a counterpart of this relationship is the relationship between particular instances of the whole and the part, more precisely – a transcendental relationship of a part to its whole.

---

[27] See Aquinas 1980, *Quodl.* 1, q. 10, art. 1, corp.; Geach 1961, 74–5: "the body of an animal is for Aquinas a single substance, so its parts cannot be distinguished in terms of attributes' belonging to different things; rather, one eye, say, is differentiated from the other because their matter is geometrically different".

The issue of the individuation of parts of substances sheds some interesting light on the various theories of individuation sketched above. Let us make five basic points.

(i) According to the Strong Self-Individuation Thesis individuality belongs to parts of substances in the same way it belongs to anything else. The only exception could be parts that are not further divisible (*simple* parts), for obviously they are individual or single in a more basic way than complexes of distinct parts (in a way the Strong Self-Individuation Thesis holds only for *simple* entities). It seems that according to Scotism as well, individuality belongs to parts of substances in the same way it belongs to anything else. Parts of substances are individual just by their haecceities, although maybe there is more room in Scotism for considerations concerning the relationships between haecceities of wholes and haecceities of their parts. By contrast, according to the other theories of individuation discussed here individuality and mutual distinction belong to parts of one and the same material substance in a way that differs from the way they belong to wholes, as I will try to show in (ii)–(v) below.

(ii) As for the Formal Individuation Thesis (including its weak version accepted by Aquinas) it is worth noting that particular forms do not play, in the individuation of parts, the role they play in the individuation of wholes. It is namely *not* the case that what is responsible for the individuation of an eye is the form of an eye, for there is no such thing as the form of an eye; what makes an eye the sort of part it is, is not a distinct form of an eye, but instead the form of the whole, namely the soul that is the only substantial form in the living being having the eye. And the difference between a hand and an eye does not have its source in the difference between forms of a hand and of an eye, but instead in the difference of ways in which one and the same form belongs to two distinct sorts of parts that are constituted by it. Similarly, the distinction between the eyes of one and the same living being does not have its source in the distinction of their forms, for their form is one and the same form of the whole. This form may be said to be responsible for the individuality of *both* eyes, but only in some indirect way; and the analysis of the sort of indirectness involved here is clearly part of a theory of parts and wholes.

(iii) As for the Subject-Individuation Thesis, particular instances of the natures of accidents have internal transcendental relationships to their subjects, and parts of substances have internal transcendental relationships to the wholes they are parts of. Transcendental relations of accidents to their subjects are different from transcendental relations of parts to their wholes, and it seems that the latter are not so essential for the individuality of parts as the former are for the individuality of accidents (according to the Instance Subject-Individuation Thesis). So, for example, there is nothing strange about one and the same substance having two exactly similar eyes, but it would be at least strange for a Thomist if one and the same proper subject had two distinct instances of one and the same accidental nature.

(iv) As for the Matter-Individuation Thesis, it seems that the argument for it (see 6.2–6.3) could be applied to parts of substances, too, to show that their non-instantiability has its source in matter as a prime subject. It should be noted, however, that the weak version of the Formal Individuation Thesis that is involved in the argument for the Matter-Individuation Thesis could not be involved here in the same way, for the reasons sketched in (ii).

(v) Quantity is responsible for the individuality of parts and the individuality of wholes in two different ways. For one thing, quantity is responsible for the individuality and distinction of *wholes* as far as it is responsible for the individuality and distinction of their *forms*; and, for the reasons presented in (ii), this is not so in the case of the individuation of parts. Secondly, in the case of the particular instances of parts there are different sorts of transcendental relationships to quantity; the distinction of parts is based on material distinction in a different way than the distinction of wholes is based on it. From a general perspective this shows that although quantity is responsible for material differences, there are two distinct sorts of material differences: on the one hand there are material differences between the parts of one and the same substance, and on the other hand, there are material differences between distinct substances (this amounts to claiming some sort of priority of substantial forms with respect to extension).

7.8 The Individuality of Human Souls. Commensuratio animae ad hoc corpus

The most significant part of the theory of the individuation of material substances is the issue of the individuation of human beings or of humanity, and the related issue of the principle of the individuation of human souls. According to the weak version of the Formal Individuation Thesis the distinction between human beings is based on the distinction of their substantial forms (their souls); and then one can ask what is responsible for the individuality of human souls.

The human soul differs on the one hand from totally immaterial forms (angels in Aquinas's metaphysics), because it is instantiated in matter as its prime subject, and it makes that matter a human body (by contrast, even if totally immaterial forms do manifest their activity in matter and henceforth being in a place can be ascribed to them, they are never *instantiated* in matter and they never make any matter a body of a living being; so angels, even if they can assume bodies, never *have* bodies in the sense in which human beings have bodies).

On the other hand, according to Aquinas the human soul differs utterly from other sorts of forms that have their instances in matter and make matter bodies of other sorts of living beings. The human soul, Aquinas says, can continue to exist even when it is not instantiated *in matter* anymore and no longer makes any matter a human body – that is to say, after bodily death. This difference between the human soul and other sorts of forms instantiated in matter has its source in the fact that the human soul is a principle of activity that is not performed by any bodily organ; it is the intellectual activity (for example, forming judgments and making proofs) and the activity of the will (for example, making decisions or intending something). After bodily death the soul preserves one and the same actual existence that it used to enjoy before death, and the body does not have this existence anymore.[28]

Now, as far as the individuality of human souls is concerned, Aquinas makes three fundamentally important claims.

(i) It is quite impossible that a soul preserves its existence, but does not preserve individuality and distinction; it is impossible that souls after death continue to exist, but cease to be distinct; actual existence and individuality are so intimately connected that it is impossible to preserve only one of them.[29] By contrast: as Anscombe remarks, it is possible that after pouring a glass of water into a bottle with some water, the water that used to be in the glass, continues to exist, but it does not preserve its distinction from the water that used to be in the bottle before; so matter, it seems, can lose its individuality while retaining its identity.[30] Here it should be remembered that matter and forms are not similar from the point of view of individuation, and three differences seem particularly relevant. (*a*) In the case in question matter does retain its identity, but this does not mean that it retains one and the same actual existence (whereas the soul retains one and the same actual existence). (*b*) The fact that matter can retain its identity while not retaining its actual existence is something specific to matter. (c) Both actual existence and individuality belong to matter in a way that is significantly different from the way they belong to forms (see 6.3.2) or to material compounds.

---

28 For a brief survey of this issue see e.g. Brower 2014, 250–254.
29 Aquinas 1980, *S. th.* I, q. 76, art. 2, ad 2; *Compendium theologiae*, c. 71; *De spiritualibus creaturis*, q. 3, corp.
30 Anscombe 1961, 48.

(ii) The second claim of Aquinas is that the individuality of human souls consists in some internal transcendental relationship to their subjects, and in particular to the human bodies they constitute. So the individuality of a human soul consists in its being the soul of a given human body, and its distinction from other human souls consists in its being the soul of a human body distinct from other human bodies. Aquinas calls this transcendental relationship *commensuratio animae ad hoc corpus*.[31]

(iii) Now the central point of Aquinas is that when a human soul ceases to make matter a human body (at the moment of bodily death) it retains that transcendental relationship and remains the soul *of that body* (that no longer exists). It should be kept in mind that when we say that a given soul is the soul *of some body*, we do not say just that it is actually instantiated in that body, but rather that there is some internal transcendental relationship of the soul to that body; and this relationship remains in the soul even when the body does not exist anymore. So, for example, Socrates's soul remains the soul of Socrates's body even when Socrates's body does not exist anymore.

Let us note that there is nothing strange about the fact that a transcendental relationship remains also when its terminus does not exist anymore (a transcendental relation does not require the actual existence of its *terminus*)[32]. Moreover, the existence of the relationship in the soul does not consist only in the fact that the soul *used* to be the soul of the given body; it consists instead in the fact that it continues to be the soul of that body.

---

31 Aquinas 1980, *De spiritualibus creaturis*, q. 9, ad 4; *Contra gent.* II, c. 7.
32 See e.g. John of St. Thomas 1933, *Logica* p. II, q. 17, art. 3: "remote et destructo termino manet transcendentalis ordo, non praedicamentalis"; Suarez 1866, *Disp. met.* 47, s. 4, n. 2: "Saepe etiam hic transcendentalis respectus, licet sit ad terminum realem, non tamen requirit realem existentiam eius".

8 Actual Existence and Individuality

8.1 The Existence-Individuation Thesis and Some Standard Arguments

The Existence-Individuation Thesis claims that

> **(The Existence-Individuation Thesis)** Actual existence (*esse, existentia actualis*) is a principle of individuation both of substances and of accidents.

The thesis is mentioned in scholastic texts on individuation quite often, but usually in a dismissive way. Scotus devotes to its rejection a very short question 3 of his treatise on individuation both in *Lectura* and in *Ordinatio*; there is a short passage devoted to it in Paulus Soncinas; it is also analysed by Fonseca, Suárez, Pasqualigo and Mastri and Belluto.[1] It is usually Henry of Ghent that is supposed to embrace the Existence-Individuation Thesis.[2] In general, however, the thesis is considered implausible and lacks serious defenders. Suárez even says that the thesis is rejected by everyone as completely false and improbable, and Pasqualigo states that it is the negation of the thesis that is *opinio communis*; Mastri and Belluto claim that this thesis was refuted a long time ago, although there are some new attempts to revive it.[3]

By contrast, some contemporary Thomists claim that it is actual existence that is a principle of individuation in the most proper sense; Joseph Owens claims (in Owens 1994) that while quantity, matter and form are principles of individuation in their ways, the actual existence of a thing is its principle of individuation in the most primitive way. This contrast seems to correspond to the diagnosis that actual existence plays a fundamental role in Aquinas metaphysics, although this

---

1 Scotus 1982, *Lect.* II, d. 3, p. 1, q. 3; 1973, *Ord.* II, d. 3, p. 1, q. 3; Soncinas 1586, *In Met.* VII, q. 32; Fonseca 1615, *In Met.* V, c. 6, q. 2; Suárez 1866, *Disp. met.* V, sect. 5; Pasqualigo 1636, *Disp. met.* 39; Mastri and Belluto 1727, *Met.*, disp. 10, q. 4.
2 Henry indeed seems to adopt some version of the Existence-Individuation Thesis in 1983, *Quodl.* 2, q. 8. It should be stressed, however, that Henry is concerned primarily with some issues concerning subsistence and *suppositum*, and these, as I have indicated in 1.2, are to be distinguished from the issues of individuation.
3 Suárez 1866, *Disp. met.* V, sect. 5, 2; Pasqualigo 1636, *Disp. met.* 39, sect. 1, 4; Mastri and Belluto 1727, *Met.*, disp. 10, q. 4.

role has been systematically diminished by the subsequent Thomist tradition. Moreover, Gracia defends the Existence-Individuation Thesis in Gracia 1988.[4]

Let us begin with some clarifications concerning actual existence. The first thing to note is that it is the object of many controversies in scholastic metaphysics, and both the adherents and the critics of the Existence-Individuation Thesis belong to various camps in these disputes. It is possible, however, to grasp what actual existence is, without a serious commitment to any of the standpoints in these disputes. The best way would be to say that actual existence is what a thing acquires when it begins to exist and what it loses when it ceases to be; we refer to actual existence when we say that something begins to exist, exists no more or continues to exist, or that something exists eternally; we may add that, according to the well-known dictum from Aristotle's *De anima*, for a living being to exist is to live: *vivere viventibus est esse*.[5] Moreover, actual existence should be distinguished from existence expressed by the existential quantifier or 'there is' construction in English. The Aristotelian thesis from *De anima* suggests that there are various kinds of actual existence corresponding to various kinds of being: so, for example, life is a kind of existence different from the existence of a stone, and a human life and a cat's life are two different sorts of existence. Moreover, within a given kind of actual existence there are individual existences of individuals; for example, the actual existence of Plato is distinct from the actual existence of Socrates, but, by contrast, the actual existence of Socrates is identical with the actual existence of his right hand (that does not exclude the possibility that the hand loses the existence while Socrates retains it).

There are at least three kinds of arguments for the Existence-Individuation Thesis. The first kind of argument is quoted by Scotus: the main premise is that actuality is the distinguishing factor (*actus determinat et distinguit*), so, the argument goes, ultimate actuality is responsible for ultimate distinction; but the actual existence of a thing is its ultimate actuality, and its ultimate distinction is its individuality.[6]

---

4 It should be noted, however, that Gracia claims that actual existence is just necessary and sufficient condition of individuality, and the scholastic concept of a principle of individuation seems different from the concept of sufficient and necessary condition.
5 See Aristotle 1961, *De an.* 415b13; Aquinas 1980, *S. th.* I, q. 18, art. 2, corp.; Wingell 1961. I think one of the best introductions to the problem of actual existence in the context of scholastic metaphysics is given in Geach 1961, 88–100, Geach 1969a and Geach 1969b; see also Geach's reply to Kenny in Geach 1991. For a discussion of Geach's standpoint see also Honnefelder 2009 and García 2012.
6 Scotus 1973, *Ord.* II, d. 3, p. 1, q. 3, n. 60. The main premise concerning actuality and distinction comes from Aristotle 1953, *Met.* 1039a7.

Another way appeals to the close connection between existence and individuality itself; Aquinas states this connection many times in the passages quoted by Owens. He says, in general, that unity (in particular individuality) and plurality belong to something in the way in which existence belongs to it (*secundum quod res habent esse, ita habent pluralitatem et unitatem* or *unumquodque enim secundum quod habet esse, habet unitatem et individuationem*)[7].

The third sort of argument is to be found in Owens himself; he says that actual existence has some unifying feature which is realized in various ways in various sorts of beings. In the case of material substances, Owens says (1994, 174–175) that actual existence "makes into a single unit" a human person and his various accidents (like his tallness and musical skills) so that they are "one real existent", namely the tall musician he is.

It seems to me that the first two arguments do show something really important, although I am not sure whether they show that existence is a principle of individuation; I focus on them in 8.2 and 8.3, beginning with the second one. The third argument, however, seems to me mistaken; I try to show this in 8.4. Finally (8.5) I present some reasons for which existence is *not* a principle of the individuation of a thing it is the existence of.

8.2 Actual Existence and Individuality

As for the second line of argument, it appeals to the general principle that

> **(The Existence Thesis)** Actual existence belongs to something precisely in the same way in which individuality belongs to it (*unumquodque secundum idem habet esse et individuationem*).

The Existence Thesis is closely related to another fundamental thesis of Aristotelian metaphysics that plays a prominent role in the debate on the principles of individuation, namely the principle *ens et unum convertuntur* (see 2.3). The Existence Thesis seems also to be the ground of the idea that everything that actually exists *must* be individual (although this idea may be defended also in other ways, for example those adopted by nominalists (see 2.5)); everything that actually ex-

---

[7] Aquinas 1980, *Responsio ad fr. Joannem Vercellensem de articulis XLII*, q. 108; *Compendium theologiae*, c. 71; *Quaestio de anima*, art. 1, ad 2; *S. th.* I, q. 3, art. 5.

ists must be individual because as far as actual existence belongs to it, individuality also belongs to it. So, for example, Pasqualigo says that just by the very making something actually exis one makes it individual.[8]

There are two senses of the Existence Thesis, corresponding to the two senses of the Subject-Individuation Thesis (see 5.2.1 and 5.2.4). So, on the one hand, we may focus on the way actual existence and individuality belong to instantiable natures:

> **(The Nature Existence Thesis)** Individuality and plurification belong to the nature of F in the same way in which actual existence belongs to it.

On the other hand, we may consider the way in which actual existence and individuality belong to particular instances of natures:

> **(The Instance Existence Thesis)** individuality and distinction belong to instances of the nature of F in the same way in which actual existence belongs to them.

It seems that Aquinas's formulation in *Responsio ad fratrem Joannem Vercellensem* corresponds to the former thesis, since Aquinas considers unity and plurality here (*habere unitatem et multitudinem*), and they can be ascribed to a nature and not to its instance; by contrast, his formulation in the *Summa* concerns the way in which actual existence belongs to individuals.

Here one might raise a crucial objection: actual existence can be ascribed *to individuals* as opposed to natures; what we ascribe to natures is having some instances, and we ascribe it by using the existential quantifier or some parallel construction in natural languages;[9] so it may seem that ascribing actual existence to *natures* is a form of Platonic realism treating instantiable natures as objects or individuals of some curious sorts.

This seems to be a serious objection, but I think there is a good response to it. Consider a uniformly white square on a chessboard. Now obviously (at least within Thomistic metaphysics) the realization of whiteness in the square and the realization of colour in it are *one and the same realization*; so, in other words, two natures have one and the same realization in the square (within the function

---

[8] Pasqualigo 1636, *Disp. met.* 39, sect. 1, 2: "productio, quae communicat esse actuale, et facit existens eo ipso communicat esse individuum".

[9] See e.g. Geach who says in 1961, 90: "An individual may be said to 'be', meaning that it is at present actually existing; on the other hand, when we say that 'there is' an X (where 'X' goes proxy for a general term), we are saying concerning a kind or description of things, Xs, that there is at least one thing of that kind or description".

analogy, this corresponds to two functions having one and the same value for some argument). So it seems that we can ask whether the actual existence of whiteness in the square and the actual existence of colour in it are one and the same actual existence or not. Now the point is that such a question cannot be asked concerning existence that is expressed by the existential quantifier or 'there is' construction. So it seems that asking the question we assume that actual existence can be ascribed in a way to natures, although obviously it is ascribed to them in a way that is utterly different from the way in which it is ascribed to individuals. Individuality, too, is ascribed to natures in a way that is utterly different from the way in which it is ascribed to their individual instances (see 5.2.4). More precisely: one and the same actual existence is the actual existence of some individual and actual existence of the nature the individual is an instance of.

In this way, I think, it is possible to ascribe actual existence to natures, and not only to individuals; yet there is still something serious about the objection in question; I return to it in the very end of 8.5.

Some of the arguments concerning individuation discussed in this book appeal to intuitions close to the Existence Thesis. So, for example, the standard argument for the Subject-Individuation Thesis is that if the actual existence of an accident depends on its subject, the individuality of that accident depends on the subject, too (see 5.1 and 5.2). In other words, the subject is responsible for the individuality of an accident insofar as it is responsible for the actual existence of that accident. And the standard argument for the Formal Individuation Thesis is based on a premise that what is a principle of the existence of a thing, is also a principle of its individuality.

There are also other interesting applications of the Nature Existence Thesis. For example, we can argue that if some nature expressed by a general term has different sorts of instances or realizations, individuality will belong to it in a number of different ways. Both Avicenna and Aquinas assume that natures have their instances on the one hand in sensible matter, and, on the other hand, in cognitive powers; these are deeply different sorts of instantiation and there are different ways the natures are individuated corresponding to these sorts of instantiation. So, for example, the structure of a building may be instantiated in stone or bricks as well as in the mind of the architect; in both sorts of instantiation, individuality belongs to the structure, but the way in which the structure is individuated in the former case is different from the way in which it is individuated in the latter one. Similarly, there could be a version of Platonism claiming that besides the usual sensible instances of whiteness there is a distinct and eternal instance of whiteness in the Platonic idea of whiteness; now the way whiteness would be individuated in the latter case would correspond to this peculiar mode of instantiation and would be different from the way in which whiteness is individuated in the sensible world; ascribing this peculiar sort of instance to whiteness we ascribe a peculiar sort of individuation to it.

As for the Instance Existence Thesis: it seems convincing that the individuality of a particular instance of an accident is based on its internal transcendental relationship to its subject just because the very actual existence of that instance also involves such an internal relationship.

Besides these two senses of the Existence Thesis there are also other interesting ones. So, for example, we could plausibly claim that individuality belongs to *matter* in the way in which actual existence belongs to it (see 6.3.2). We ascribe actual existence to matter when we say that it is actualized as the material being of a given sort (e.g. a bell); and we ascribe individuality to it when we say that it actually is an individual bell. Now it is peculiar to the way in which existence belongs to matter that matter may lose some existence while retaining its identity. The point is that according to the Existence Thesis this peculiarity is mirrored in the way in which individuality belongs to matter; so, for example, matter can lose its individuality while retaining its identity.

All this shows, I think, that the Existence Thesis in its various senses grasps something very important about the connection between existence and individuation. Is it enough to show that actual existence is *a* principle of the individuation of what it is the existence of? Clearly it is not *the* principle of individuation; the problem is whether the Existence Thesis is a sufficient reason for claiming that existence is just *a* principle of individuation: something that is responsible for the individuality of the thing in some specific and irreducible way. Now the arguments showing that form, matter or quantity are principles of individuation always try to identify something in these principles that makes them responsible in some peculiar and irreducible way for the individuality of the thing. By contrast, it seems to me, the very Existence Thesis does not yet show any special feature of the actual existence that makes it responsible for the individuality of the thing in some irreducible way. The two other arguments in favour of the Existence-Individuation Thesis, however, do try to single out such a feature of actual existence; so I focus on these two arguments in turn.

8.3 Ultimate Actuality, Ultimate Distinction, and Noninstantiability Again

The main premise of the first argument for the Existence-Individuation Thesis is the principle:

(Actuality-Distinction Thesis) Actuality is the source of distinction *(actus distinguit)*.

There are two senses of the Actuality-Distinction Thesis corresponding to the two senses of the Subject-Individuation Thesis. On the one hand it may be understood as a thesis about the way in which distinction belongs to *individuals*, on the other hand – as a thesis concerning the way in which plurality or number belong to instantiable *natures*. I focus first on the former sense of the Actuality-Distinction Thesis and then on the latter one.

From the historical point of view, the Actuality-Distinction Thesis comes from Aristotelian considerations concerning parts and wholes. A substance, Aristotle claims, cannot be composed of a number of substances inhering in it *actually*; if there were two substances in it *actually*, we would have two substances there, and not something actually one. It is possible, by contrast, that a substance is composed of a number of substances that are contained in it *potentially*. So it is in this sense that actuality is the source of distinction.[10]

It seems that what Aristotle says can be paraphrased in the following way: if actuality belongs to a whole, what we have is a single substance the parts of which are not actual. And when, by contrast, actuality belongs to the parts, what we have is a number of actually distinct substances that do not actually compose a single one. So when a part becomes actual, it is its actuality that distinguishes it from other parts; and when a whole becomes actual, it is its actuality that distinguishes it, as some unit, from its surrounding as well as from its parts.

This might be illustrated by the following example. Suppose we have a piece of wood that splits at some time into two parts. In general what is altered in such a change is the number of pieces of wood: there are two pieces now instead of one; in other words, the change is just a generation of some new distinction.[11] Now there are two ways in which such a change may be analysed. On the one hand, it might be analysed in terms of (dis)continuity or generation of new surfaces. On the other hand, however, the change may be analysed in terms of actuality: before the change, actuality belonged primarily to the whole and only in a derivative way to the parts; after the change, by contrast, actuality belongs primarily or immediately to the parts. So when actuality begins to belong to some piece immediately and primarily, it makes it something distinct from others; it is actuality that is the source of distinction.

---

10 Aristotle 1953, *Met.* 1039a3–7.
11 In Brower's terminology it is a one-many change (2014, 64–66), but its peculiarity consists in the fact that it consists basically in nothing else than introducing some discontinuity; it might be called a *pure* one-many change.

Now one might wonder whether the pieces are now distinct because actuality belongs to each of them immediately or rather because of their present discontinuity; and whether one of these things (and which one) is the ground of the other. This seems to be just another formulation of the difficult issue of the relationship between substance and quantity or extension (see 7.5). So it is possible that the Actuality-Distinction Thesis is just the Aristotelian solution of the issue – a solution favouring actuality rather than discontinuity.

It is also important to note, however, that division into pieces is a very peculiar example of distinction; and it may seem dubious whether conclusions concerning this peculiar sort of distinction may be generalized for other sorts of distinction that are not connected with division into pieces. I cannot go into the details of this issue now; anyway, it seems to me that the example of division of some stuff into pieces gives a good illustration of the way in which actual existence or actuality is the source of distinction.[12]

In the example of division into pieces we focus on the way in which distinction belongs to some instances of natures; the point is that actuality may belong to them immediately or not immediately, and when it belongs to them immediately, it makes them distinct.

The Actuality-Distinction Thesis, however, may be understood in another way, too, namely as a thesis concerning the way in which actuality (and henceforth distinction or plurality) belongs to instantiable natures. Now the first thing to note is that we talk about the *instantiation* of a nature in a weaker and a stronger sense. The weaker sense is relevant when we say that the nature of colour or being a colour is instantiated both in being red and in being green, more generally – in something that is instantiable itself. By contrast, we have the stronger sense corresponding to the *ultimate* actuality when we say that the nature of colour or being a colour is instantiated in some particular instance of whiteness. The difference is that what is an instance of some nature in the weaker sense (for example being red or being green) is itself instantiable; and what is an instance of some nature in the stronger sense, does not have its instances and is the *ultimate* realization, *actus ultimus*. There are no instances of a particular instance of being white in the sense in which there are realizations of being green or being white. Now it seems plausible that the ultimate realization or ultimate actuality in this sense is just the actual existence.

---

[12] It is worth noting that Henry of Ghent (1983, *Quodl.* 2, q. 8) considers the example of division into pieces as a model of plurification of natures; and he says that it is thanks to *subsistentia* that the parts are actually separated ("per subsistentiam actualem appositam separantur ab invicem").

From this perspective the Actuality-Distinction Thesis claims that the instantiation of a nature is always connected with a possible plurification of it. And the argument for the Existence-Individuation Thesis is the following: each instantiation of a nature is a source of some distinction; so the ultimate realization of a nature, that is the actual existence, is a source the ultimate distinction an plurification, that is: individual distinction.

Now such a line of arguments poses at least one interesting problem. In the argument for the Matter-Individuation Thesis it is a prime subject, and prime matter in particular, that is said to be a principal source of noninstantiability. It seems clear that noninstantiability that is referred to in the argument for the Matter-Individuation Thesis and noninstantiability referred to here are closely related. In general, there seem to be two ways of arriving to what is noninstantiable: on the one hand, *via* non-ultimate instantiations, and here the ultimate actuality or actual existence is noninstantiable; on the other hand, via the primary subjects, and here prime matter is noninstantiable.

Finally, actual existence as the ultimate actuality seems something similar to the Scotistic haecceity which Scotus himself calls the ultimate reality of form, *ultima realitas formae* (see 3.7). There seem to be, however, two differences between them. The first is that here ultimate actuality or realization is ascribed to *instantiable natures*; by contrast, in the analysis of the Scotistic haecceity in 3.7 I focused on ascribing ultimate actuality to instances of natures or to natures considered as parts of their instances. Another difference is that the actual existence of an individual is the actual existence of its form as well as the actual existence of the matter in which the form is instantiated. This identity does not seem to hold for Scotistic haecceities, or at least it is not something Scotus is much interested in.

8.4 Actual Existence, Accidental Unity, and Individuality

Let us now turn to the third line of argument which is to be found in Joseph Owens. The main premise is the claim that it is actual existence that is responsible for some special sort of unity illustrated by the example of a tall musician – that is a man who happens to be a musician and a tall man at the same time. Now this sort of unity, Owens claims, is not grounded in some necessary connections between being a man, being tall and being a musician, but it is something specific to individuality. This is supposed to show that it is the actual existence that is responsible in some important way for the unity of individuals.

I think this line of argument is invalid for two reasons. The first reason is that the unity specific for a tall musician is traditionally classified as accidental unity (*unitas per accidens*); it is radically different from singleness and individuality, and, moreover, it is derivative from it. The other reason is that actual existence is *not* a principle or ground of accidental unity. I focus on these two reasons below.

8.4.1 *Per se* Unity, Accidental Unity, and Individuality

The unity of a tall musician consists in the fact that one and the same man happens to be both a musician and a tall man; the existence of a tall musician consists in the fact that one and the same man remains a musician and remains tall for some time. In Aristotelian terminology a tall musician is a transcategorial compound of various entities and so a being *per accidens* (*ens per accidens*) having accidental unity. Beings like a tall musician are to be contrasted with *entia per se* belonging to a single category – both substances like men and cats *and* accidents like the musical skill of Johann Sebastian Bach are *entia per se* in this sense.[13]

The contrast between beings *per accidens* and beings *per se* is one of the most important traits of the Aristotelian metaphysics of categories. Let us note four aspects of this contrast.

The first thing is that the unity of a tall musician, as I have already said, consists in the fact that one and the same man happens to be both a musician and tall for some time. So the ground of this unity is the unity of the man (a *per se* being) in whom both the accidents are instantiated. The latter kind of unity, the unity of the man, does not consist in the fact that some distinct properties are instantiated in one and the same subject. In particular, as far as man is a rational living being, we could say that the unity of man involves some connection of life and rationality, but this connection does *not* consist in the fact that life and rationality belong to one and the same subject; it consists instead in the fact that we have here a single form which is immediately and of itself (see 4.3) both a form of living being and a form of rational being. One could also say that being rational is an instance of being a living being in the weak sense introduced in 8.3, while being tall is not a realization of being a musician (neither in the strong nor in the weak sense).

Secondly, a particular man instantiates something one, namely the human nature, while a particular tall musician does not instantiate as such anything one,

---

13 See e.g. Aristotle 1953, *Met.* 1017a7–22. Anscombe 1961, 21–23; Brower 2014, 42–43. Of course beings *per accidens* or accidental unities are to be sharply distinguished from accidents or accidental forms.

but is instead a compound of instances of two utterly different instantiable things, namely of being tall and of being a musician. Let us note in passing that the claim that the musical skill of Johann Sebastian Bach (or at least the compositional skill of Johann Sebastian Bach) is an instance of something one (some instantiable nature), and not a compound of instances of various things – that is, an entity *per se* as opposed to a *per accidens* one – is a non-trivial claim belonging to the metaphysics of skills, substantiated both by metaphysical speculation and by the musical experience of mankind.

Thirdly, Aristotle notes that there is not such thing as coming to be and passing away of beings *per accidens*.[14] A being *per accidens* like a tall musician begins to exist either when a musician becomes tall or when a tall man becomes a musician; the fact that a tall musician begins to exist is in a way a side effect of distinct processes like becoming tall or becoming a musician. By contrast, becoming tall and becoming a musician are distinct kinds of real changes, and the first one is investigated in physiology or medicine.

Finally, in some respects beings *per accidens* are similar to arbitrarily singled out mereological sums of various entities (for example of my right hand and one of the moons of Jupiter). They may be unambiguously singled out or identified by identifying their components, and in a way they are something real in the sense of being mind-independent entities. We do not think of them, however, as being distinct subjects of actuality or wholes of some sort. In the case of beings *per accidens* the connection between the components is admittedly stronger than in the case of arbitrary mereological sums; but in neither case can we think that there is a single distinct actuality specific to such a kind of being.

Now the main question is this: what is the relationship between beings *per accidens* or accidental unities like a tall musician and individuality or singleness? To see this, let us make four points.

(i) As far as individuality or singleness belonging to *natures* is concerned, we do ascribe individuality or singleness to being a man, to being tall and to being a musician. But we cannot ascribe (at least in a similar way) individuality or singleness to being a tall musician, because being a tall musician is not an instantiable nature at all; being a tall musician does not have instances in the sense in which being a musician or being tall do.

(ii) As far as individuality or singleness belonging to *particular instances* of natures is concerned, for similar reasons we cannot ascribe individuality or singleness to some tall musician in the way in which we ascribe it to some particular

---

14 Aristotle 1953, *Met.* 1026b21–24.

instance of being tall or of being a musician. In some respect this is comparable to our not ascribing individuality or singleness to arbitrary mereological sums, like the sum of my right hand and the given moon of Jupiter. To sum up, individuality and singleness may be ascribed only to beings *per se*.

(iii) Perhaps there is a being *per accidens* or an accidental unity which is a combination of *all* the accidents some man has simultaneously for a given time; but even if there is such a thing it is clear that, on some fundamental Aristotelian assumptions, that being is *not* identical with the man in question.

(iv) Finally, it is clear that the transcategorial connections which are essential for beings *per accidens* do belong primarily to particular instances of natures of various categories. If they may be ascribed to natures, they are always to be ascribed to them only in virtue of their particular instances. It is in this sense (and I am inclined to think that *only* in this sense) that there is some important relationship between accidental unity and individuality or singleness.

8.4.2 *Per se* Unity, Accidental Unity, and Existence

So what precisely is the relationship between beings *per accidens* or accidental unity and actual existence? Is Owens right in claiming that it is actual existence that in some important way is responsible for accidental unity? To answer these questions let me make four points.

(i) While (at least in some interpretations of Aquinas) there is such a thing as the distinct existence of a particular instance of musical skill, and there is such a thing as the actual existence of a man (which is his life), there is no such thing as the actual existence of a tall musician as such; more generally, actual existence cannot be ascribed to *per accidens* beings – for reasons at least partly similar to the reasons for which actual existence is not ascribed to arbitrary mereological sums.[15] In other words: the existence that may be ascribed to *per accidens* beings (that is: the existence of a given transcategorial connection) is *not* what is called actual existence in Aquinas.

---

15 In the first three points I assume that accidents have a distinct actual existence of their own; this, however, was a topic of a big debate within Thomistic scholars (see e.g. Brown 1985, Wippel 2000, 238–294, Wippel 1981, 209–224 and the literature cited there). Although I think that accidents do have a distinct actual existence of their own, I think also that some of the points here may be reformulated so as not to require this assumption. As for the debate, I offer only one reason in favour of distinct *esse* of accidents at the very end of 8.5.

(ii) The components of a *per accidens* unity do not have any *common* actual existence; so, for example, the actual existence of Johann Sebastian Bach is not the actual existence of his musical skill. Similarly, if a common actual existence might be ascribed to the components of some mereological sum, this sum would not be just an arbitrary mereological sum, and the components should be parts of a single whole – according to the first sense of the Actuality-Distinction Thesis sketched above (see 8.3).

(iii) The existence of a *per accidens* unity like that of a tall musician requires the actual existence of the man in question, the actual existence of his being a musician as well as the actual existence of his being tall. Moreover, to grasp a transcategorial connection one has to refer to the actual existence of the natures of its components. This, however, seems not enough to conclude that the actual existence is a principle of accidental unity; anyway, *per accidens* entities, unlike *per se* ones, in some important sense do *not* have principles at all.

(iv) Owens's line of argument may seem plausible as far as we treat *per accidens* beings as a sort of wholes and think that the role of actual existence is comparable to its role in the case of the single piece of wood as discussed in 8.3. The point, however, is that this sort of similarity between wholes and *per accidens* beings is an illusion, as is shown by the other points concerning accidental unity, individuality, and actual existence.

8.5 Is Actual Existence a Principle of Individuation?

So my claim is that Owens's argument is inconclusive; as for the two other arguments based on the Existence Thesis and the Actuality-Distinction Thesis, I think they show some deep connection between actual existence and individuality, but this connection does not seem enough to draw the conclusion that actual existence is the only or sufficient *principle* of individuation. There are at least three reasons to think so.

(i) It seems that the argument against the strong version of the Formal Individuation Thesis (see 4.3 and 5.5) can also be applied against the Existence-Individuation Thesis. If a form is not the form of a given individual in the same way it is a form of a given species or genus, some actual existence may be the actual existence of a given individual in a way that differs from the way in which it is the actual existence of some genus and species. It is possible, of course, that there is a deep difference between form and existence precisely in this respect, but such a difference would require a thorough investigation of the way in which some actual existence belongs to a given individual. For example, one might wonder whether actual existence is ultimate actuality in some way similar to the Scotistic haecceity. A *prima facie* reason against it is that there are *various kinds* of actual existence, and so a particular actual existence is, unlike a haecceity, an instance of some instantiable nature.

(ii) It also seems that the arguments for the Subject-Individuation Thesis and the Matter-Individuation Thesis may be applied to the case of actual existence to show that not only accidents and substantial forms, but also actual existence do depend on their subjects as far as individuality is concerned. Existence clearly can be said to be in some subject, although not in the sense in which we say that form is in some subject. Again it is possible that there is some fundamental difference between form and existence precisely in this respect; but it would require a thorough investigation to show this.

(iii) Finally, it seems that the argument for the Quantity-Individuation Thesis may also be applied to actual existence to show that not only forms, but also actual existence do require, in some way, dimensive quantity as a sort of basis of their numerical distinction. Again there is a possibility of some fundamental difference between existence and forms in this respect, but it would take a thorough investigation to show that there is indeed such a deep difference.

There is another well-known objection to the idea that existence is the principle of individuation; one might namely claim that we want to find principles of individuation for non-existent *possibilia*.[16] Now at least *prima facie* the Existence Thesis might be used against this objection: something that does not actually exist is not individual. Of course it may be disputed whether the individuation of *possibilia* offers a genuine counterexample or a reason to reject the Existence Thesis. Here, however, I cannot enter that dispute, because it would involve much work in the metaphysics of possibility.[17]

Another question is whether the actual existence of a thing is *a* principle of individuation responsible, in some way, for some aspect of the individuality of that thing. Here, I think, we encounter still another fundamental problem of scholastic metaphysics. Too see the problem, let us note first that we have been considering the ways in which both individuality and actual existence belong, on the one hand, to instantiable natures expressed by general terms, and on the other hand to particular instances of these natures. So, for example, individuality and actual existence are ascribed to being white, being a bell or being a man, and, on the other hand, to some particular being white, some particular being a bell or some particular humanity.

---

16 See e.g. Oderberg 2002, 128–129.
17 For some introduction see e.g. Wippel 1984, Wolter 1993 and King 2001.

Now the point is that even when we describe in some detail the ways in which individuality belongs to natures and their instance, we leave one fundamental question unanswered. Note first that it is clear within the Aristotelian metaphysical framework that a white thing, for example a white square on a chessboard, is distinct from its own whiteness (the square and its whiteness belong to two distinct categories in the Aristotelian sense). But what about being a bell? Is a bell, for example the Royal Sigismund Bell in Cracow, distinct from its being a bell? And, moreover, what about humanity? Is a man, for example Socrates, distinct from his own humanity? Surely Socrates and his humanity do *not* differ in the way in which the square differs from its whiteness: Socrates and his humanity do *not* belong to distinct categories in the Aristotelian sense of the term; but this does not settle the question whether they are distinct at all or not.

There are also some related questions concerning the relationship between Socrates and his humanity. Is it possible in any sense at all that one and the same man has two distinct humanities, and if this is impossible, what kind of impossibility is it, and what is its source? Note that the Subject-Individuation Thesis does not settle this question, since it concerns accidents, and humanity clearly is not an accident of Socrates. Moreover, the Matter-Individuation Thesis does not settle this question, because it concerns the way in which form is instantiated in matter, and not the way in which humanity is instantiated in a man. Finally, the Quantity-Individuation Thesis does not settle the question, too, because it concerns the way in which forms are realized in pieces of matter.

Socrates here is just an example of what used to be called a substantial subject or a *suppositum*; the difficult questions mentioned above belong to the issue of the relationship between a *suppositum* and the instance of the relevant nature.

In general many theories focusing on individuation may consider issues of individuality without settling these difficult questions concerning the relationship between a *suppositum* and its own instance of its substantial nature. In a way these questions do not belong to the issue of individuation at all – although they are much discussed in the scholastic metaphysics. To sum up: what we are after in the theory of individuation is the way in which individuality belongs to natures and their instances, and the relationship between a nature and its instances; here, by contrast, we encounter another problem which concerns the relationship between (instances of) natures and their *supposita* (for more about *suppositum* see 1.2 (x)).

Now the point is that the questions focusing on the relationship between substantial subjects and instances of their substantial natures are immediately related to the issue of actual existence. To see this connection note that the paradigmatic example of actual existence is *life* (*vivere viventibus est esse*), and it seems intuitively clear that life belongs to Socrates in a more primitive way than it belongs to his own humanity. In other words, it is Socrates who lives in the strongest and most appropriate sense; parts of Socrates's body, for example his right hand, live too, but in some secondary sense; similarly Socrates's humanity: it lives, but in some other secondary sense. More generally, the actual existence of a thing belongs primarily to the substantial subject (*suppositum*), and only in a secondary way to its parts or to its instance of its substantial nature. In other words, in some strong sense of 'exist' it is the *suppositum* that exists, and not the instance of its substantial nature in it.[18]

I think, moreover, that it is precisely this intuition that makes it plausible that actual existence is what is ascribed to *individuals* as opposed to instantiable natures expressed by general terms (see 8.2). Again, there is some strong and intuitively very appealing sense of 'exist' in which existence is ascribed to *supposita* as opposed to natures or particular instances of natures. This shows that there is some strong connection between the issues of actual existence and the issue of *suppositum*. The latter, however, is distinct from the issue of individuality and individuation; and it would have to be investigated thoroughly if we were to grasp the relationship between actual existence and individuality or singleness.

In spite of this negative conclusion I think there are several very important lessons to be learned from the arguments for the Existence-Individuation Thesis. They concern primarily the issues of self-individuation and noninstantiability. To begin with, the ultimate actuality as something noninstantiable might be contrasted, on the one hand, with the noninstantiability of matter, and, on the other hand, with the nonistantiability of Scotistic *haecceitates*; as far as the latter are concerned, a haecceity is not an instance of anything instantiable, but the ultimate actuality in the sense of actual existence seems to be an instance of a kind. Moreover, there is some intimate connection between the division into pieces and the Actuality-Distinction Thesis; so there is a close connection between quantity and actual existence, especially as far as self-individuation is concerned.

---

18 See in particular Aquinas 1980, *In Sent.* III, d. 6, q. 2, art. 2, corp.: "unde nec natura rei nec partes eius proprie dicuntur esse, si esse praedicto modo accipiatur; similiter autem nec accidentia". I think that the fact that there is some special strong sense of '*esse*' and that this strong sense is closely related to *suppositum* is the key to settling the issue whether accidents have a distinct esse of their own.

9 Concluding Remarks: The Thomistic Theory of Individuation

9.1 Main Features of the Thomistic Theory of Individuation

The Thomistic theory of individuation sketched in the chapters 5–8 deserves to be called the classical theory of individuation; it is also so recognized by its critics. There are at least eight traits specific to this theory.

(i) Various kinds of beings have different principles of individuation or sources of individuality. In other words, the differences between kinds of beings concern also the ways in which individuality belongs to them. In particular, there are different ways in which individuality belongs to material substances, immaterial substances, and accidents; there are different ways in which individuality belongs to various sorts of accidents; and there are different ways in which individuality belongs to forms, to matter, and to compounds of matter and substantial form. Moreover, there is a difference between the ways in which individuality belongs to particular *instances* of natures and to instantiable *natures* themselves. By contrast, the Scotistic theory focuses on three main ways in which individuality belongs to something: the way it belongs to haecceities, the way it belongs to particular instances of natures, the way it belongs to natures as *parts* of their instances. Nominalism distinguishes at most the ways in which individuality belongs to simple and to complex entities.

(ii) Even in the case of a single sort of entity it is possible that there is no single principle of individuation or *the* principle of individuation of this sort of entity; for example, forms of material substances, matter as well as quantity, are all principles of the individuation of material substances. So the individuation of material compounds is a matter of the interplay of a number of principles. In some cases this interplay is to be analysed in terms of various aspects of individuality (in particular: noninstantiability and numerical unity) that distinct principles of individuation are responsible for.

(iii) There are many ways of being a principle of individuation or something responsible for some aspect of individuality. In some cases what is (in some way) a principle of individuation is *not* self-individuated (prime matter is noninstantiable and is thought to be the source of noninstantiability of forms, but it does not mean that it is individual by itself or self-individuated). Moreover, in some cases what is a principle of individuation is not anything specific to it (again, prime matter is a principle of the individuation of material substances, although one and the same prime matter can successively constitute various material individuals).

(iv) There are things that are self-individuated or individual by themselves; individuality belongs to them in an immediate way, and they are distinct from one another just *by themselves* (dimensive quantity has this feature, so, for example, two exactly similar squares are distinct just by themselves). Being self-individuated, however, is grounded in some features specific to the kind in question that can be described not only in the context of individuality (for example, two exactly similar squares are distinct by themselves, because they are distinct by their position which is not something distinct from them). More generally, the way Thomists understand self-individuation is in many aspects different from the way it is understood by nominalists and Scotists.

(v) There are also (*pace* nominalists) many different ways in which individuality may belong to something *not immediately*, but in virtue of something else – ways in which something is made individual by something distinct from it. For example, individuality belongs to material substances in virtue of their forms, and it belongs to accidents in virtue of their subjects, and the connection between an accident and its subject that is responsible for its individuality does vary from one sort of accident to another; moreover, individuality belongs to forms in virtue of matter and its dimensive quantity. Finally, the way in which individuality belongs to instantiable natures differs from the way in which it belongs to instances of these natures. In some cases the distinction between something that is individual and what *makes* it individual is very strong: for example, in the case of the individuation of accidents by their subjects it is a distinction of categories in the Aristotelian sense. At any rate, the key to understanding derivative individuality is not to be looked for in a peculiar sort of part-whole relation postulated by Scotism, but instead in various sorts of transcendental relations.

(vi) Noninstantiability seems close to self-individuation. The point is, however, that there are various ways of being noninstantiable; in particular, although prime mater, substantial forms instantiated in matter and substantial forms of immaterial beings are all noninstantiable, they are noninstantiable in utterly different ways; moreover, prime matter, although noninstantiable, is not individual.

(vii) Some of ultimate sources of individuality are not instances of anything; prime matter is a good example. What is not an instance of anything is not necessarily self-individuated, and what is self-individuated might still be an instance of some instantiable nature (quantity is a good example).

(viii) The Thomistic theory of individuation focuses on instantiation in a subject as opposed to instantiation in general; instantiable natures are instantiated *in subjects* and this circumstance is crucial for the understanding of instantiation.

9.2 The Thomistic Theory of Individuation, Scotism, and Nominalism

The seven points sketched above contradict some intuitions developed within Scotism and nominalism. These intuitions include, in particular, the following seven ideas.

(i) There must be a single general answer to the question of the principle of individuation holding for *any* sort of entity whatsoever; as Suárez says, we should look for a uniform principle of individuation (*quaeri debet uniforme principium individuationis*).

(ii) There must be a single principle of individuation for a single entity, responsible for all the aspects of the individuality of that entity.

(iii) The principle of the individuation of a given thing must be something specific to that thing only (something *maxime proprium*), and, in particular, something that cannot enter the constitution of any other thing.

(iv) A thing cannot be made individual or single by a distinct thing.

(v) An ultimate source of individuality must be something that is self-individuated or individual by itself. Being self-individuated cannot be explicated in general terms and is in some way primitive.

(vi) Ultimate sources of individuality must be noninstantiable and cannot be instances of anything instantiable. A study of some features specific to prime matter, forms or quantity is not necessary for a good understanding of noninstantiability and not being an instance of anything instantiable.

(vii) The theory of individuation should focus on instantiation in general as opposed to instantiation *in a subject*; subjects are not essential for the instantiation of what is instantiated in them.

9.3 The Thomistic Theory of Individuation from a Historical Point of View

The debate between the classical theory of individuation and the Scotistic and nominalistic ones is one of the main strands of the whole discussion on principles of individuation. In particular, there have been massive criticisms of the classical theory originating from some of the seven crucial nominalistic and Scotistic intuitions sketched above. From a historical point of view it seems that the defence against this criticism has become more and more difficult. Typically it has required a good and more developed grasp of what was briefly sketched in Aquinas's succinct remarks concerning individuation. A symptom of the growing difficulty of this task is the fact that some eminent authors of the second scholasticism belonging to the Thomist tradition (in the broad sense) either embraced the nominalist (as Suárez did) or the Scotist (as Fonseca did) theories of individuation. Another symptom is the lack of clarity concerning the very notion of *materia signata*.

Another aspect of the growing difficulty of the defence of the Thomistic standpoint is a deterioration of the understanding of some key differences referred to in Thomistic theories of individuation. Some clear examples of such differences are the difference between the concept of matter and a sortal concept, the difference between substance and accidents, and the difference between dimensive quantity and other kinds of accidents.

The heart of the problem seems to be the relationship between self-individuation, noninstantiability and not being an instance of anything – the issues fundamental for individuality – and some special features of prime matter, forms, and quantity.

9.4 The Problem of Individuation: a General Framework

By way of concluding remarks, I would like to offer a sketch of the issue of individuation that emerges from the considerations in this book.

(i) *Prima facie* the nominalistic Strong Self-Individuation Thesis that everything is individual by itself might well seem a plausible answer to the problem of individuation both because of its simplicity and because of serious reasons in favour of it. It seems clear, however, that the Strong Self-Individuation Thesis is false (at least for some reasons belonging to the metaphysics of number), and the efforts not to give it up make one postulate some *simple* and sometimes otherwise unknown entities to play the role of individuals in the strict sense. Once you reject the Strong Self-Individuation Thesis you encounter a number of interesting issues concerning individuation. And it is not quite clear how much one has to reject if one rejects the Strong Self-Individuation Thesis.

(ii) There are two basic ways in which individuality or singleness is ascribed to something. On the one hand, we ascribe individuality or singleness and number to instantiable *natures* expressed by general terms, in the way in which we ascribe to them having instances. On the other hand, we ascribe individuality or singleness and distinction to particular instances of these natures. So the issue of individuation is basically the issue of the way in which individuality belongs to instantiable natures and to their particular instances. As for the former, there are some fundamental ideas expressed in the Avicennian Instance Ascription Thesis and in Frege's distinction of *Merkmal* and *Eigenschaft*, and a number of detailed problems related to the relationship between instantiable natures and their instantiations.

(iii) Natures are instantiated *in subjects* in a very general sense of the term. The relationship between an instance of nature and the subject the nature is instantiated in depends on the nature as well as on the sort of subject. In general the way in which a subject is essential for the instantiation of a nature, it is also essential for the individuality (and multiplication) ascribed to the nature in question. That is the point of the Nature Subject-Individuation Thesis, the Nature Quantity-Individuation Thesis, and the Matter-Individuation Thesis. In general, *pace* Scotism, to grasp the nature of instantiation one has to take subjects of instantiation into account.

(iv) In the case of particular instances of natures there is an internal transcendental relationship of an instance to its subject; that relationship is reflected in the fact that a given instance of whiteness is the whiteness *of* the given subject, and the given instance of patience is *someone's* patience. Individuality and distinction belong to a particular instance of a nature in virtue of the internal transcendental relationship to its subject. For various sorts of natures and subjects there are various sorts of the transcendental relationship. That is the point of the Instance Subject-Individuation Thesis, the Instance Quantity-Individuation Thesis, and the Matter-Individuation Thesis.

(v) If individuality and distinction belong to an instance of a nature in virtue of its relationship to *something else*, the instance in question is *not* individual just by itself, and is not individual immediately. In another important sense a nature is not individual by itself or as such, according to the Instance Ascription Thesis. So, *pace* the nominalists, there are many different ways in which something may be individual *not* by itself or *not* immediately.

(vi) According to a suggestion of Geach's (inspired both by Frege and by Aquinas), natures instantable in subjects may be compared to functions (understood in a Fregean way) having subjects as their arguments and instances as values. The relationship of an instance to its subject is comparable to being the value *of* a given function *for* a given argument. The key point of the analogy is that an instantiable nature has not just instances, but rather *instances in subjects* – just like a function does not just have values, but rather has values for arguments.

(vii) The composition of a function sign and an argument sign (in 'the square root of 2' or 'the whiteness of the B5 square on the chessboard') does *not* have to reflect – *pace* Avicenna and Scotus – some metaphysical composition within the instance of the nature or the value of the function for a given argument. A nature is *not* any peculiar sort of *part* of its instance – a part distinct from another one which is individuality of that instance itself. What the composition of 'the whiteness of _' and 'the B5 square on the chessboard' reflects is instead some internal transcendental relationship of an instance of whiteness to its subject; the very instantiable nature is in a way involved in this relationship, but is not a part of the instance. To repeat, the key to understanding derivative individuality is *not* (*pace* Scotism) a peculiar sort of the part–whole relation.

(viii) Noninstantiability is closely related do individuality. What is noninstantiable is an important source of individuality. *Pace* nominalism, noninstantiability is not a primitive feature of reality. There are, moreover, two different ways of arriving to what is noninstantiable: on the one hand, *via* the notion of an ultimate realization or ultimate actuality (it is reflected in Scotus's considerations on haecceities and in some considerations on actual existence as a source of individuality); on the other hand – *via* the notion of a prime subject (it is reflected in Aquinas's arguments for the Matter-Individuation Thesis).

(ix) There are various sorts of prime subjects. So, for example, among prime subjects there are (within Aquinas's metaphysics) both separated forms (created immaterial substances) that cannot be instantiated in matter and prime matter.

(x) The concept of prime matter is not a general concept under which various pieces of matter fall; pieces of matter are *not* instances of prime matter, and prime matter as such, *pace* Scotus and many Thomists, is nonistantiable. Moreover, the noninstantiability of matter is *not* individuality. It seems that neglecting this fact is one of the main sources of the difficulties concerning *materia signata*. Admittedly, the noninstantiability of prime matter is a difficult topic; I would argue, however, that it offers a better perspective of understanding noninstantiability (and henceforth individuality) than the Scotistic strategy of *ultima realitas*.

(xi) Noninstantiability distinguishes numerical unity in the strict sense from numerical unity in the broad sense; it is not, however, the only aspect of individuality, because a manifold of co-existing instances of some nature, for example all the instances of whiteness on a given chessboard, is in some way noninstantiable, and in some way instantiates the relevant nature – but it contrasts with a *single* instance of that nature.

(xii) What is a prime subject is also the principle of noninstantiability of what is instantiated in it. Within function analogy: adding the sign of a prime subject to a function sign results in an expression that is not a function sign. More precisely, it is the transcendental relationship to the relevant prime subject (and not adding some saturating part) that makes the instance of a nature noninstantiable.

(xiii) If, on the other hand, one approaches noninstantiability *via* the notion of an ultimate actuality or ultimate reality, there is an interesting contrast between the Scotistic *haecceitas* and actual existence (at least if you accept the principle *vivere viventibus est esse*).

(xiv) Various theories of individuation pose items that are *not* instances of anything instantiable as a sort of ultimate sources of individuality. For the nominalist, nothing at all is an instance of anything instantiable (there is no room for instantiation in the ontological sense); for the Scotist, haecceities are not instances of anything instantiable. In the Thomistic theory, by contrast, it is prime matter that is not an instance of anything instantiable. Admittedly, the topic of prime matter is a difficult one; I would argue, however, that it offers a better perspective for understanding what is not an instance of anything than the Scotistic strategy of postulating haecceities or the nominalistic strategy of rejecting any ontological sense of instantiation.

(xv) In particular, according to the Thomistic theory of individuation, both prime matter which is not an instance of anything *and* geometrical attributes which *are* instances of instantiable natures, are sources of individuality, although in different ways: they are responsible for various aspects of individuality.

(xvi) There are various sorts of entities that, for various reasons, are individual by themselves or immediately – are *self-individuated*. Self-individuated items are usually thought to be ultimate sources of individuality. In the Thomistic theory, in particular, instances of geometrical attributes are self-individuated: two exactly similar squares are distinct just *by themselves*, because they are differentiated by their position (*situs*) which is not something distinct from them. Here we appeal to some specific features of an instantiable nature of a geometrical attribute to explain *why* its instances are self-individuated. This contrasts both with the nominalistic thesis that *everything* that is individual is bound to be self-individuated and with the Scotistic thesis that there must be some entities, namely haecceities, that are self-individuated.

(xvii) It is important to note that geometrical attributes are self-individuated although they are instances of some instantiable natures. On the other hand, it is important to note that prime matter is noninstantiable, but is not self-individuated (and is not individual at all). Finally, manifolds of co-existing material objects are noninstantiable, but are not individual. So the relationships between being self-individuated, being noninstantiable and not being an instance of anything are quite complex.

(xviii) As an analysis of pure one-many changes (or of division into pieces) show, there is some sort of close relationship between quantity and actual existence. This relationship is important because both actual existence and quantity are in their ways related to self-individuation or noninstantiability: actual existence as ultimate actuality is thought to be noninstantiable, and instances of quantity are self-individuated in the sense indicated above.

(xix) Many theories of individuation postulate *simple* entities as ultimate sources of individuality: this is particularly clear in the case of nominalism. It is also a fundamental thesis of Aristotelian theories of parts and wholes that substantial forms are basically simple or not composed of parts. The connection between simplicity of a form and singleness, however, is, in light of the Subject-Individuation Thesis, quite a complex issue. Although a form is just by itself a simple unifying factor and a principle of the internal unity of a thing, forms of material substances and accidental forms are individuated by their subjects.

(xx) The way in which actual existence belongs to something corresponds to the way in which individuality belongs to it; this correspondence is one of the key aspects of the principle *ens et unum convertuntur*. The actual existence, however, belongs primarily to the *suppositum* and not to the instance of its substantial nature in it; and there is some sort of distinction between a *suppositum* and its instance of substantial nature. To grasp the relationship between actual existence and actuality one has to grasp the relationship between a *suppositum* and the particular instance of its substantial nature in it.

(xxi) To sum up: on the one hand, there is a close relationship between self-individuation, noninstantiability, not being an instance of anything instantiable, and being simple; most of these interrelated issues are evoked in most of the theories of individuation as key aspects of *primitive* individuality. According to the Thomistic theory, the key to understand the relations between them (and primitive individuality in general) is a good grasp of noninstantiability of prime matter, of self-individuation of quantity or simplicity of forms. The Thomistic picture of primitive individuality contrasts in many respects with the nominalistic and the Scotistic views postulating various sorts of primitive thisness.

On the other hand, various aspects of the function analogy are the key to understand *derivative* individuality. An instantiable nature is not any sort of part of its instances. It is essential, however, for a given instance that it is an instance *of* some nature *in* some subject; there is a sort of internal transcendental relationship of an instance of a given nature to its subject of instantiation – or, more precisely, there is a wide spectrum of such relationships particular to various sorts of subjects and instantiable natures.

Bibliography

Ancient and Scholastic Texts

Aquinas, Thomas (1947), *Summa Theologica*, trans. By the Fathers of the English Dominican Province, New York: Benziger Bros.

Aquinas, Thomas (1980), *S. Thomae Aquinatis Opera Omnia*, ed. R. Busa SI, Stuttgart-Bad Cannstatt: Frommann-Holzboog.

Aristotle (1908), *Metaphysica*, trans. D. Ross (*The Works of Aristotle*, t. 8), Oxford: Clarendon Press.

Aristotle (1953), *Aristotle's Metaphysics. A Revised Text with Introduction and Commentary by W.D. Ross*, Oxford: Clarendon 1953.

Aristotle (1961), *De anima*, Edited with Introduction and commentary by W.D. Ross, Oxford: Clarendon Press.

Aristotle (1983), *Physics. Books III and IV*. Translated with Introduction and Notes by E. Hussey, Oxford: Clarendon Press.

Auriol, Peter (1605), *Commentaria in Secundum librum Sententiarum*, Romae: Ex Typographia Aloysii Zanetti.

Avicenna (1980), *Avicenna Liber de philosophia prima sive scientia divina. Édition critique de la traduction latine médiévale* ed. S. van Riet, t. 2: V–X (*Avicenna Latinus*, 1.4), Louvain: Peeters.

Baconthorpe, John (1526), *Super quatuor Sententiarum libros*, Venetiis.

Buridan, John (1588), *Quaestiones in Metaphysicam Aristotelis*, Parisiis (reprint: Frankfurt: Minerva 1964).

Buridan, John (1987), *Tractatus de differentia universalis ad individuum*, ed. S. Szyller, in *Przegląd Tomistyczny*: 3, 135–178.

Cajetan (Thomas de Vio) (1888), *Commentaria in Summam theologiae*, in *S. Thomae Aquinatis Opera Omnia*, iussu impensaque Leonis XIII P.M., t. 4, Romae: Ex Typographia Polyglotta.

Cajetan (Thomas de Vio) (1907), *Commentarium in opusculum De ente et essentia*, Romae: Ex Pontificia Officina Typographica.

Capreolus, John (1902), *Defensiones theologiae Divi Thomae Aquinatis*, ed. C. Paban, T. Pègues, Turonibus: Sumptibus Alfred Cattier, Bibliopolae Editoris

Collegium Complutense Fratrum Discalceatorum B. Mariae de Monte Carmeli (1693), *Artium cursus*, t. 3, Coloniae Agrippinae: Sumptibus Huguetan.

Collegium Salamanticense Fratrum Discalceatorum B. Mariae de Monte Carmeli (1679), *Cursus theologicus*, t. 1, Lugduni: Sumptibus Joannis Antonii Huguetan et Soc.

Dominic of Flandria (1621), *In duodecim libros Metaphysicae Aristotelis*, Coloniae Agrippinae: Typis Arnoldi Kempensis, Sumptibus Ordnis.

Duns Scotus, John (1959), *Ordinatio*, lib. I, dist. 11–25 (*Ioannis Duns Scoti Opera Omnia*, ed. Commissio Scotistica, t. 5), Civitas Vaticana.

Duns Scotus, John (1973), *Ordinatio*, lib. II, dist. 1–3 (*Ioannis Duns Scoti Opera Omnia*, ed. Commissio Scotistica, t. 7), Civitas Vaticana.

Duns Scotus, John (1982), *Lectura*, lib. II, dist. 1–6 (*Ioannis Duns Scoti Opera Omnia*, ed. Commissio Scotistica, t. 18), Civitas Vaticana.

Durand of Saint-Pourçain (1537), *In Petri Lombardi Sententias theologicas commentariorum libri IV*, Venetiis: Apud Gulielmum Rovillium.
Ferrara, Francis (1898), *Commentaria in libros quatuor Contra gentiles s. Thomae de Aquino*, ed. I. Sestili, Romae: Orphanotropii a S. Hieronymo Aemiliani.
Fonseca, Peter (1615), *Commentaria in Libros Metaphysicorum Aristotelis Stagiritae*, Coloniae: Sumptibus Lazarii Zetzner (reprint: Hildesheim: Olms 1964).
Godfrey of Fontaines (1914), *Les quodlibet cinq, six et sept de Godefroid de Fontaines (texte inédit)*, ed. M. de Wulf, J. Hoffmans (Les Philosophes Belges, t. 3), Louvain: Institut Supérieur de Philosophie de l'Université.
Henry of Ghent (1983), *Quodlibet* II, ed. R. Wielockx (*Henrici de Gandavo Opera omnia*, t. 6), Leuven: Leuven University Press.
Henry of Lübeck (1975), *Quaestio de principio individuationis*, ed. W. Bucichowski, in *Mediaevalia Philosophica Polonorum*: 21, 105–113.
Javelli, Chrysostom (1676), *Quaestiones in Aristotelis XI Metaphysices Libros*, Lugduni: Apud Carolum Pesnot.
John of St. Thomas (1884), *Cursus theologicus in Summam theologicam D. Thomae*, Parisiis: Vivès.
John of St. Thomas (1933), *Cursus philosophicus thomisticus*, ed. B. Reiser, Taurini: Marietti.
John of St. Thomas (1949), *Cursus theologicus in Iam–IIae, De habitibus*, ed. A. Mathieu, H. Gagné, Quebeci.
John of Naples (1951), "Zwei unedierte Artikel des Johannes von Neapel über das Individuationsprinzip", ed. P. Stella, in *Divus Thomas* (Freiburg): 29, 129–166.
John of Paris (Quidort) (1974), *Quaestio de principio individuationis*, ed. J.P. Müller OSB, in *Virtus Politica. Festgabe zum 75. Geburtstag von Alfons Hufnagel*, ed. J. Müller und H. Kohlenberger, Stuttgart-Bad Cannstatt: Frommann-Holzboog, 335–356.
Leibniz, Gottfried Wilhelm (1930), "Disputatio metaphysica de principio individui", in G.W. Leibniz, *Sämtliche Schriften und Briefe*, Sechste Reihe, Erste Band, Darmstadt: Otto Reich Verlag.
Marius Victorinus (2014), *Commenta in Ciceronis Rhetorica: Accedit incerti auctoris tractatus de attributis personae et negotio*, ed. T. Riesenweber, Berlin/Boston: Walter de Gruyter.
Mastri, Bartholomew and Belluto, Bonaventure (1727), *Philosophiae ad mentem Scoti cursus integer*, Venetiis: Apud Nicolaum Pezzana.
Ockham, Wilhelm (1970), *Scriptum in librum primum Sententiarum. Ordinatio (Dist. II and III)*, ed. S. Brown, G. Gál (*Guillelmi de Ockham Opera Theologica*, t. 2), St. Bonaventure: The Franciscan Institute.
Ockham, Wilhelm (1977), *Scriptum in librum primum Sententiarum. Ordinatio (Dist. IV-XVIII)*, ed. G.J. Etzkorn (*Guillelmi de Ockham Opera Theologica*, t.3), St. Bonaventure: The Franciscan Institute.
Pasqualigo, Zaccaria (1636), *Disputationes metaphysicae*, t. 2, Romae: Typibus Francisci Caballi.
Peter of Auvergne (1934), "Une Quaestion Inédite de Pierre d'Auvergne sur l'individuation", ed. E. Hocedez, in *Revue Néoscolastique de Philosophie*: 36, 355–386.
Punch, John (1672), *Philosophiae ad mentem Scoti cursus integer*, Lugduni:Sumptibus LAurenti Arnaud and Petri Borde.
Soncinas, Paul (1588), *Quaestiones metaphysicales acutissimae*, Venetiis (reprint: Frankfurt: Minerva, 1967).

Suárez, Francis (1866), *Disputationes metaphysicae* (*Opera omnia*, ed. C. Berton, t.25–26), Parisiis (reprint: Hildesheim: Olms 1965).

Modern Texts

Angelelli, Ignacio (1967), *Studies on Gottlob Frege and Traditional Philosophy*, Dordrecht: D. Reidel Publishing Company.

Angelelli, Ignacio (1994), "The Scholastic Background of Modern Philosophy: *Entitas* and Individuation in Leibniz, in in *Individuation in Scholasticism: The Later Middle Ages and the Counter-Reformation, 1150–1650*, ed. J.J.E. Gracia, Albany: State University of New York Press, 535–541.

Anscombe, Gertrude Elizabeth Margaret (1961), "Aristotle. The Search for Substance", in G.E.M. Anscombe, P.T. Geach, *Three Philosophers*, Oxford: Blackwell 1961, 1–64.

Anscombe, Gertrude Elizabeth Margaret (1981a), "The Principle of Individuation", in *The Collected Philosophical Papers of G.E.M. Anscombe*, t. 1, Oxford: Blackwell, 57–65.

Anscombe, Gertrude Elizabeth Margaret (1981b), ""Under a Description"", in *The Collected Philosophical Papers of G.E.M. Anscombe*, t. 2, Oxford: Blackwell, 208–219.

Bäck, Allan (1996), "The *Triplex Status Naturae* and its Justification", in *Studies in the History of Logic. Proceedings of the IIIrd Symposium on the History of Logic*, ed. I. Angelelli, M. Cerezo, Berlin/New York: Walter de Gruyter, 133–153.

Beuchot, Mauricio (1994), "Chrysostom Javellus and Francis Sylvester Ferrara", in *Individuation in Scholasticism: The Later Middle Ages and the Counter-Reformation, 1150–1650*, ed. J.J.E. Gracia, Albany: State University of New York Press, 457–473.

Bos, Egbert P. (2003), "Francis of Meyronnes on Relations and Transcendentals", in *Die Logik des Transzendentalen. Festschrift für Jan A. Aertsen zum 65. Geburtstag*, ed. M. Pickavé, Berlin/New York: Walter de Gruyter, 320–336.

Brower, Jeffrey E. (2012), "Matter, Form, and Individuation", in *The Oxford Handbook of Aquinas*, ed. B. Davies, Oxford: Oxford University Press, 85–100.

Brower, Jeffrey E. (2014), *Aquinas's Ontology of the Material World: Change, Hylomorphism, and Material Objects*, Oxford: Oxford University Press.

Brown, Barry F. (1985), *Accidental Being. A study in the Metaphysics of St. Thomas Aquinas*, Lanham, MD: University Press of America.

Chisholm, Roderick (1989), "Boundaries", in R. Chisholm, *On Metaphysics*, Mineapolis: University of Minnesota Press.

Denkel, Arda (1991), "Principia Individuationis", in *The Philosophical Quarterly*: 41, 212–228.

Donati, Silvia (1998), "Materie und Räumliche Ausdehnung in einigen ungedruckten Physikkomentaren aus der Zeit von etwa 1250–1270", in *Raum und Raumvorstellungen in der Mittelaterlichen Philosophie*, ed. J.A. Aersten, A. Speer, Berlin/New York: Walter de Gruyter, 17–51.

Elders, Leo (1993), *The Metaphysics of Being of St. Thomas Aquinas in a Historical Perspective*, Leiden: Brill.

Frege, Gottlob (1987), *Die Grudlagen der Arithmetik*, Stuttgart: Reclam.

Frege, Gottlob (2008a), "Funktion und Begriff", in *Funktion, Begriff, Bedeutung. Fünf logische Studien*, ed. G. Patzig, Göttingen: Vandenhoeck & Ruprecht, 1–22.

Frege, Gottlob (2008b), "Über Begriff und Gegenstand", in *Funktion, Begriff, Bedeutung. Fünf logische Studien*, ed. G. Patzig, Göttingen: Vandenhoeck & Ruprecht, 47–60.

García, Marcela (2012), "*Vivere viventibus est esse?* The Relevance of Life for the Understanding of Existence", in *Philosophisches Jahrbuch*: 119, 347–374.
Geach, Peter Thomas (1956), "Good and Evil", in *Analysis*: 17, 32–42.
Geach, Peter Thomas (1961), "Aquinas", in G.E.M. Anscombe, P.T. Geach, *Three Philosophers*, Oxford: Blackwell, 65–126.
Geach, Peter Thomas (1969a), "Form and Existence", in P.T. Geach, *God and the Soul*, 42–64.
Geach, Peter Thomas (1969b), "What Actually Exists", in P.T. Geach, *God and the Soul*, 65–74.
Geach, Peter Thomas (1972), "Nominalism", in P.T. Geach, *Logic Matters*, Berkeley and Los Angeles: University of California Press, 189–301.
Geach, P.T. (1980), *Reference and Generality. An Examination of Some Medieval and Modern Theories*, Ithaca: Cornell University Press
Geach, Peter Thomas (1991), "Reply to Kenny", in *Peter Geach: Philosophical Encounters*, ed. H.A. Lewis, Dordrecht: Kluwer, 254–258.
Głowala, Michał (2013), "Indywidua, *modi, supposita*. Jan od św. Tomasza o indywiduacji cnót", "Filo-Sofija": 23, 99–116.
Gracia, Jorge J.E. (1983), "Individuals as Instances", in *The Review of Metaphysics*: 37, 37–59.
Gracia, Jorge J.E. (1984), *Introduction to the Problem of Individuation in the Early Middle Ages*, München: Philosophia Verlag.
Gracia, Jorge J.E. (1988), *Individuality. An Essay on the Foundations of Metaphysics*, Albany: State University of New York Press.
Gracia, Jorge J.E. (1991), "Individuality, Individuation", in H. Burkhardt, B. Smith (eds), *Handbook of Metaphysics and Ontology*, München: Philosophia Verlag.
Gracia, Jorge J.E. (1994a), "Prologue", in *Individuation in Scholasticism: The Later Middle Ages and the Counter-Reformation, 1150–1650*, ed. J.J.E. Gracia, Albany: State University of New York Press, ix–xiv.
Gracia, Jorge J.E. (1994b), "Introduction: The Problem of Individuation", in *Individuation in Scholasticism: The Later Middle Ages and the Counter-Reformation, 1150–1650*, ed. J.J.E. Gracia, Albany: State University of New York Press, 1–20.
Gracia, Jorge J.E. (1994c), "Francis Suárez", in *Individuation in Scholasticism: The Later Middle Ages and the Counter-Reformation, 1150–1650*, ed. J.J.E. Gracia, Albany: State University of New York Press, 475–510.
Gracia, Jorge J.E. (1994d), "Epilogue: Individuation in Scholasticism", in *Individuation in Scholasticism: The Later Middle Ages and the Counter-Reformation, 1150–1650*, ed. J.J.E. Gracia, Albany: State University of New York Press, 543–549.
Gracia, Jorge J.E. and Kronen, John (1994), "John of St. Thomas", in *Individuation in Scholasticism: The Later Middle Ages and the Counter-Reformation, 1150–1650*, ed. J.J. E. Gracia, Albany: State University of New York Press, 511–534.
Heider, Daniel (2014), *Universals in Second Scholasticism. A Comparative Study with focus on the theories of Francisco Suárez S.J. (1548–1617), João Poinsot O.P. (1589–1644) and Bartolomeo Mastri da Meldola O.F.M. Conv. (1602–1673)/Bonaventura Belluto O.F.M. Conv. (1600–1676)*, Amsterdam/Philadelphia: John Benjamins Publishing Company.
Honnefelder, Ludger (2009), "Time and Existence", in *Unity and Time in Metaphysics*, ed. L. Honnefelder, E. Runggaldier, B. Schick, Berlin/New York: Walter de Gruyter, 199–209.
King, Peter O. (1992), "Duns Scotus on the Common Nature and the Individual Difference", in *Philosophical Topics*: 20, 51–76.

King, Peter O. (1994a), "Bonaventure", in *Individuation in Scholasticism: The Later Middle Ages and the Counter-Reformation, 1150–1650*, ed. J.J.E. Gracia, Albany: State University of New York Press, 141–172.
King, Peter O. (1994b), "Jean Buridan", in in *Individuation in Scholasticism: The Later Middle Ages and the Counter-Reformation, 1150–1650*, ed. J.J.E. Gracia, Albany: State University of New York Press, 397–430.
King, Peter O., (2000), "The Problem of Individuation in the Middle Ages", in *Theoria* 66: 159–184.
King, Peter O. (2001), "Duns Scotus on Possibilities, Powers, and the Possible", in *Potentialität und Possibilität*, ed. T. Buchheim, C.H. Kneepkens, K. Lorenz, Stuttgart-Bad Cannstatt: Frommann-Holzboog, 175–199.
King, Peter O. (2005), "Duns Scotus on Singular Essences", in *Medioevo*: 30, 111–138.
Kraus, Johannes (1936), "Die Lehre von der realen spezifischen Einheit in der älteren Skotistenschule", in *Divus Thomas* (Freiburg) 14, 353–378.
Lloyd, A.C. (1962), "Genus, Species, and Ordered Series in Aristotle", in *Phronesis*: 7, 67–90.
Lowe, E. Jonathan (2004), "Some Formal Ontological Relations", in *Dialectica*: 58, 297–316.
Lowe, E. Jonathan (2005), "Individuation", in *Oxford Handbook of Metaphysics*, ed. M.J. Loux and D.W. Zimmermann, Oxford: Oxford University Press, 75–95.
Lowe, E. Jonathan (2009), *More Kinds of Being: A Further Study of Individuation, Identity, and the Logic of Sortal Terms*, Malden, Ma and Oxford: Wiley-Blackwell.
Lowe, E. Jonathan (2013), *Forms of Thought: A Study in Philosophical Logic*, Cambridge: Cambridge University Press.
Maier, Anneliese (1955), "Das Problem der räumlichen Ausdehnung", in A. Maier, *Metaphysische Hintergründe der spätscholastischen Naturphilosophie*, Roma: Edizioni di storia e Letteratura.
Maurer, Armand A. (1994), "Wilhelm of Ockham", in *Individuation in Scholasticism: The Later Middle Ages and the Counter-Reformation, 1150–1650*, ed. J.J.E.Gracia, Albany: State University of New York Press, 373–396.
McCullough, Laurence B. (1996), *Leibniz on Individuals and Individuation. The Persistence of Premodern Ideas in Modern Philosophy*, Dordrecht: Kluwer.
Mulligan, Kevin, Simons, Peter, Smith, Barry (1984), "Truth-Makers", in *Philosophy and Phenomenological Research*: 44, 287–321.
Noone, T.B., (2003), "Universals and Individuation", in *The Cambridge Companion to Duns Scotus*, Cambridge: Cambridge University Press, 100–128.
Oderberg, David (2002), "Hylomorphism and Individuation", in *Mind, Metaphysics, and Value in the Thomistic and Analytical Traditions*, ed. J. Haldane, Notre Dame: University of Notre Dame Press, 125–142.
Oderberg, David (2007), *Real Essentialism*, New York: Routledge.
Owens, Joseph (1967), "Common Nature: A Point of Comparison between Thomistic and Scotistic Metaphysics", in *Inquiries into Medieval Philosophy: A Collection in Honor of Francis P. Clarke*, ed. J.F. Ross, Westport: Grenwood Pub. Co., 185–209.
Owens, Joseph (1994), "Thomas Aquinas", in *Individuation in Scholasticism: The Later Middle Ages and the Counter-Reformation, 1150–1650*, ed. J.J.E. Gracia, Albany: State University of New York Press, 173–194.
Park, Woosuk (1990a), "Haecceitas and the Bare Particular", in *The Review of Metaphysics*: 44, 375–397.

Park, Woosuk (1990b), "Scotus, Frege, and Bergmann", in *The Modern Schoolman*: 67, 259–273.
Park, Woosuk (1996), "Understanding the Problem of Individuation: Gracia Vs Scotus", in *John Duns Scotus: Metaphysics and Ethics*, ed. L. Honnefelder, R. Wood, M. Dreyer, Leiden: Brill, 273–289.
Parsons, Terence (2014) *Articulating Medieval Logic*, Oxford: Oxford University Press.
Pasnau, Robert (2011), *Metaphysical Themes 1274–1671*, Oxford: Clarendon Press.
Peterson, Linda (1994), "Cardinal Cajetan and Giles of Rome", in *Individuation in Scholasticism: The Later Middle Ages and the Counter-Reformation, 1150–1650*, ed. J.J.E. Gracia, Albany: State University of New York Press, 431–455.
Pickavé, Martin (2007), "The Controversy over the Principle of Individuation in Quodlibeta (1277– ca. 1320): A Forest Map, in *Theological Quodlibeta in the Middle Ages: The Fourteenth Century*, ed. Ch. Schabel, Leiden: Brill, 17–80.
Pini, Giorgio (2005), "Scotus on Individuation", in *Proceedings of the Society for Medieval Logic and Metaphysics*: 5, 50–69.
Riesenweber, Thomas (2015), *C. Marius Victorinus, Commenta in Ciceronis Rhetorica. Prolegomena und Kritischer Kommentar*, Berlin/Boston: Walter de Gruyter.
Rind, Miles and Tillinghast, Lauren (2008), "What is an Attributive Adjective?", in *Philosophy*: 83, 77–88.
Rudavsky, Tamar (1977/1980), "The Doctrine of Individuation in Duns Scotus", in *Franciskanische Studien:* 59, 328–377 and 62, 63–83.
Wingell, Albert E. (1961), "Vivere viventibus est esse in Aristotle and St. Thomas", in *The Modern Schoolman*: 38, 85–120.
Wippel, John F. (1981), *The Metaphysical Thought of Godfrey of Fontaines. A Study in Late Thirteenth-Century Philosophy*, Washington: The Catholic University of America Press.
Wippel, John F. (1994), "Godfrey of Fontaines, Peter of Auvergne and John Baconthorpe", in *Individuation in Scholasticism: The Later Middle Ages and the Counter-Reformation, 1150–1650*, ed. J.J.E. Gracia, Albany: State University of New York Press, 221–255.
Wippel, John F. (2000), *The Metaphysical Thought of Thomas Aquinas. From Finite Being to Uncreate Being*, Washington, D.C.: The Catholic University of America Press.
Wolter, Allan B. (1993), "Scotus on the divine origin of possibility", in *American Catholic Philosophical Quarterly*: 67, 95–107.
Wolter, Allan B. (1994), "John Duns Scotus", in *Individuation in Scholasticism: The Later Middle Ages and the Counter-Reformation, 1150–1650*, ed. J.J.E. Gracia, Albany: State University of New York Press, 271–297.
Wood, Rega (1996), review of *Individuation in Scholasticism: The Later Middle Ages and the Counter-Reformation, 1150–1650*, ed. J.J.E. Gracia, in *The Philosophical Review*: 105, 112–116.

Index

accident 5, 12, 15, 19, 20, 21, 66, 73, 74, 75, 76, 77, 78, 80, 81, 82, 83, 85, 86, 87, 88, 90, 91, 92, 93, 97, 110, 111, 117, 119, 121, 123, 124, 126, 127, 128, 131, 133, 135, 136, 140, 142, 144, 145, 146, 147, 148, 150
actual distinction 91, 92, 115
actuality 5, 62, 69, 100, 103, 104, 119, 132, 136, 137, 138, 139, 141, 143, 146, 152, 153
Angelelli, I. 41, 46, 47, 52, 54, 119
Anscombe, G.E.M. 2, 10, 14, 52, 91, 98, 100, 103, 123, 129, 140
Aquinas, Thomas 3, 4, 8, 12, 15, 16, 17, 27, 35, 56, 57, 72, 73, 74, 75, 76, 78, 80, 82, 84, 87, 93, 94, 95, 96, 97, 99, 100, 104, 105, 109, 111, 113, 114, 115, 116, 117, 118, 119, 120, 122, 124, 126, 127, 128, 129, 130, 131, 132, 133, 134, 135, 142, 146, 151, 152
Aristotle 4, 5, 27, 28, 31, 35, 43, 67, 69, 93, 100, 109, 113, 132, 137, 140, 141
Auriol, Peter 23, 25, 26
Avicenna 46, 47, 49, 50, 51, 52, 53, 54, 55, 56, 57, 59, 66, 77, 78, 79, 135, 151

Bäck, A. 46
Baconthorpe, John, 67, 68
bare particular 14, 63
Begriff 14, 20, 41, 47, 48, 57
Belluto, Bonaventure 60, 61, 75, 88, 90, 131
Bergmann, G. 14
Beuchot, M. 122
Boethius 10
Bos, E.P. 29
Brower, J. 33, 78, 96, 97, 98, 99, 105, 120, 129, 137, 140
Brown, B.F. 142
Buridan, John 23, 25, 30

Cajetan (Thomas de Vio) 73, 84, 93, 102, 110, 122, 123
Capreolus, John 73, 93, 94, 96, 110, 123, 124
Chisholm, R. 110

Denkel, A. 23
diafora 31, 32, 37, 40
Dominic of Flandria 93, 94, 96, 102, 124
Donati, S. 121
Durand of Saint-Pourçain 83

Eigenschaft 47, 57, 151
Elders, L. 29
Eustachius a S. Paulo 119
exemplification 12, 77
existence 19, 37, 47, 55, 69, 75, 99, 100, 104, 129, 130, 131, 132, 133, 134, 135, 136, 138, 139, 140, 142, 143, 144, 145, 146, 152, 153, 154
extension 2, 3, 5, 19, 21, 67, 73, 93, 94, 95, 110, 112, 113, 121, 122, 128, 138

Ferrara, Francis 93, 96, 110, 123, 124
Fine, K. 46
Fonseca, Peter 15, 19, 39, 40, 63, 64, 131, 150
form 3, 5, 8, 19, 20, 24, 32, 33, 46, 57, 60, 61, 62, 63, 64, 66, 67, 68, 69, 70, 71, 72, 88, 89, 91, 94, 95, 96, 97, 98, 99, 101, 103, 104, 105, 106, 107, 109, 111, 112, 113, 114, 121, 122, 123, 124, 125, 127, 128, 129, 131, 134, 136, 139, 140, 143, 144, 145, 147, 148, 150, 152, 153
Formal Individuation Thesis 67, 68, 69, 70, 71, 72, 75, 88, 89, 90, 92, 95, 106, 127, 128, 135, 143
Frege, G. 14, 20, 35, 37, 41, 47, 48, 49, 55, 56, 57, 96, 105, 151
function 14, 55, 56, 60, 61, 76, 78, 79, 92, 96, 100, 105, 106, 107, 124, 134, 135, 151, 152, 152, 154

García, M. 132
Geach, P.T. 4, 8, 11, 14, 15, 16, 20, 31, 35, 41, 46, 47, 55, 56, 59, 60, 61, 67, 76, 78, 91, 96, 97, 98, 99, 100, 103, 115, 116, 123, 126, 132, 134, 151
Gegenstand 14, 20, 41, 56, 105

Głowala, M. 83
Godfrey of Fontaines 12, 13, 19, 67, 68, 69, 72
Gracia, J.J.E. 3, 6, 7, 9, 13, 14, 15, 17, 24, 25, 122, 125, 132

haecceitas 9, 19, 39, 63, 64, 65, 66, 100, 101, 104, 105, 107, 118, 119, 127, 139, 144, 146, 147, 152, 153
Heider, D. 42
Henry of Ghent 131, 138
Henry of Lübeck 64, 68, 110, 123, 124
Honnefelder, L. 132
Hussey, E. 31
hypostasis 11, 12, 13

Instance Ascription Thesis 47, 48, 49, 52, 54, 57, 59, 65, 66, 76, 78, 80, 81, 85, 117, 150, 151
Instance Composition Thesis 52, 53, 54, 55, 56, 57, 72, 78, 81, 92
instantiability 9, 10, 42, 46, 48, 49, 64, 65, 76, 79, 80, 81, 91, 92, 95, 96, 98, 99, 100, 101, 102, 104, 106, 107, 111, 117, 118, 119, 124, 134, 137, 138, 141, 144, 146, 147, 148, 149, 150, 151, 152, 153, 154
instantiation 11, 12, 46, 47, 51, 52, 56, 59, 68, 72, 74, 75, 76, 77, 80, 81, 84, 85, 86, 87, 88, 91, 92, 93, 95, 96, 98, 99, 100, 102, 104, 105, 106, 111, 112, 113, 114, 117, 120, 121, 125, 128, 129, 130, 135, 138, 139, 140, 145, 148, 149, 151, 152, 153, 154

Javelli, Chrysostom 93, 102, 123
John of Naples 23, 25, 27, 28, 68
John of Paris (Quidort) 96
John of St. Thomas 73, 76, 79, 84, 85, 90, 91, 93, 110, 130

Kenny, A. 132
King, P.O., 3, 4, 5, 14, 25, 41, 53, 56, 63, 144
Kraus, J. 42
Kronen, J. 3, 7, 122

Leibniz, G.W. 6, 21, 23, 27, 37, 38, 114
life 132, 140, 142, 145, 146
Lloyd, A.C. 43

Lowe, E.J. 4, 5, 6, 9, 10, 12, 14, 20, 23, 29, 46, 77

Maier, A. 121
manifold 34, 87, 89, 114, 123, 124, 125, 152, 153
Mastri, Bartholomew 60, 61, 74, 88, 90, 131
matter 5, 19, 20, 21, 24, 60, 61, 63, 64, 66, 67, 68, 69, 72, 93, 94, 95, 96, 97, 98, 99, 100, 101, 102, 103, 104, 105, 106, 107, 109, 110, 111, 112, 113, 114, 118, 120, 121, 122, 123, 124, 125, 126, 128, 129, 130, 131, 135, 136, 139, 145, 147, 148, 150, 152
Maurer, A.B. 25, 26
McCullough, L.B. 14
mereological sum 8, 141, 142, 143
Merkmal 47, 57, 151
Mulligan, K. 26

nature 12, 13, 19, 20, 39, 40, 41, 42, 45, 46, 47, 48, 49, 52, 53, 54, 56, 57, 58, 59, 60, 61, 62, 63, 64, 65, 66, 68, 72, 74, 75, 76, 77, 78, 79, 80, 81, 82, 84, 85, 86, 91, 92, 96, 98, 99, 100, 104, 107, 111, 112, 117, 118, 119, 124, 125, 126, 127, 128, 134, 135, 138, 139, 141, 142, 143, 144, 145, 146, 147, 148, 150, 151, 152, 153, 154
nominalism 19, 20, 23, 24, 25, 26 34, 37, 60, 65, 69, 74, 79, 118, 119, 147, 148, 149, 150, 151, 152, 153, 154
noninstantiability 9, 20, 21, 93, 95, 96, 98, 101, 102, 103, 104, 105, 106, 107, 123, 124, 125, 128, 136, 139, 146, 147, 148, 149, 150, 152, 153, 154
number 2, 5, 13, 14, 34, 35, 36, 37, 46, 47, 50, 56, 73, 80, 82, 89, 91, 100, 114, 115, 117, 123, 124, 137, 150

Ockham, Wilhelm 6, 23, 25, 26, 28, 30, 34, 36, 37, 83, 84, 118
Oderberg, D. 14, 46, 101, 122, 144
Olivi, Peter 17, 18
ontological square 12, 14, 77
Owens, J. 57, 66, 131, 133, 139, 142, 143

Park, W. 14, 41, 46, 48, 55, 63

Parsons, T. 51
part 2, 8, 11, 12, 13, 20, 34, 36, 52, 53, 55, 59, 61, 64, 65, 66, 69, 78, 79, 81, 84, 88, 89, 92, 96, 100, 102, 107, 109, 110, 111, 112, 113, 114, 115, 116, 117, 126, 127, 128, 137, 138, 139, 143, 146, 147, 148, 151, 152, 154
Pasnau, R. 110, 121
Pasqualigo, Zaccaria 77, 87, 88, 101, 102, 131, 134
person 11, 12, 13, 14, 96, 133
Peter of Auvergne 19, 67, 68, 69, 70, 71, 72, 96
Peterson, L. 122
Pickavé, M. 15
piece 34, 88, 89, 90, 99, 100, 104, 109, 111, 112, 113, 114, 115, 117, 118, 120, 121, 122, 123, 137, 138, 143, 145, 146, 152, 153
prime subject 96, 98, 99, 101, 102, 103, 104, 105, 106, 107, 109, 123, 124, 125, 128, 139, 152
Punch, John 10, 40, 64

quantity 19, 20, 21, 67, 93, 94, 95, 96, 109, 110, 111, 112, 114, 115, 117, 119, 120, 121, 122, 123, 124, 125, 126, 128, 131, 136, 138, 144, 145, 146, 147, 148, 149, 150, 151, 153, 154

Richard Rufus of Cornwall 17
Riesenweber, T. 10
Rind, M. 8
Ross, D. 27, 31, 35
Rudavsky, T. 39

saturatedness 14, 96, 105, 106, 107
Scotus, John Duns 4, 6, 17, 18, 19, 26, 39, 40, 41, 42, 43, 44, 45, 48, 49, 52, 55, 56, 57, 58, 59, 60, 61, 62, 63, 64, 66, 77, 79, 83, 84, 101, 104, 107, 111, 121, 131, 132, 139, 151, 152
Simons, P. 26
simple entities 11, 19, 20, 29, 34, 35, 36, 37, 53, 66, 89, 92, 127, 147, 150, 154
Smith, B. 26
Soncinas, Paul 93, 96, 101, 103, 104, 105, 131

soul, 4, 14, 67, 68, 70, 87, 96, 106, 112, 127, 128, 129, 130
Strong Formal Individuation Thesis 71, 72, 89, 92
Strong Self-Individuation Thesis 23, 24, 25, 26, 27, 28, 29, 36, 39, 45, 48, 65, 68, 118, 127, 150
Suárez, Francis 3, 6, 9, 13, 19, 23, 27, 30, 36, 64, 67, 68, 74, 75, 93, 96, 101, 118, 130, 131, 149, 150
subject 2, 3, 7, 11, 15, 19, 21, 28, 32, 33, 37, 55, 63, 67, 73, 74, 75, 76, 77, 79, 80, 81, 83, 84, 85, 86, 87, 88, 89, 90, 91, 92, 94, 95, 96, 97, 98, 100, 102, 104, 105, 106, 107, 109, 110, 116, 117, 118, 119, 120, 127, 128, 130, 135, 136, 140, 144, 145, 146, 148, 149, 151, 152, 153, 154
Subject-Individuation Thesis 73, 74, 75, 79, 80, 81, 82, 84, 86, 87, 88, 89, 90, 91, 92, 111, 117, 119, 120, 121, 126, 127, 134, 135, 137, 144, 145, 151, 154
substance 5, 12, 15, 20, 21, 38, 66, 67, 68, 73, 93, 94, 104, 105, 131, 133, 137, 138, 140, 147, 148, 152, 153
suppositum 11, 12, 13, 16, 131, 145, 146, 154

Tillinghast, L. 8
transcendental relation 29, 79, 80, 81, 84, 85, 88, 89, 91, 92, 107, 112, 115, 118, 120, 126, 127, 128, 130, 136, 151, 152, 154

unity 2, 5, 11, 13, 26, 27, 28, 29, 40, 41, 42, 43, 44, 45, 46, 48, 56, 57, 68, 69, 70, 71, 75, 76, 78, 80, 89, 92, 112, 125, 133, 134, 139, 140, 142, 143, 147, 152, 153
universals 2, 5, 6, 13, 26, 48
unsaturatedness 14, 49, 96, 106, 124

Victorinus, Marius 10

Weak Formal Individuation Thesis 66, 72, 78, 95, 106, 128, 152
Weak Self-Individuation Thesis 61, 74
Wippel, J. 13, 67, 120, 142, 144
Wolter, A.B. 39, 41, 144
Wood, R. 17, 18

www.ingramcontent.com/pod-product-compliance
Lightning Source LLC
Chambersburg PA
CBHW030656230426
43665CB00011B/1113